JUDICIAL AND LEGAL
SYSTEMS IN AFRICA

Butterworth's African Law Series

No. 1. Essays in African Law, by A. N. Allott, M.A., Ph.D.

No. 2. Law and Justice in Buganda, by E. S. Haydon, B.A.

No. 3. The Native Law of Succession in South Africa, by A. J. Kerr, B.A., LL.M.

No. 4. Judicial and Legal Systems in Africa, edited by A. N. Allott, M.A., Ph.D.

JUDICIAL AND LEGAL SYSTEMS IN AFRICA

EDITED BY

A. N. ALLOTT, M.A., Ph.D.

Reader in African Law in the University of London;
Director, Restatement of African Law Project, School
of Oriental and African Studies.

LONDON
BUTTERWORTHS
1962

ENGLAND:	BUTTERWORTH & CO. (PUBLISHERS) LTD. LONDON: 88 Kingsway, W.C.2.
AFRICA:	BUTTERWORTH & CO. (AFRICA) LTD. DURBAN: 33–35 Beach Grove
AUSTRALIA:	BUTTERWORTH & CO. (AUSTRALIA) LTD. SYDNEY: 6–8 O'Connell Street MELBOURNE: 473 Bourke Street BRISBANE: 240 Queen Street
CANADA:	BUTTERWORTH & CO. (CANADA) LTD. TORONTO: 1367 Danforth Avenue, 6
NEW ZEALAND:	BUTTERWORTH & CO. (NEW ZEALAND) LTD. WELLINGTON: 49–51 Ballance Street AUCKLAND: 35 High Street
U.S.A.:	BUTTERWORTH INC. WASHINGTON, D.C.: 7235 Wisconsin Avenue, 14

PRINTED IN GREAT BRITAIN BY PAGE BROS. (NORWICH) LTD.

PREFACE

It may be helpful to the reader if I explain in a few words the genesis, purposes and limitations of this work. It is sometimes exceptionally difficult to discover from the printed sources how the courts are composed, what are the channels of appeal, and how the courts' powers and jurisdiction vary; accordingly the Department of Law at the School of Oriental and African Studies offered to compile, as one of the papers available to delegates at the London Conference on the Future of Law in Africa, 28th December, 1959 to 8th January, 1960,* a statement in brief of the systems of courts in the African territories represented and of the kinds of law that they were empowered to administer.

This compilation was well received by those attending the Conference and, in pursuance of hopes expressed there, a thoroughly revised and amplified version is now offered in printed form. The drafts of each Chapter were submitted for comment to distinguished experts in each territory, and were amended in the light of their suggestions (those who so kindly aided with this task of revision, and whose names are given below, do not of course bear any responsibility for anything contained in this work).

Each chapter (other than that specially contributed on Liberia by Professor Konvitz) follows a similar lay out (though with adaptations to fit the peculiarities of each system). As a result the volume is self-indexing. The types of courts are broadly indicated by letters and numbers, A. generally signifying courts whose primary law is the law of the land (" English " or Roman-Dutch, as the case may be), B. courts primarily administering " native law and custom ", and C. Islamic and other special courts. The composition and powers of each court are set out under the following heads:—

CONSTITUTION AND POWERS
    (1) Establishment
    (2) Composition
    (3) Jurisdiction—original
    (4) Jurisdiction—appellate

CONTROL OF COURTS
    (5) Appeals from the court
    (6) Review/revision of proceedings in the court
    (7) Transfer of proceedings from the court
    (8) Inspection, supervision, etc. of the court

LAW TO BE ADMINISTERED
    (9) General law
    (10) Customary l aw
    (11) Islamic or other law

---

* For the Conference Record, see *The Future of Law in Africa*, edited by A. N. Allott, London, Butterworths, 1960.

This book is not meant to be a complete statement on the functions and jurisdiction of courts in Africa, since certain matters are taken for granted and others are not dealt with here. The general law of every African territory, for instance, not only includes the received law of England or elsewhere as set out below, but also territorial legislation by a colonial or independent legislature, which may have incidentally modified the received law or in its turn adopted more recent enactments from overseas; no attempt is made in this introduction to African legal systems to chart the extent to which territorial legislation has thus contributed to the legal system. Nor is any attempt made to estimate how far the general or English law applies in practice, where it has to compete with the co-existing systems of customary or Islamic law. All these matters fall to be dealt with in works dealing in detail with the law of a particular territory. We must hope that detailed guides to the laws of each territory will be prepared in due course under the stimulus of the movement for law revision and legal research and instruction in Africa. Furthermore, the legal systems summarized here are restricted to those which either have the common law as their basis, or at least have been strongly influenced by it. (The legal system of the Republic of South Africa has not been summarized here, as there already exist many excellent guides to it.) It would be most convenient to have in English and in a readily accessible form descriptions of the legal systems of the North African states, of the former French and Belgian territories, and of the Portuguese possessions in Africa; but these must await the preparation of a companion volume.

The statements of the law and judicial systems refer, so far as possible, to the position as it was on 1st July, 1960. Exceptionally some of the chapters (*e.g.*, those dealing with Nigeria and the Somali Republic) deal with the position at a later date, in order to take account of recent definitive and fundamental changes in the constitutional and legal position.

A. N. ALLOTT

Department of Law,
School of Oriental and African Studies.
October, 1961.

ACKNOWLEDGEMENTS

We desire to thank the following persons who very kindly looked over the appropriate portions of the manuscript:—

The Gambia—The Hon. Mr. Justice J. A. L. Wiseham.
Sierra Leone—The Hon. Mr. C. O. E. Cole, Solicitor-General.
Ghana—The Hon. Mr. Justice N. A. Ollennu; F. A. R. Bennion, Esq.
Nigeria—Dr. F. A. Ajayi, Legal Draftsman, W. Region; Mr. M. O. Ajegbo, Attorney-General, E. Region; the Hon. Mr. Justice Brett, Federal Supreme Court; S. S. Richardson, Esq., Commissioner for Native Courts, N. Region.
Southern Cameroons—The Hon. Mr. Justice G. B. A. Coker.
Kenya—The Hon. Mr. Justice D. W. Conroy (formerly Solicitor-General, Kenya, now Chief Justice, Northern Rhodesia).

Tanganyika—The Hon. Mr. J. S. R. Cole, Attorney-General, Tanganyika.

Uganda—H. F. Morris, Esq., Native Courts Adviser; J. S. Read, Esq., Lecturer in African Law, School of Oriental and African Studies, University of London.

Zanzibar—The Hon. Mr. Justice Mahon, Chief Justice of Zanzibar.

Sudan—W. L. Twining, Esq., Faculty of Law, University of Khartoum.

Somali Republic—The Hon. Mr. Justice Greene (formerly Chief Justice of the Somaliland Protectorate).

Federation of Rhodesia and Nyasaland—The Hon. Mr. J. M. Greenfield, C.M.G., Q.C., Federal Minister of Law; R. D. M. Davidson, Esq., Registrar, Federal Supreme Court.

Northern Rhodesia—The Hon. B. A. Doyle, Esq., Q.C., Attorney-General; W. M. McCall, Esq., Solicitor-General.

Southern Rhodesia—E. W. G. Jarvis, Esq., Attorney-General, Southern Rhodesia.

Nyasaland—The Hon. Sir T. C. Spenser-Wilkinson, Chief Justice of Nyasaland; J. B. Pine, Esq., Solicitor-General.

Basutoland—W. A. Ramsden, Esq., Registrar, High Court.

Bechuanaland—R. A. Tilbury, Esq., Legal Secretary.

Swaziland—T. B. Brinkman, Esq., Legal Secretary.

We particularly desire to thank Miss J. A. Hall, of the School of Oriental and African Studies, who was responsible for the typing and preparation of the manuscript.

CONTENTS

		page
Preface	. . . .	v
Acknowledgements	. . . .	vi
Guide to Statutes	. . . .	xi

PART I.—WEST AFRICA

By W. C. DANIELS, LL.M., Dipl. O.A.S.; *of the Middle Temple Barrister-at-Law; Research Officer, Restatement of African Law Project, School of Oriental and African Studies.*

THE GAMBIA	. . . .	1
SIERRA LEONE	. . . .	13
GHANA	. . . .	20
FEDERATION OF NIGERIA	. . . . . .	44
SOUTHERN CAMEROONS	. . . .	76

LIBERIA (By MILTON R. KONVITZ, *Professor, Cornell University, Director, Liberian Codification Project; Member of New Jersey Bar*). 82

PART II.—EAST AFRICA

By E. COTRAN, LL.B., Dipl. I.L.; *of Lincoln's Inn, Barrister-at-Law; Research Officer, Restatement of African Law Project, School of Oriental and African Studies.*

KENYA	. . . .	89
TANGANYIKA	. . . .	98
UGANDA	. . . .	106
ZANZIBAR	. . . .	118
SUDAN	. . . .	125
SOMALI REPUBLIC	. . . .	136

Contents

PART III.—CENTRAL AFRICA

By W. T. McClain, LL.B., LL.M., *of the Bar of Indiana;
Research Officer, Restatement of African Law Project,
School of Oriental and African Studies.*

page

Federation of Rhodesia and Nyasaland 147

Northern Rhodesia 150

Southern Rhodesia 160

Nyasaland 169

PART IV.—HIGH COMMISSION TERRITORIES

By W. T. McClain.

High Commission Territories 179

Basutoland 181

Bechuanaland 191

Swaziland 199

APPENDIX

Diagrams of Court Systems 207

Index to Diagrams 208

Explanation of Symbols 208

GUIDE TO STATUTES

(Including Acts, Ordinances, Proclamations, etc.)

Notes: (1) Each territory has a periodical *revision* and consolidation of its laws (*e.g.*, that for Sierra Leone is dated 1959); in the revision each principal law is given a *chapter number* (usually abbreviated to " cap."), by which number the law is often cited. In addition *annual volumes* of legislation are issued, containing the principal laws made during the previous year; each such law is given a serial number (*e.g.*, " No. 22 of 1959 "), by which it is sometimes cited.

(2) Certain territories (*e.g.*, Ghana, Northern Rhodesia) have abandoned the system of periodical revision in favour of a loose-leaf system involving the issue of annual *editions* of all the laws in force. Chapter numbers are usually retained from one edition to the next.

(3) For ease of reference, the appropriate revisions or editions of the laws of each territory are listed below.

WEST AFRICA

THE GAMBIA
    Laws of the Gambia, 1955 Revision, and subsequent annual volumes.

SIERRA LEONE
    Laws of Sierra Leone, 1959 Revision, and subsequent annual volumes.

GHANA
    Laws of the Gold Coast, 1951 Revision.
    Laws of the Gold Coast, 1952–56 (annual volumes).
    Ordinances and Acts of Ghana, 1957.
    Acts of Ghana, 1958–60 (annual volumes).
    Acts of the Republic of Ghana, 1960–current (loose-leaf: in continuous revision).

NIGERIA
    FEDERATION AND LAGOS
        Laws of the Federation of Nigeria and Lagos, 1958 Revision, and subsequent annual volumes.
    WESTERN REGION
        Laws of the Western Region of Nigeria, 1959 Revision, and subsequent annual volumes.
    EASTERN REGION
        Laws of the Eastern Region of Nigeria, 1954–current (annual volumes).
    NORTHERN REGION
        Laws of the Northern Region of Nigeria, 1954–current (annual volumes).

SOUTHERN CAMEROONS
Laws of Southern Cameroons, 1954–60 (annual volumes).

LIBERIA
Liberian Code of Laws, 1956, and subsequent annual volumes.

EAST AFRICA

KENYA
Laws of Kenya, 1948 Revision.
Colony and Protectorate of Kenya Ordinances, New Series, 1948–59 (Vols. 27–38).

TANGANYIKA
Tanganyika Revised Laws, 1959 Revision (loose-leaf: in continuous revision).

UGANDA
Laws of Uganda, 1951 Revision, and subsequent annual volumes.

ZANZIBAR
Laws of Zanzibar, 1934 Revision.
1935–38 Supplements, and subsequent annual volumes.

SUDAN
Laws of the Sudan, 1955 Revision, and subsequent annual volumes.

SOMALILAND PROTECTORATE
Laws of the Somaliland Protectorate, 1950 Revision.
Laws of the Somaliland Protectorate, 1950–60 (annual volumes).

CENTRAL AFRICA

FEDERATION OF RHODESIA AND NYASALAND
Statute Laws of the Federation of Rhodesia and Nyasaland, 1955–current (annual volumes).

NORTHERN RHODESIA
Laws of Northern Rhodesia, 1961 Edition (loose-leaf: in continuous revision).

SOUTHERN RHODESIA
Statute Law of Southern Rhodesia, 1939 Revision, and subsequent volumes.

NYASALAND
Laws of Nyasaland, 1958 Revision (loose-leaf: in continuous revision).

HIGH COMMISSION TERRITORIES

BASUTOLAND
Laws of Basutoland, 1949 Revision, and subsequent annual volumes.

BECHUANALAND PROTECTORATE
Laws of Bechuanaland, 1959 Revision.
Note: These contain nothing on African courts, but an African Courts Proclamation has since been issued.

SWAZILAND
Laws of Swaziland, 1951 Revision, and subsequent annual volumes.

PART I

WEST AFRICA

By

W. C. DANIELS, LL.M., Dipl.O.A.S.,

*of the Middle Temple, Barrister-at-Law; Research
Officer, Restatement of African Law Project,
School of Oriental and African Studies.*

SUMMARY

		PAGE
THE GAMBIA		1
SIERRA LEONE		13
GHANA		20
FEDERATION OF NIGERIA		44
SOUTHERN CAMEROONS		76

LIBERIA (By MILTON R. KONVITZ, *Professor, Cornell University, Director, Liberian Codification Project; Member of New Jersey Bar*). 82

THE GAMBIA[1]

The Territory consists of the Colony and the Protectorate. Thus a description of the legal and judicial system of the two parts of the Gambia must distinguish between the Colony system and the Protectorate system.

A. 1(a) THE PRIVY COUNCIL

Appeals lie from decisions of the Gambia Court of Appeal to Her Majesty in Council both as of right and with the leave of the Court of Appeal [The Gambia (Appeals to Privy Council) Order in Council, 1961. S.I. 1961 No. 744, art. 3].

A. 1(b) THE GAMBIA COURT OF APPEAL

CONSTITUTION AND POWERS

(1) Establishment.—Established by the Gambia Court of Appeal Order in Council, 1961 [S.I. 1961 No. 743, art. 3].

(2) Composition.—The judges of the Court comprise a President and such number of other judges as may be appointed by the Governor [S.I. 1961 No. 743, art. 3(2)].

(3) Jurisdiction.—" The Court shall have such jurisdiction and powers as may be conferred upon it by this Order or any other law " [S.I. 1961 No. 743, art. 3(1)]. The West African Court of Appeal Ordinance, which provides for appeals from the superior courts of the Gambia to the West African Court of Appeal, " shall until repealed continue in force after the commencement of this Order" [S.I. 1961 No. 743, art. 21; Laws of the Gambia, 1955, Cap. 6].

I. THE COLONY

It comprises the Island of St. Mary, most of which is occupied by Bathurst, and the Kombo St. Mary Administrative Division. The judicial system consists of:—

A. Courts primarily administering the general law, viz.:—

 (a) The Supreme Court of the Colony;
 (b) the Bathurst Magistrate's Court;
 (c) the Court of Requests;
 (d) the Kombo Saint Mary Magistrate's Court;
 (e) the Juvenile Court;

and C. Courts primarily administering Mohammedan law, viz.:—

 (f) the Mohammedan Court (Bathurst);
 (g) the Kombo Saint Mary Mohammedan Court.

There are no African or Native Courts in the Colony.

---

[1] For diagram of courts system see p. 209, *post.*

A. 2 THE SUPREME COURT

CONSTITUTION AND POWERS

(1) Establishment.—The Supreme Court of the Colony of the Gambia was first established by the Supreme Court Ordinance, No. 5 of 1888, since amended [Laws of the Gambia, 1955, cap. 5, s. 14].

(2) Composition.—It is constituted by the Chief Justice [S.C.O., s. 4].

(3) Jurisdiction—original.—The Supreme Court is a superior Court of Record, and possesses:—

    (a) Unlimited jurisdiction and powers similar to those vested in the High Court of Justice in England [S.C.O., s. 15].

    (b) Admiralty jurisdiction [Colonial Courts of Admiralty Act, 1890 (53 & 54 Vict., c. 27)].

    (c) All the powers and authorities vested in the Lord High Chancellor of England as regards lunatics and others [S.C.O., s. 17].

    (d) (Subject to the Ordinance) jurisdiction " in probate, divorce, and matrimonial causes . . . to be exercised in conformity with the law and practice for the time being in England " [S.C.O., s. 17].

All criminal causes are tried before the Chief Justice with a jury of twelve men [S.C.O., 1888, s. 33]. Civil causes are triable before the Chief Justice without a jury [S.C.O., s. 64].

(4) Jurisdiction—appellate.—Under the Criminal Procedure Code, cap. 23, s. 283(1), " any person convicted on a trial held by any subordinate court may appeal to the Supreme Court ". By The Court of Requests Ordinance, cap. 9, s. 31(1), a party aggrieved by the decision of that Court (which hears all personal pleas to the limit of £50), may appeal to the Supreme Court.

Appeals lie from the decisions of the Bathurst Mohammedan Court to the Supreme Court [Mohammedan Law Recognition Ordinance, cap. 31, s. 8(1)].

Finally, appeals from the Kombo Saint Mary Mohammedan Court lie to the Supreme Court [The Kombo Saint Mary Division Ordinance, cap. 103, s. 76(1)].

CONTROL OF COURT

(5) Appeals from.—Appeals from the Supreme Court lie to the Gambia Court of Appeal [S.I. 1961 No. 743, art. 19].

LAW TO BE ADMINISTERED

(9) General law.—(a) By the Law of England (Application) Ordinance, cap. 3, s. 2, the Supreme Court is empowered to administer " the common law, the doctrines of equity and the statutes of general application in force in England on the 1st November, 1888 ".

(b) " All Acts of Parliament declared to extend or apply to the Gambia shall be in force so far only as the limits of the local jurisdiction and local circumstances permit and subject to any existing or future local Ordinance " [L. of E.(A.)O., s. 3(1)].

(c) Law and equity are to be concurrently administered, but in case of conflict, the rules of equity are to prevail [L. of E.(A.)O., s. 41(1), (3)].

(d) The courts are under a duty to administer the Ordinances passed by the local Legislature.

(10) Customary law.—" (*i*) Nothing in this Ordinance shall deprive the courts of the right to observe and enforce the observance, or shall deprive any person of the benefit, of any native law or custom existing in the Gambia, such law or custom not being repugnant to natural justice, equity and good conscience, nor incompatible either directly or by necessary implication with any law, for the time being in force.

(*ii*) Such laws and customs shall be deemed applicable in causes and matters where the parties thereto are natives, and also in causes and matters between natives and non-natives where it may appear to the Court that substantial injustice would be done to either party by a strict adherence to the rules of English law.

(*iii*) No party shall be entitled to claim the benefit of any local law or custom, if it shall appear either from express contract or from the nature of the transactions out of which any suit or question may have arisen, that such party agreed that his obligations in connection with such transactions should be regulated exclusively by English law or that such transaction is a transaction unknown to native law and custom.

(*iv*) In cases where no express rule is applicable to any matter in controversy, the court shall be governed by the principles of justice, equity and good conscience " [L. of E.(A.)O., s. 5].

(11) Islamic or other law.—The laws of the Gambia include provisions for the application of Islamic law. The earliest of these is the Mohammedan Law Recognition Ordinance, 1905, incorporated in cap. 31 of the Laws of the Gambia, 1955. For example, the Mohammedan Court at Bathurst is empowered to administer justice " according to the rules of Mohammedan law " [M.L.R.O., s. 7]; while, " subject to such restrictions as may be prescribed, appeal shall lie from any decision of the Mohammedan Court to the Supreme Court " with " a Tamsir or person learned in the Mohammedan law " sitting, for advisory purposes only, as assessor to the judge [M.L.R.O., s. 8(1), (11)]. (See also Anderson, J. N. D., *Islamic Law in Africa*, pp. 225–248).

A. 3 THE BATHURST MAGISTRATE'S COURT

CONSTITUTION AND POWERS

(1) Establishment.—This court of summary jurisdiction was established by the Bathurst Magistrate's Court Ordinance, No. 28 of 1916, since amended and now incorporated in cap. 8 of the Laws of the Gambia, 1955.

(2) Composition.—(a) The Colonial Magistrate;
(b) any two or more Justices of the Peace;
(c) any person appointed by the Governor to be a magistrate of the Court [B.M.C.O., 1916, s. 3(2)].

3

(3) Jurisdiction—original.—The Colonial Magistrate has jurisdiction and power to hear and determine all summary conviction offences [B.M.C.O., s. 12].

(4) Jurisdiction—appellate.—Nil.

Control of Court

(5) Appeals from.—Appeals lie from the judgments of the Magistrate's Court to the Supreme Court [Criminal Procedure Code, cap. 23, s. 1] (see A. 2(4), p. 2, *ante*).

(6) Review/revision.—Every subordinate court is under a duty to forward a monthly list of cases decided by such court to the Judge of the Supreme Court for review [Crim. P.C., ss. 297–299].

(7) Transfer.—The Crim. P.C., s. 65(1) provides that " if upon the hearing of any proceedings under this Code it appears that the cause or matter is outside the limits of the jurisdiction of the court, such court shall . . . direct the case to be transferred to the court having jurisdiction ".

(8) Inspection, supervision, etc.—The Court is under the supervision of the Supreme Court. The Colonial Magistrate or other officer presiding over the Court must keep a register containing all complaints and offences, and accounts of fees, fines, penalties, etc., to which book the Attorney-General, Colonial Secretary and the Principal Auditor must at all times have access [B.M.C.O., s. 5(c)–(f)].

Law to be Administered

(9) General law.—As Supreme Court, but within the jurisdiction of the Court (see A. 2(9), *ante*).

(10) Customary law

(11) Islamic or other law ⎱ Nil.

A. 4 THE COURT OF REQUESTS

Constitution and Powers

(1) Establishment.—This is one of the oldest courts. It was established by the Court of Requests Ordinance, No. 6 of 1882, now contained in cap. 9 of the Laws of the Gambia, 1955.

(2) Composition.—The Court is held in the Colony on every Friday of each week, and is presided over by the Colonial Magistrate or two Commissioners of the Court [C.R.O., s. 2(1)].

(3) Jurisdiction—original.—It has jurisdiction in all pleas of personal actions where the debt or damage involved is not more than £50, but it lacks jurisdiction in certain specified actions, viz.:—malicious prosecution, libel, slander, criminal conversation, seduction, or breach of promise of marriage. All the actions in the Court are heard and determined in a summary way [C.R.O., s. 4(1), (2)].

(4) Jurisdiction—appellate.—Nil.

CONTROL OF COURT

(5) Appeals from.—Appeals lie from the decisions of the Court of Requests to the Supreme Court, but the leave of the Court or the Supreme Court must be obtained if the value of the matter at issue does not exceed the value of £5 [C.R.O., s. 31(1) as amended by C.R. (Amendment) O., No. 6 of 1957].

(8) Inspection, supervision, etc.—This Court is under the supervision of the Supreme Court inasmuch as the Supreme Court has power to frame rules and regulate the practice of the Court [C.R.O., s. 34].

LAW TO BE ADMINISTERED

(9) General law.—As Supreme Court (see A. 2(9), p. 2, *ante*), but within the limits of jurisdiction of the Court of Requests.

(10) Customary law ⎫
(11) Islamic or other law ⎭ Nil.

A. 5 THE KOMBO SAINT MARY MAGISTRATE'S COURT

CONSTITUTION AND POWERS

(1) Establishment.—This Court is established within the Kombo Saint Mary Division, and is subordinate to the Supreme Court [The Kombo Saint Mary Division Court Ordinance, cap. 103, s. 67(1)].

(2) Composition.—In the exercise of its criminal jurisdiction, the Magistrate's Court is deemed to be:—

(a) A subordinate court of the first class when presided over by the Colonial Magistrate [K.St.M.D.C.O., s. 68(1) (a)], or by any person appointed to be a magistrate of the Bathurst Magistrate's Court [K.St.M.D. (Amendment) O., No. 9 of 1957, s. 3]; or

(b) A subordinate court of the second class when presided over by two or more justices of the peace for the Colony [K.St.M.D.O., s. 68(1)(b)].

By s. 69(1) of the K.St.M.D.O., in the exercise of its civil jurisdiction, the Magistrate's Court is deemed to be duly constituted when it is presided over by the Colonial Magistrate, or by any person appointed to be a magistrate of the Bathurst Magistrate's Court [K.St.M.D.(A.)O., No. 9 of 1957, s. 4].

(3) Jurisdiction—original.—(*a*) *Criminal.*—Same jurisdiction as that of the Bathurst Magistrates' Court. It is expressly stipulated that " the practice and procedure to be observed in the Magistrates' Court in the exercise of its criminal jurisdiction shall . . . be assimilated as nearly as circumstances will permit to the practice and procedure observed in the Bathurst Magistrates' Court . . ." [K.St.M.D.C.O., s. 62(2)].

(*b*) *Civil.*—All pleas of personal actions where the debt or damage claimed does not exceed £50, " provided that the Court shall not have

5

cognizance of any action for malicious prosecution, or for libel or slander, or for criminal conversation or for seduction or for breach of promise of marriage " [K.St.M.D.C.O., s. 69(2)(a), (d)]. The practice and procedure are similar to those of the Court of Requests [K.St.M.D.C.O., s. 69(3)].

(4) Jurisdiction—appellate.—Nil.

CONTROL OF COURT

(5) Appeals from.—Appeals, in both criminal and civil cases, lie from the decisions of the Court to the Supreme Court; except that in civil cases, where the value of the matter at issue does not exceed the sum of £5, the leave of the Court or of the Supreme Court must be obtained [K.St.M.D.(A.)O., 1957, s. 5].

(6) Review/revision

(7) Transfer

(8) Inspection, supervision, etc.

(9) General law

(10) Customary law

(11) Islamic or other law

As Bathurst Magistrate's Court and the Court of Requests (see A.3, A.4, pp. 3, 4, *ante*).

A. 6 JUVENILE COURTS

CONSTITUTION AND POWERS

(1) Establishment.—Established by the Children and Young Persons Ordinance, [cap. 20, s. 6(1)].

(2) Composition.—The C.Y.P.O., s. 6(1) stipulates: " A juvenile court for the purpose of the hearing and determination of cases relating to children or young persons shall be constituted by a magistrate (sitting with such other person or persons as the Judge of the Supreme Court shall appoint) or by two justices of the peace."

(3) Jurisdiction—original.—Exclusive jurisdiction over children or young persons. (" Young person " means a person who has attained the age of fourteen years and is under the age of seventeen [C.Y.P.O., s. 2].)

(4) Jurisdiction—appellate.—Nil.

CONTROL OF COURTS

(5) Appeals from.—Appeals lie to the Supreme Court.

(6) Review/revision

(7) Transfer

(8) Inspection, supervision, etc.

Under the supervision, etc. of the Supreme Court.

LAW TO BE ADMINISTERED

(9) General law.—As Supreme Court, but within jurisdictional limit.

(10) Customary law
(11) Islamic or other law } Nil.

C. 1 THE MOHAMMEDAN COURT
(Bathurst)

CONSTITUTION AND POWERS

(1) Establishment.—Established by the Mohammedan Law Recognition Ordinance, No. 10 of 1905 now embodied in cap. 31 of the Laws of the Gambia, 1955. This Court is established at Bathurst, and is to be known as the Mohammedan Court [M.L.R.O., 1905, s. 4].

(2) Composition.—It is " constituted by a Cadi to be appointed by the Governor; provided that:—

    (a) Whenever in the opinion of the Governor the Cadi is not a man of uncontested ability the Court shall be constituted by the Cadi and two assessors;

    (b) whenever the office of Cadi is vacant, or the Cadi is unable . . . to perform the duties of his office the court shall be constituted by two or more Assessors and the Senior Assessor shall give the judgment of the court." [M.L.R.O., 1905, s. 5(1)].

(3) Jurisdiction—original.—The Court has " jurisdiction in all causes and matters, contentious or uncontentious, between or exclusively, affecting Mohammedan natives, relating to civil status, marriage, succession, donations, testaments, and guardianship " [M.L.R.O., s. 6]. The recognition by this Ordinance granted to Mohammedan Law does not extend to criminal law, civil contracts other than marriage, or religious trusts [M.L.R.O., 1905, s. 9].
" . . . Save insofar as may be prescribed, the procedure and practice of the Court shall be according to the rules of Mohammedan law " [M.L.R.O., 1905, s. 7].

(4) Jurisdiction—appellate.—Nil.

CONTROL OF COURT

(5) Appeals from.—Appeals lie from any decision of the Mohammedan Court to the Supreme Court with a Tamsir or person learned in the Mohammedan law sitting for advisory purposes only, as assessor to the judge [M.L.R.O., 1905, s. 8(1), (2)].

(8) Inspection, supervision, etc.—By the Supreme Court [M.L.R.O., 1905, s. 10, by implication].

LAW TO BE ADMINISTERED

(9) General law
(10) Customary law } Nil.

(11) Islamic or other law.—In Bathurst and the Colony, the two Cadis' Courts (i.e. the Bathurst Mohammedan Court and the Kombo

Saint Mary Mohammedan Court) administer Shari'a law of the Maliki School in all causes and matters between or exclusively affecting Moslem Africans relating to civil status, marriage, donations, testaments and guardianship [M.L.R.O., s. 6; K.St.M.D.C.O., s. 72].

C. 2 THE KOMBO SAINT MARY MOHAMMEDAN COURT

Under this heading it is not intended to follow the usual pattern, since a quotation from *Islamic Law in Africa* by Professor J. N. D. Anderson, is considered sufficient. He remarks (p. 226):

"Again, the Kombo Saint Mary Division Ordinance, 1946, which provides *inter alia*, for the establishment of a Quadi's Court at Kombo Saint Mary, now an integral part of the Colony, contains the same provisions, almost verbatim, in a slightly different order, [*sc.* to the Mohammedan Law Recognition Ordinance, No. 10 of 1905] except that an additional section enacts that the ' Governor in Council may by order confer upon the Mohammedan Court jurisdiction to enforce within the limits of its jurisdiction all or any of the provisions of any Ordinance or Ordinances specified in such Order and to impose penalties on persons subject to the jurisdiction of the Court who offend against such provisions '." [See the K.St.M.D.O., ss. 71 *et seq.*]

II. THE PROTECTORATE

The Protectorate consists of strips of territory on either bank of the River Gambia. The judicial system comprises:—

A. Courts primarily administering the general law, viz.:—
    (a) The High Court of the Protectorate;
    (b) Subordinate Protectorate courts.

B. Courts primarily administering African customary law, viz.:—
    (c) District Tribunals.

A. 2 THE HIGH COURT

Constitution and Powers

(1) Establishment.—Established by Ordinance No. 13 of 1944, now embodied in the Protectorate Courts Ordinance, cap. 7; it is the principal Court of Judicature for the Protectorate of the Gambia.

(2) Composition.—The Judge of the Supreme Court of the Colony is also the Judge of the High Court [P.C.O., s. 4(1)]. The Deputy Judge of the Supreme Court where appointed, is the Deputy of the High Court [P.C.O., s. 4(2)].

(3) Jurisdiction—original.—It has in respect of matters occurring in the Protectorate, the same jurisdiction, civil and criminal, as is exercised by the Supreme Court in respect of matters occurring in the Colony [P.C.O., s. 3(2)]; " provided that except insofar as the Governor in Council may by order otherwise direct, the High Court shall not exercise original jurisdiction in any suit which shall raise any issue as to the title to land, or as to the title to any interest in land which is subject to the jurisdiction of a District Tribunal, nor in any matter which is subject to the jurisdiction of a District Tribunal, relating to marriage, family status, guardianship of children, inheritance or disposition of property on death " [P.C. (Amendment) O., 1958, s. 3].

(4) Jurisdiction—appellate.—There is jurisdiction to hear and determine appeals from the decisions of the subordinate Protectorate court, if the matter at issue does not exceed the value of £5. The court's leave must be obtained [P.C.O., s. 20]. The High Court may order a new trial [P.C.(A.)O., No. 7 of 1957, s. 4].

CONTROL OF COURT

(5) Appeals from.—Appeals from the decisions of the High Court lie to the Gambia Court of Appeal [S.I. 1961 No. 743, art. 3].

LAW TO BE ADMINISTERED

(9) General law.—" So far as is consistent with the Protectorate system, and without prejudice to any such reasonable native laws and customs . . . all laws Statutes, Ordinances and Rules for the time being in force in, and being of general application throughout the Colony, shall extend and apply to the Protectorate, and to all matters, civil and criminal arising therein, and shall be so extended and applied in all courts of law, whether within the Colony or the Protectorate " [P.C.O., s. 29].

(10) Customary law.—" All native laws and customs existing in the Protectorate whether relating to matters of succession, marriage, divorce, dowry, the rights and authorities of parents, the tenure of land or any other matter, shall, where not repugnant to natural justice, nor incompatible with the principles of the law of England or with any law or Ordinance of the Colony applying to the Protectorate . . . continue and remain in full force and effect, and shall be taken cognizance of and enforced in all courts of law, whether in the Colony or the Protectorate in all causes and matters whatsoever arising in or relating to the Protectorate " [P.C.O., s. 30].

(11) Islamic or other law.—The phrase " all native laws and customs " in the above quotation in this context is presumably intended to include Mohammedan law (see Anderson, J. N. D., *Islamic law in Africa*, p. 228, note 1).

A. 3 SUBORDINATE COURTS

CONSTITUTION AND POWERS

(1) Establishment.—Established by Ordinance No. 13 of 1947, now embodied in the P.C.O., cap. 7 of the Laws of the Gambia, 1955. Section 11 stipulates that such a Court is to be established in every division of the Protectorate.

(2) Composition.—Constituted when presided over by a magistrate [P.C.O., s. 11(1)]. Magistrates are of two classes, and their powers and jurisdiction in criminal matters are determined by the class of their appointment [P.C.O., s. 21(1)]. Thus the Colonial Magistrate, the Senior Commissioner and a Divisional Commissioner are first class magistrates, whilst every other administrative officer is, *virtute officii*, a second class magistrate [P.C.O., s. 21].

(3) Jurisdiction—original.—Empowered to exercise both civil and criminal jurisdiction throughout the Protectorate. Their jurisdiction is concurrent with that of any District Tribunal unless provision is made to the contrary [P.C.O., s. 12(1)]. On the criminal side, the powers and the jurisdiction of a magistrate are limited according to the class of such magistrate [P.C.O., s. 12(2)]. The sentences which may be passed are as follows:—

First class magistrate—
 (a) imprisonment for a term not exceeding 2 years;
 (b) fine not exceeding £200;
 (c) corporal punishment—when confirmed by the Supreme Court.

Second class magistrate—
 (a) imprisonment not exceeding 6 months;
 (b) fine not exceeding £50;
 (c) corporal punishment—when confirmed.

The civil jurisdiction of the Court is limited to £100 suit value [P.C.O., s. 14].

(4) Jurisdiction—appellate.—Nil.

CONTROL OF COURTS

(5) Appeals from.—Appeals lie from the subordinate Protectorate courts to the High Court. Where the value of the matter at issue does not exceed the sum of £5, the leave of the Protectorate court or the High Court must first be obtained [P.C.O., s. 20].

(6) Review/revision.—Subordinate courts are under a duty to forward to the High Court such returns of cases tried as may be required from time to time [P.C.O., s. 26].

(7) Transfer.—With respect to any civil causes pending or proceeding in any Protectorate court, the High Court may order that the cause or matter be transferred to another court of equal or superior jurisdiction or to the Court of Requests [P.C.O., s. 19]. Any court in any civil and criminal proceedings at any stage may order such proceedings to be transferred for trial to any District Tribunal having power to entertain such proceedings [P.C.O., s. 13(1)].

(8) Inspection, supervision, etc.—" The High Court shall exercise general powers of supervision over all Protectorate courts and may . . . inspect or direct the inspection of all records and may give such directions as it may in any case consider necessary in the interests of justice " [P.C.O., s. 27].

LAW TO BE ADMINISTERED

(9) General law.—As High Court, within the limits of their jurisdiction.

(10) Customary law.—The subordinate Protectorate courts have jurisdiction in native law and custom as courts of first instance [P.C.O., s. 12(1)]. In practice it is hardly ever exercised.

(11) Islamic or other law. See A. 2(11), p. 9, *ante.*

B. DISTRICT TRIBUNALS

CONSTITUTION AND POWERS

(1) Establishment.—The Governor may by warrant establish a Tribunal in each District [District Tribunals Ordinance, cap. 49, s. 3(1)].

(2) Composition.—A Tribunal consists of the Chief himself who sits as President and such number of members as is set out in the warrant appointing the Tribunal. They are appointed by the Senior Commissioner (by powers delegated by the Governor, s. 4) on the advice of the District Authority concerned [District Tribunal Rules, cap. 49, r. 4; Subsidiary Legislation of Gambia, p. 446].

(3) Jurisdiction—original.—Every District Tribunal has full jurisdiction to the extent set forth in its warrant over causes and matters in which all the parties are natives resident or being within the area of the jurisdiction of the Tribunal [D.T.O., s. 7]. " Native " means any member of an African race [D.T.O., s. 2]. The Governor may exclude certain persons from the jurisdiction of the District Tribunal [D.T.O., s. 8]. The criminal jurisdiction of a District Tribunal extends to the hearing, trial and determination of all criminal charges in which any native is accused of having committed an offence within the jurisdiction of the Tribunal [D.T.O., s. 9]. The civil jurisdiction extends to all civil suits in which the defendant is ordinarily resident within the area of the jurisdiction of the Tribunal.

There are two grades of Tribunals, namely Group and District; the extent of the jurisdiction of each Tribunal depends on its grade:—

Group Tribunals: criminal causes punishable by imprisonment for a period not exceeding 12 months, or by a fine not exceeding £25, or both; civil actions in which the debt does not exceed £50.

District Tribunals: criminal causes punishable by imprisonment for a period not exceeding 6 months, or by a fine not exceeding £10, or both; civil actions in which the debt does not exceed £25 [D.T.R., r. 6].

(4) Jurisdiction—appellate.—Nil.

CONTROL OF COURTS

(5) Appeals from.—By s. 5 of the D.T.(A.)O., no. 13 of 1958, appeals now lie from the decisions of District Tribunals or of a Commissioner exercising powers under s. 23(a) of the Principal Ordinance of cap. 49, both in civil and criminal jurisdiction, to the High Court, in the same manner as appeals from a Protectorate court to the High Court.

(6) Review/revision.—The decisions of District Tribunals both in their criminal and civil jurisdiction are subject to review by the Commissioner of that Division [D.T.O., s. 23].

11

(7) Transfer.—The Commissioner in exercising his powers of review, may also transfer a case or suit to a Protectorate court on his own motion, or that of a party [D.T.O., s. 25]. This may be done either before trial or at any stage of the proceedings for trial. After sentence has been passed or judgment given, he may order the case to be retried [D.T.O.(A.)O., s. 8].

(8) Inspection, supervision, etc.—Every Commissioner has at all times access to any District Tribunal in his division, and to their records [D.T.O., s. 23].

LAW TO BE ADMINISTERED

(9) General law.—(a) The provisions of all rules and orders made by a District Authority or a Commissioner [D.T.O., s. 11(c)].

(b) The provisions of any Ordinance or regulation which the Tribunal may be authorised to administer [D.T.O., s. 11(d), (e)].

(10) Customary law.—" The native law and custom prevailing in the area of the jurisdiction of the Tribunal, so far as it is not repugnant to justice and morality or inconsistent with the provisions of any Order of the Queen-in-Council or with any other law in force in the Protectorate " [D.T.O., s. 11(a)].

(11) Islamic or other law.—" The Mohammedan law relating to civil status, marriage, succession, divorce, dowry, the rights and authorities of parents and guardianship whenever the parties are Mohammedans " [D.T.O., s. 11(b)].

SIERRA LEONE[1]

Sierra Leone comprises:—(a) an area consisting of Freetown and its immediate environs, formerly known as the "Colony"; and (b) an area formerly known as the "Protectorate". The country became independent on April 27, 1961, and the former Colony and Protectorate thereupon ceased to exist as such. However, the existing laws of the former Colony and Protectorate of Sierra Leone continue in force in Sierra Leone until repealed [Sierra Leone (Constitution) Order in Council, 1961 S.I. 1961/741, art. 4], and references in such laws to the "Colony" and "Protectorate" are to be taken as references to the areas comprised in the former Colony and Protectorate respectively [S.L.(C.) O-in-C, First Schedule, Part V].

The courts consist of:—

    A. Courts primarily administering the general law, viz.:
      (a) the Privy Council;
      (b) the Court of Appeal of Sierra Leone;
      (c) the Supreme Court of Sierra Leone;
      (d) the Magistrates' Courts in the (former) Colony and Protectorate.

    B. Courts primarily administering African customary law, viz.:
      (e) Native Courts
      (f) Combined Courts.

A. 1(a) THE PRIVY COUNCIL

The Judicial Committee of the Privy Council is the final court of appeal. Appeals lie from decisions of the Court of Appeal to Her Majesty in Council both as of right and with the leave of the Court of Appeal [S.L.(C.) O-in-C, 1961, S.I. 1961/741, 2nd Sched., Constitution, art. 84]. The pre-existing Orders in Council, including the Sierra Leone and the Gambia (Appeals to Privy Council) Order in Council, 1959, are thereby revoked [S.I. 1961/742, art. 21].

A. 1(b) COURT OF APPEAL

CONSTITUTION AND POWERS

    (1) Establishment.—Established by the Constitution [S.I. 1961/741, 2nd Sched., Constitution, s. 79]. (Note that this Court of Appeal replaced the former Sierra Leone and the Gambia Court of Appeal.)

    (2) Composition.—It consists of:—
      (a) a President;
      (b) the persons for the time being holding or acting in the offices of the Chief Justice and the Puisne Judges of the Supreme Court, who are judges of the Court of Appeal *ex officio*; and

---

[1] For diagram of courts system see p. 210, *post.*

13

(c) such number, if any, of other judges as may be prescribed by Parliament [S.I. 1961/741, 2nd Sched., Constitution, art. 79(2)].

(3) Jurisdiction.—" The Court shall have such jurisdiction and powers as may be conferred upon it by the Constitution or any other law " [S.I. 1961/741, 2nd Sched., Constitution, art. 79(1)].

A. 2 THE SUPREME COURT

CONSTITUTION AND POWERS

(1) Establishment.—Established by S.I. 1961/741, 2nd Sched., Constitution, art. 75(1). See also the Courts Ordinance, cap. 7, Laws of Sierra Leone, 1959, which applies to the former Colony and the former Protectorate.

(2) Composition.—The Supreme Court is a superior court of record and consists of the Chief Justice and such number of Puisne Judges as may be prescribed by Parliament [S.I. 1961/741, 2nd Sched., Constitution, art. 75(2)].

(3) Jurisdiction—original.—The Court has such jurisdiction and powers as are conferred upon it by the Constitution or any other law [S.I. 1961/741, 2nd Sched., Constitution, art. 75(1)].

The Court has no jurisdiction in regard to:—

(a) Any question arising exclusively between natives which—

(*i*) involves title to land situated within the Protectorate; or

(*ii*) relates to marriage or divorce by native customary law, or any matrimonial claim founded on such a marriage; or

(*iii*) where the claim or matter in dispute does not exceed £50 in value;

(b) the administration of estates of deceased persons who are natives where such estates lie within the jurisdiction of any native court [C.O., s. 11].

In civil matters the Court is constituted by a Judge sitting alone in the former Colony, and by a Judge sitting with the aid of two or more assessors in the former Protectorate, especially where matters of native law and custom are involved [C.O., ss. 17, 18].

A person charged with a criminal offence at any sessions of the Supreme Court held in the former Colony, if the offence is punishable by death, is tried before a judge sitting with a jury of twelve persons. If the offence is not punishable by death, he is tried by a jury unless he elects to be tried by the Court with the aid of assessors [C.(A.)O., No. 2 of 1960, s. 2]. In criminal proceedings before the Supreme Court held in the former Protectorate, the trial judge is assisted by two or more natives as assessors [C.O., s. 15].

The Supreme Court has also all the powers and authorities of the Lord High Chancellor with regard to lunatics [C.O., s. 13].

(4) Jurisdiction—appellate.—The Supreme Court has jurisdiction to hear and determine all appeals from the Magistrates' Courts [C.O., s. 23; see also Courts (Appeals) Ordinance, No. 18 of 1960, ss. 3 and 4].

CONTROL OF COURT

(5) Appeals from.—Appeals from the decisions of the Supreme Court lie to the Court of Appeal [S.I. 1961/741, 2nd Sched., Constitution, art. 79; Courts (Appeals) Ordinance, No. 18 of 1960, Parts IV and V].

LAW TO BE ADMINISTERED

(9) General law.—" Subject to the provisions of this and any other Ordinance, the Common Law, the doctrines of equity, and the statutes of general application in force in England on the 1st day of January, 1880, shall be in force in Sierra Leone " [C.O., s. 37].

Certain Acts of the United Kingdom Parliament, enacted after 1880, have been expressly adopted, e.g., the Settled Land Act, 1884; the Larceny Act, 1916; the Supplies and Services (Transitional Powers) Act, 1945.

(10) Customary law.—" Nothing in this Ordinance shall deprive the Supreme Court and the Magistrates' Courts when determining matters arising in the Protectorate in their civil jurisdiction, of the right to observe and enforce the observance of, or shall deprive any person of the benefit of, any law and custom existing in the Protectorate and not being repugnant to natural justice, equity and good conscience, nor incompatible, either directly or by necessary implication, with any Ordinance applying to the Protectorate. Such native customary law shall, except where the circumstances, nature or justice of the case shall otherwise require, be deemed applicable in all causes and matters where the parties thereto are natives, and also in causes and matters between natives and non-natives where it shall appear to the Court that substantial injustice would be done to any party by a strict adherence to the rules of any law other than native customary law.

Provided that no party shall be entitled to claim the benefit of any local law or custom if it shall appear either from the express contract, or from the nature of the transaction out of which any cause or matter may have arisen that such party agreed that his obligations in connection with such transactions should be regulated exclusively by English law; and in cases where no express rule is applicable to any matter in controversy, the Court shall be governed by the principles of justice, equity and good conscience " [C.O., s. 38].

(11) Islamic or other law.—The only specific mention of Islamic law in the Ordinances of Sierra Leone is in the Mohammedan Marriage Ordinance, No. 20 of 1905 [now cap. 96 of the Laws of Sierra Leone, 1959]. The relevant provision is that of s. 3 which stipulates that " proof according to Mohammedan Law of the existence, past or present, of a Mohammedan marriage, or of the dissolution of a Mohammedan marriage, shall be received in evidence by all the Courts in the Colony and by any person having, by law or consent of parties, authority to hear and examine witnesses ".

A. 3 MAGISTRATES' COURTS

CONSTITUTION AND POWERS

(1) Establishment.—These are also established under the Courts

Ordinance [ss. 26–35, as subsequently amended]. Sierra Leone is divided into Judicial Districts and a Magistrate's Court is established in each of such Districts [C.O., ss. 26, 27,].

(2) Composition.—Duly constituted when presided over by a Police Magistrate, a Provincial or a District Commissioner [C.O., s. 28].

(3) Jurisdiction—original.—The Criminal Procedure Ordinance, cap. 39, applies to the Magistrates' Courts in the exercise of their criminal jurisdiction, whereby cases are tried summarily. Subject to the provisions of s. 29 every Magistrate's Court has jurisdiction to hear and determine all civil and criminal matters arising within the district, or transferred to it by the Supreme Court, provided that:—

    (a) " the jurisdiction conferred by this section may be exercised in the Sherbro Judicial District by any Magistrate exercising jurisdiction therein, in respect of any civil or criminal matter arising in the Bonthe Judicial District ";

    (b) " the jurisdiction . . . may . . . be exercised in the Police District of Freetown by any Magistrate exercising jurisdiction therein, in respect of any civil or criminal matter arising within the area of the Lungi Airport in the Port Loko Judicial District . . . " [C.O., s. 30].

In addition to any other civil jurisdiction conferred upon Magistrates' Courts, every such Court has jurisdiction to hear and determine:—

    (a) *In the [former] Colony.*—Any cause other than an action founded upon libel, slander, false imprisonment, malicious prosecution, seduction, or breach of promise of marriage wherein the claim does not exceed £200 in value.

    (b) *In the [former] Protectorate.*—Any cause or matter other than libel, slander, etc., where such cause or matter is between:—

        (*i*) non-natives, or

        (*ii*) a native and a non-native, or

        (*iii*) a native and the holder of a trading licence although a native and arises out of the latter's trading, " wherein the claim . . . does not exceed £200, or, in claims for the recovery of possession, other than those under the Summary Ejectment (Protectorate) Ordinance, where the annual rental value does not exceed £100 " [C.O., s. 29 (1), (2)].

" No cause or matter which is within the civil jurisdiction of Magistrates' Courts or of the combined courts established under the Native Courts Ordinance, and to which one of the parties is a non-native, shall be instituted in any other court " [C.O., s. 29(3)].

(4) Jurisdiction—appellate.—Nil.

CONTROL OF COURTS

(5) Appeals from.—Appeals from the decisions of the Magistrates' Courts are heard and determined by the Supreme Court [C.O., s. 23; and Courts (Appeals) Ordinance, 1960, Part II].

(6) Review/revision.—Nil.

(7) Transfer.—The Supreme Court has power to transfer any civil cause before a Magistrate's Court either to the Supreme Court itself, or to another Magistrate's Court. Any criminal proceedings before a Magistrate's Court can be transferred from that Court to any other Magistrate's Court for hearing and determination there [C.O., s. 33(a), (b)].

(8) Inspection, supervision, etc.—Nil.

LAW TO BE ADMINISTERED

(9) General law

(10) Customary law } As for Supreme Court (see A. 2(9–11), p. 15, *ante*).

(11) Islamic or other law

B. NATIVE COURTS

CONSTITUTION AND POWERS

(1) Establishment.—Established under the Native Courts Ordinance, No. 40 of 1932, as amended and re-enacted as cap. 8 of the Laws of Sierra Leone, 1959. It must be read as one with the Protectorate Ordinance, cap. 60.

By s. 3 of the N.C.O., cap. 8, Native Courts have been established in each district of the former Protectorate and recognised for the administration of justice. (Note that there are no Native Courts in the former Colony.) These are:

(*i*) *The Native Appeal Courts.*—There appear to be two types:—

(a) The Chiefdom Court which hears and determines appeals from a Native Court constituted by a Section Chief [N.C.O., s. 12];

(b) Group Native Appeal Courts established under s. 14, which states that the Governor may, at the request of the tribal authorities of two or more chiefdoms, establish a Group Native Appeal Court for these chiefdoms.

(*ii*) *The Courts of the Native Chiefs* (hereinafter referred to as Native Courts).—Established by s. 3(1) of the N.C.O.

(*iii*) *Combined Courts.*—The establishment of the Combined Courts is provided for by s. 4 of the N.C.O., which stipulates that any Paramount Chief in whose Chiefdom a considerable number of non-natives have settled, may ask the District Commissioner to establish such a Court. The expression " non-native " means any person other than a native (i.e., any person who is a member of a race, tribe or community settled in Sierra Leone [Interpretation Ordinance, cap. 1]).

(2) Composition.—A Group Native Appeal Court consists of the Paramount Chief and one or more representatives of each Chiefdom of the group [N.C.O., s. 15].

Native Courts consist of the Native Courts as now existing according to native law and custom, and such other Native Courts as may be established under the Ordinance. Examples of the first are (a) Town

17

Headman's Court; (b) Sub-Chief's Court; (c) Chief's Court. [Fenton, J. S., *Outlines of Native Law in Sierra Leone*, p. 9].

The Combined Court comprises the Paramount Chief of the Chiefdom, and one non-native sitting as joint judge with him, or some other chief assistant [N.C.O., s. 4].

(3) Jurisdiction—original.—(*i*) *Group Native Appeal Court.*—Nil, but it has the same jurisdiction and powers exercised according to native law and custom by Native Courts generally [N.C.O., s. 17].

(*ii*) *Native Courts.*—Such Courts have jurisdiction according to law and custom:—

(a) to administer the estates of deceased persons, so far as they are situate within the jurisdiction of the Native Courts, where such deceased persons are natives, and

(b) to hear and determine:—(*i*) all civil cases triable by native law, arising exclusively between natives, other than a case between two or more Paramount Chiefs or Tribal Authorities about land, or a case in which a debt owing to him in connection with his trade is claimed by the holder of any trading licence; (*ii*) all criminal cases where the accused person, etc., is a native, except e.g., cases of murder and offences relating to unlawful societies; (*iii*) any cause or matter arising out of the provisions of any Ordinance which the Courts may be authorised to enforce [N.C.O., s. 7].

(*iii*) *Combined Courts.*—All civil cases between natives and non-natives where the value of the subject matter does not exceed £5, other than land cases and rent cases. All cases between natives and non-natives arising out of e.g., common assault, or the use of abusive language [N.C.O., s. 23].

(4) Jurisdiction—appellate.—(*i*) *Group Native Appeal Courts.*— These have the same jurisdiction and powers as the Native Courts generally, but an appeal court may pass such sentence as " the chiefdom of first instance could have done, or order such cause to be re-heard before the Chiefdom Court of first instance, or refer the cause to the District Commissioner " [N.C.O., s. 17].

(*ii*) *Native Courts* ⎫
(*iii*) *Combined Courts* ⎬ Nil.

CONTROL OF COURTS

(5) Appeals from.—There is no right of appeal from the Native Courts in civil cases, but the District Commissioner has power to review (see (6), *infra*). In criminal cases provision is made for all sentences exceeding 14 days' imprisonment to be reported to the District Commissioner by a method which is to operate as an appeal [N.C.O., s. 22(1), (2)].

In the case of a Combined Court, the Ordinance states that the judgment of such a Court should be binding on all parties if the judges are unanimous, but subject to review; if such judgment is not unanimous, then the matter may be brought before the Magistrate's Court [N.C.O., s. 24].

(6) Review/revision.—The District Commissioner is empowered to review and revise the decisions of Native and Combined Courts [N.C.O., s. 27(2)].

(7) Transfer.—The District Commissioner has access to all the Native Courts and Combined Courts, and in exercising his power, may transfer any cause or matter, either before trial or at any stage of the proceedings, to the Magistrate's Court [N.C.O., s. 27(2)(b)].

Where any cause or matter within the jurisdiction of a Native Court or a Combined Court:—

  (a) is refused hearing or determination by such Court, or
  (b) is unlikely in the opinion of the District Commissioner to receive a fair trial,

the District Commissioner must transfer that cause or matter to the Magistrate's Court in the district [N.C.O., s. 35].

(8) Inspection, supervision, etc.—The power of inspection of Native Courts' and Combined Courts' records is also vested in the District Commissioner [N.C.O., s. 27].

LAW TO BE ADMINISTERED

(9) General law.—Native Courts and Combined Courts can administer, *inter alia*, the provisions of any Ordinance which they may be authorised to do by an Order in Council under s. 11 of the N.C.O. [N.C.O., s. 7].

(10) Customary law.—" The Native Courts and the Combined Courts shall administer justice in accordance with native law and custom so far as the same is not repugnant to natural justice, equity and good conscience, or incompatible, either directly or indirectly, with any Ordinance applying to the Protectorate, but subject always to the provisions of this Ordinance " [N.C.O., s. 5].

GHANA[1]

It is necessary to set out both the previous legal and judicial system of Ghana, as it was before the introduction of the Republican Constitution on July 1, 1960, and the present system, because (a) the reported decisions of Ghana (and Gold Coast) courts, which form the basis of the present " common law " of Ghana, cannot be understood without a study of the statutory provisions upon which they were based, and (b) some of the pre-existing institutions and laws have been saved by the new Courts Act, 1960; e.g., by s. 154, the jurisdiction relating to Admiralty, probate, matrimonial, custody of infants and persons of unsound mind and other matters governed by the Courts Ordinance, ss. 15, 16 and 17, and the application of English statutes of general application under s. 83 of the Courts Ordinance, continue in conformity with the Ordinance until modified.

I. BEFORE JULY 1, 1960

For the purposes of the administration of justice, the whole of Ghana was divided into seven Judicial Divisions, namely Eastern, Central and Western Divisions, Southern Ghana, Ashanti Division, Brong-Ahafo Division and the Northern Region and Volta Divisions.

The courts established were—

A. Courts primarily administering the general law, viz.:—
    1. The Supreme Court, which consisted of:—
        (a) The High Court of Justice, and
        (b) The Court of Appeal.
    2. Magistrates' Courts.
    3. Juvenile Courts.
B. Courts primarily administering African customary law, viz.:—
    4. Native Courts.
    5. Local Courts.

The Supreme Court of Ghana was first established by Ordinance, No. 4 of 1853. It was brought up to date by the Courts Ordinance, cap. 4, No. 7 of 1935, which has subsequently been amended. The most recent and relevant ones were the Courts (Amendment) Ordinance, 1957; and the Courts (Amendment) Act, 1958. By the provisions of s. 2 of the Courts (Amendment) Ordinance, 1957, the Supreme Court was constituted a Court of Record and consisted of—

    (a) The Court of Appeal;
    (b) The High Court of Justice.

A. 1(a) THE PRIVY COUNCIL

The Privy Council was the final court from the decisions of the Court of Appeal.

---

[1] For diagram of courts system see p. 211, *post.*

A. 1(b) THE COURT OF APPEAL

CONSTITUTION AND POWERS

(1) Establishment.—The Court of Appeal was established in 1957 by (*i*) The Court of Appeal Ordinance, No. 35 of 1957; (*ii*) The Courts (Amendment) Ordinance, No. 17 of 1957; (*iii*) The Courts (Amendment) Act, No. 8 of 1957.

(2) Composition.—It consisted of the Chief Justice and not more than two Justices of Appeal, and of the Puisne Judges of the Supreme Court. It was duly constituted when presided over by not less than three of the judges of the Court of Appeal, of whom one must be the Chief Justice or a Justice of Appeal [C.(A.)A., s. 4].

(3) Jurisdiction—original.—Nil.

(4) Jurisdiction—appellate.—(*a*) *Civil.*—An appeal lay to the Court of Appeal from a Divisional Court (sitting in its original jurisdiction) in, e.g., the following cases:—

- (*i*) Claims exceeding £100, matrimonial matters, interlocutory matters.
- (*ii*) Appeals from the decisions of a Divisional Court on appeal from a Magistrate's or a Native Court [C.A.O., 1957, s. 4]. However, upon judicial interpretation of the words " where an appeal lies therefrom under any Ordinance ", it has been held that no appeal lies from such decisions of the Divisional Court, except in land suits. See, e.g. *Shippi and anor.* v. *Adjini* (1949), 12 W.A.C.A. 472.

(*b*) *Criminal.*—(*i*) A person convicted by or in a Divisional Court, or by any Judge, might appeal to the Court of Appeal on, e.g., the following grounds:

- (a) against conviction;
- (b) against sentence (with the Courts' leave) [C.A.O., 1957, ss. 9–12].

(*ii*) Further, the Court of Appeal could hear and determine appeals from the decisions of the Supreme (Divisional) Court in its appellate jurisdiction on a question of law (not including severity of sentence). The Appeal Court's permission must be obtained in the case of an appeal on question of fact [Criminal Procedure Code, cap. 10, s. 338].

CONTROL OF COURT

(5) Appeals from.—Appeals from the decisions of the Court of Appeal lay to the Privy Council. The appealable amount was £500 [Privy Council Appeals O-in-C, 1957, L.N. 215/57].

LAW TO BE ADMINISTERED

(9) General law.—As High Court (see A. 2(9), p. 24, *post*).

A. 2 THE HIGH COURT OF JUSTICE

CONSTITUTION AND POWERS

(1) Establishment.—The Supreme Court of Ghana was established by the Courts Ordinance, 1935 which was incorporated into the Courts Ordinance, 1951, cap. 4, as amended.

By the various provisions of the Courts (Amendment) Ordinance, 1957, the word " High " was substituted for the word " Supreme ".

(2) Composition.—By s. 3 of the Courts (Amendment) Act, 1957, the High Court of Justice consisted of the Chief Justice of Ghana, and so many Puisne Judges of the Supreme Court as the Governor General might from time to time appoint.

For the purposes of the administration of justice, the whole of Ghana was divided into Judicial Divisions, in each of which there was at least one Divisional Court [C.O., s. 22; C.(A.)A., 1958, s. 7]. A Divisional Court was constituted by one or two Puisne Judges.

In 1945 steps were taken to form a special division of the Supreme Court to deal with the problems of litigation over land. Such a Division was known as the " Lands Division ", and a Court of the Lands Division was called a " Land Court " [C.O., s. 24]. By the Commissioners of Assize and Civil Pleas Act, 1958, and in accordance with s. 56 of the Ghana (Constitution) Order in Council, 1957, the Governor-General might appoint persons to be known as Commissioners of Assize and Civil Pleas, who were to be attached to the High Court [Commissioners of Assize and Civil Pleas Act, No. 12 of 1958, s. 2(1)].

(3) Jurisdiction—original.—The High Court was a superior court of record, and had throughout Ghana power to exercise:—

(a) All the civil and criminal jurisdiction, powers and authorities vested in the High Court of Justice in England [C.O., s. 15, as amended, e.g., by the C.(A.)O., 1957, s. 5];

(b) Admiralty jurisdiction;

(c) All the powers and authorities vested in the Lord High Chancellor of England, e.g., with liberty to appoint guardians;

(d) (Subject to the C.O., 1951) jurisdiction " in Probate, Divorce and Matrimonial Causes . . . in conformity with the law and practice for the time being in force in England " [C.O., s. 17].

(e) Original jurisdiction in all proceedings in which the validity of any law is called in question [the Ghana (Constitution) O-in-C, 1957, s. 31(5)].

(f) It had jurisdiction in land cases between the chiefs of Southern Ghana, Ashanti, and the Northern Territories [C.O., s. 20].

The inherent jurisdiction of the Supreme Court was, however, removed in the following cases by special provisions in the Native Court Ordinances. Thus the Supreme Court was precluded from exercising jurisdiction:—

(a) In any civil cause or matter which the Court considered to be " properly cognizable " by a Native Court (e.g., in accordance with s. 58 of the Native Courts (Colony) Ordinance, Laws of the Gold Coast, 1951], or by a Local Court [the Local Courts Act, 1958, s. 55];

(b) In any cause affecting a person who appeared to the Court to be a juvenile [C.O., s. 65 as amended by the Juvenile Offenders Act, 1958, s. 2]; or

(c) to entertain causes and matters relating to elections and the constitutional relations of chiefs [C.O., s. 88].

Land Courts.—Land Courts had exclusive original jurisdiction in all causes and matters relating to the ownership, possession, or occupation of lands, e.g.:—

(a) where there was no Native Court competent to try the cause or matter;

(b) where the cause or matter had been transferred to the Land Court from a Native Court.

Commissioners of Assize and Civil Pleas.—The jurisdiction of a Commissioner of Assize and Civil Pleas was largely similar to that of a High Court Judge, subject to the following limitations. He was not required:—

(a) to try any criminal case where the maximum penalty on conviction was death or life imprisonment;

(b) to try any civil case where the amount claimed by the plaintiff exceeded £2,500;

(c) to entertain any application by way of *habeas corpus, certiorari, mandamus,* prohibition or information in the nature of *quo warranto;* or

(d) to hear any cause or matter in which the validity of any Act of Parliament was called in question [C.A.C.P.A., s. 4(1)].

(4) Jurisdiction—appellate.—The High Court in its appellate jurisdiction had power to hear and determine all appeals from the decisions of the Magistrates' Courts in civil and criminal causes [C.O., s. 39]. It could also hear and determine appeals from the decisions of the Juvenile Courts [C.O., ss. 68 and 73]. A Commissioner of Assize and Civil Pleas had no jurisdiction to hear any appeal from the Magistrates' Courts in any criminal cause or matter [C.A.C.P.A., s. 4(d)].

(*a*) *Civil.*—Appeals in civil causes lay to the Divisional Court of the High Court in the Judicial Division where the Magistrate's Court was exercising jurisdiction [C.A.C.P.A., s. 40].

(*b*) *Criminal.*—Appeals in criminal causes lay to the Divisional Courts in accordance with the provisions of the Criminal Procedure Code [C.A.C.P.A., s. 43].

CONTROL OF COURT

(5) Appeals from.—Appeals from the High Court of Justice lay to the Court of Appeal (see A. 1(b)(4), p. 21, *ante*).

(7) Transfer.—(*i*) Under s. 34 of the C.O., the Chief Justice had power to transfer, at any time and without application from any of the parties thereto, any cause or matter from:—

(a) a Judge to any other judge of the High Court;

(b) a Judge to any other Magistrate's Court. Such power is not to be exercised in any cause before a Magistrate sitting in an appellate capacity from a decision of a Native Court [C.O., s. 36].

(*ii*) Any Divisional Court might of its own motion, or on application, report any cause or matter for transfer to any other court.

(*iii*) A Judge of the Divisional Court was empowered to transfer any civil cause or matter to any other Magistrate's Court [C.O., s. 38], or he might also remit a civil cause or matter in any Magistrate's Court in the judicial division in which he was exercising jurisdiction, to any other Magistrate's Court in the same judicial division [C.(A.)O., 1954, s. 3].

(*iv*) A Judge of the Divisional Court had power to remit civil cases which he considered could be suitably tried by a Magistrate's Court C.(A.)O., 1954, s. 3].

(8) Inspection, supervision, etc.—The High Court had full power of supervision in respect of all proceedings in the subordinate courts [C.O., s. 58].

Law to be Administered

(9) General law.—" Subject to the terms of this or any other Ordinance, the common law, the doctrines of equity, and the statutes of general application which were in force in England on the 24th day of July, 1874, shall be in force within the jurisdiction of the Courts " [C.O., s. 83].

" All Imperial laws declared to extend or apply to the jurisdiction of the Courts shall be in force, so far only as the limits of local jurisdiction and local circumstances permit, and subject to any existing or future ordinances of the Colonial Legislature; and for the purpose of facilitating the application of the said Imperial laws, it shall be lawful for the said Courts to construe the same with such verbal alterations, not affecting the substance as may be necessary to render the same applicable to the matter before the Court; and every Judge, or person exercising judicial powers, Magistrate or officer of the Supreme Court having or exercising functions of the like kind, or analogous to the functions of any Judge or officer referred to in any such law, shall be deemed to be within the meaning of the enactments thereof relating to such last-mentioned Judge or officer; and whenever the Great Seal or any other seal is mentioned in any such statute it shall be read as if the seal of the Supreme Court or the seal of a Magistrate's Court were substituted therefor: and in matters of practice all documents may be written on ordinary paper, notwithstanding any practice or directions as to printing or engrossing on vellum, parchment or otherwise " [*ibid.*, s. 85].

" In every civil cause or matter . . . in any of the Courts, law and equity shall be administered concurrently . . . and in all matters in which there is any conflict or variance between the rules of equity and the rules of the common law with reference to the same matter, the rules of equity shall prevail " [*ibid.*, s. 86].

The effect of these three provisions was that " Courts " (i.e., the Supreme Court and Magistrates' Courts) were empowered to administer English law, etc. which was in force in England as at a particular date, and Ordinances and Acts of the local legislature. On the criminal side, the Supreme Court administered the Criminal Code.

(10) Customary law.—" Nothing in this Ordinance shall deprive the courts of the right to observe and enforce the observance or shall deprive any person of the benefit of any native law or custom existing in the Gold Coast, such law or custom not being repugnant to natural justice, equity and good conscience, nor incompatible either directly or by necessary implication with any ordinance for the time being in force. Such laws and customs shall be deemed applicable in causes and matters where the parties thereto are natives, and particularly, but without derogating from their application in other cases, in causes and matters relating to the tenure and transfer of real and personal property, and to inheritance and testamentary dispositions, and also in causes and matters between natives and non-natives where it may appear to the Court that substantial injustice would be done to either party by a strict adherence to the rules of English law. No party shall be entitled to claim the benefit of any local law or custom, if it shall appear either from express contract or from the nature of the transactions out of which any suit in question may have arisen, that such party agreed that his obligations in connection with such transactions should be regulated exclusively by English law; and in such cases where no express rule is applicable to any matter in controversy, the court shall be governed by the principles of justice, equity and good conscience " [C.O., s. 87(1)].

The effect of this provision was that the Supreme Court was empowered to enforce the observance of customary law in cases where the parties were Africans, and it was not contrary to natural justice, equity and good conscience, or to any express enactment. Indeed, even where one party was not an African, the strict enforcement of the English law was not required where substantial injustice would be done. On the other hand, where it appeared that parties, even though African, intended their obligations to be governed by English law, the customary law was inapplicable.

(11) Islamic or other law.—In Ghana there is no legislation expressly authorising the application of Islamic law as such, except within the terms of the Marriage of Mohammedans Ordinance [Laws of the Gold Coast, 1951, cap. 129], s. 9 of which stipulates:—

' No marriage contracted or divorce effected in the Gold Coast by persons professing the Mohammedan faith shall be valid unless registered under this Ordinance."

This provision is regularly disregarded. In the Supreme Court Islamic law might on occasion be applied, not as native law but as required by " justice, equity and good conscience ". (For a detailed account, see Anderson, J. N. D., *Islamic Law in Africa*, pp. 249–286.)

A. 3 MAGISTRATES' COURTS

CONSTITUTION AND POWERS

(1) Establishment.—Throughout Ghana there were local courts of summary jurisdiction subordinate to the Supreme Court established under the Courts Ordinance. The word " Magistrate " included in this context a Senior Magistrate, a District Magistrate, and a Government Agent when performing any of the functions of a District Magistrate, or any other officer when performing any of the magisterial functions of such a Commissioner [C.(A.)O., 1954, s. 2].

(2) Composition.—A Magistrate's Court was duly constituted when presided over by a Magistrate, in some places by a Stipendiary Senior

Magistrate, or a District Magistrate; and in others by a Government Agent sitting as a Magistrate [C.O., s. 44, as amended by the Courts (Jurisdiction of Government Agents) Order, No. 109 of 1951].

(3) Jurisdiction—original.—Magistrates' Courts exercised summary jurisdiction throughout Ghana. Under s. 48 of the C.O., 1951, every District Magistrate within his magisterial district had jurisdiction original and appellate, e.g., in all civil suits in which the matter involved did not exceed the value of £150. In the case of a Senior Magistrate the maximum amount was £300 [C.(A.)O., 1954].

On the criminal side, District Magistrates or certain Government agents had jurisdiction to hear and determine, e.g., all offences punishable under any Ordinance, or under certain sections of the Criminal Code, by fine not exceeding £100, or imprisonment for twelve months or both [C.O., s. 49, Order No. 27 of 1942]. In the case of Senior Magistrates' Courts the maximum punishment was by fine not exceeding £500, or imprisonment not exceeding five years or by both [C.(A.)O., 1954, s. 6].

In addition to the jurisdiction conferred by any other Act, every District Magistrate had and exercised the jurisdiction of the High Court to hear and determine offences under s. 468 of the Criminal Code (which relates to poisons intended for any illegal purpose) any rule of law to the contrary notwithstanding. This did not apply to Government Agents sitting as Magistrates [District Magistrates (Extended Jurisdiction) Act, No. 60 of 1959, s. 2(1)(2)].

(4) Jurisdiction—appellate.—Under s. 51 of the C.O. and s. 48 of the Local Courts Act, 1958, District Magistrates' Courts had power to hear and determine appeals from Native Courts and the Local Courts respectively [see (5), *infra*], in civil causes other than land and succession causes, in which the subject matter of the cause was valued at £10 or more; and in criminal causes in which a sentence or imprisonment, or a fine exceeding £10 was imposed [Local Courts Act, 1958, s. 48(1)].

CONTROL OF COURTS

(5) Appeals from.—Appeals lay from Magistrates' Courts to the High Court (see A. 2(4), p. 23, *ante*).

(6) Review/revision.—Under s. 39 of the C.O., the High Court had authority to exercise full power of supervision and revision in respect of all proceedings in the Magistrates' Courts. Upon receipt of the monthly list of criminal cases from the Magistrates' Courts, a Judge might if he thought fit revise the decisions of such courts [C.O., ss. 57 and 58].

(7) Transfer.—Every Magistrate's Court might report causes, whether civil or criminal to be transferred to another court [C.O., s. 36]. No court of summary jurisdiction other than a Juvenile Court was to hear any charge against a person who appeared to the Court to be a juvenile. In every such case, the Court was to make an order transferring the charge to the Juvenile Court [C.O., s. 65].

LAW TO BE ADMINISTERED

(9) General law

(10) Customary

(11) Islamic or other law

} As High Court(see A.2 (9–11), pp. 24–25, *ante*), but within the limits of their jurisdiction.

B. 1 NATIVE COURTS

CONSTITUTION AND POWERS

(1) Establishment.—There were also Native Courts established under the following Ordinances (to be found in the Laws of the Gold Coast, 1951, revised), namely:—

(*i*) Native Courts (Colony) Ordinance, cap. 98.

(*ii*) Native Courts (Ashanti) Ordinance, cap. 99.

(*iii*) Native Courts (Northern Territories) Ordinance, cap. 104.

(*iv*) Native Courts (Southern section of Togoland) Ordinance, cap. 106.

As can be seen, these separate Ordinances operated within each of the seven Judicial Divisions in Ghana mentioned earlier. There was thus no uniform system of native courts extending throughout the country. These courts were traditional institutions which were controlled and developed to meet the needs of the present times. The organisation of the courts was in the past closely linked with that of the Native Authorities.

(2) Composition.—Until recently, the Court members were almost exclusively chiefs and their elders. This system still operated in Northern Ghana, where the personnel of the Court consisted of " Head Chiefs, sub-divisional Chiefs or a sub-divisional Chief, or chiefs of a chief, or any other person or persons, or a combination of any such authorities and persons " [Native Courts (Northern Territories) Ordinance, cap. 104, s. 4(1)].

In Ashanti and Brong-Ahafo the position was similar, but in Southern Ghana and Southern Togoland non-chiefs were increasingly and extensively appointed as members of courts.

(3) Jurisdiction—original.—Native Courts had jurisdiction over the following persons:—

(a) Persons of African descent who were normally subject to African customary law.

(b) Persons whether of African descent or not whom the Governor-General had directed to be subject to the jurisdiction of a Native Court.

(c) Persons, whether of African descent or not, who had at any time instituted proceedings in any Native Court [N.C.(C.)O., cap. 98, Laws of the Gold Coast (1951), s. 10].

Public officers acting in their official capacity were not subject to the jurisdiction of Native Courts [N.C.(C.)O., s. 12].

The area of jurisdiction roughly coincided with the area of the Local Council Authority.

Every Native Court had full jurisdiction in all civil and criminal causes in which the parties were subject to their jurisdiction. On the civil side they had exclusive jurisdiction in suits between Africans concerning marriage, customary rights in land and succession of property, and in some other personal suits where the highest amount involved did not exceed £100. Their criminal jurisdiction included offences under a number of Ordinances, local authority by-laws as well as customary offences.

Courts in each of the territories were usually divided into four grades, namely grades A, B, C and D (in the Northern Territories there were only three). In comparing the powers of the Courts it should be noted that the grades did not directly correspond. The extent of the jurisdiction was usually set out in the Schedule to the Native Court Ordinances. To take an example from the N.C.(C.)O., cap. 98 as amended:

Criminal	Grade A	Grade B	Grade C	Grade D
Putting any person into fetish	A fine not exceeding £50 or by imprisonment for a term not exceeding 6 months	£25 or 3 months imprisonment	£10 or 2 months imprisonment	£2 or 1 month imprisonment

Civil	Grade A	Grade B	Grade C	Grade D
Suits relating to occupation of land	Unlimited	Unlimited	No jurisdiction	No jurisdiction
Personal suits	Where the debt or damage does not exceed £100	£50	£25	£10

As a rule, Native Courts were not allowed to hear causes of a constitutional nature (e.g., N.C. (Ashanti) O., cap. 99, s. 8).

(4) Jurisdiction—appellate.—The Governor-General had power to appoint any Native Court to be a court of appeal within the area of its jurisdiction, (e.g., N.C. (Ashanti) O., s. 24), to which appeals lay from the lower courts. On the civil side the channel of appeal depended on whether the cause was about land or not.

Where there was no Native Court, appeals from the lower courts lay to the Magistrate's Court and then to the Divisional Courts. Where the suit was a land suit, an appeal lay in such a case to the Land Court, and then to the Court of Appeal.

CONTROL OF COURTS

(5) Appeals from.—The system of appeals is detailed below. The example taken from p. 12 of the *Report of the Commission on Native Courts*, 1951, and modified, will clarify the position.

Southern Ghana and Southern Togoland :—

- (a) *Civil cases not about land.*—Native Court (grade A, B, C or D): Native Appeal Court (if any, and if court below is of grade B, C or D).
- (b) *Civil cases about land.*—Native Court (grade A or B): Native Appeal Court (if any, and if court below is of grade B): Land Court: Court of Appeal: Privy Council.
- (c) *Criminal cases.*—Native Court (grade A, B, C or D): Native Appeal Court (if any, and if court below is of grade B, C or D): Magistrate's Court: Divisional Court of the High Court.

In criminal cases, an appeal from a Native Court of first instance in the Colony of Southern Togoland lay to the Native Appeal Court (if any), thence to the Magistrate's Court, thence to the High Court. In Ashanti and the Northern Territories, Native Appeal Courts had no appellate jurisdiction in criminal cases, otherwise the ladder of appeal was the same.

In civil cases not about land, the right of appeal in all regions was the same as that in criminal cases in Southern Ghana. In civil land cases, an appeal lay from a Native Court of first instance to a Native Court of Appeal, thence to the Supreme Court, and to the Court of Appeal, and, finally to the Privy Council.

(6) Review/revision.—The Registrars of Native Courts were under a duty to submit monthly returns of all causes decided by him to the Senior Government Agent of the district for review [e.g. Native Courts (Southern Section of Togoland Ordinance), cap. 106, ss. 59 and 61].

Mention must also be made of the Judicial Adviser. The office was introduced in 1944. A Judicial Adviser was appointed to each of the territories. In Togoland, for example, a Judicial Adviser might of his own motion review any cause or matter determined by a Native Court [N.C.(S.S. of T.)O., s. 60].

(7) Transfer.—The power of transfer was vested in different authorities. The system operating in Southern Ghana, and Southern Togoland seems to be the most clearly defined. For example:—

(*i*) Under s. 54 of the N.C.(C.)O., " A Magistrate's Court [" Magistrate's Court " means in this context a Magistrate's Court constituted by the Government Agent] may either of its own motion or on the application of either party to a cause or matter by order stop the hearing of any cause, matter or question before any Native Court " and transfer it to the appropriate court under certain conditions. Note that in the case of land suits or suits within the jurisdiction of the Divisional Court, the Magistrate's Court did not transfer it, but reported the pendency and the circumstances to the land judge in the case of a land suit, or to the Chief Justice in a non-land suit and the land judge or the Chief Justice might then transfer and direct where it should be tried.

(*ii*) A grade A Native Court had power to remit causes to a lower grade Native Court within its territorial jurisdiction, or to transfer it to a higher grade Native Court [N.C.(C.)O., ss. 56 and 57].

(*iii*) Whenever it appeared to any court that any civil cause or matter brought before it was one properly cognizable by a Native

Court, the court was required to stop it and refer the parties to a competent Native Court [N.C.(C.)O., s. 58].

(8) Inspection, supervision, etc.—This work was specifically assigned to the Judicial Advisers. Their full duties were described in Gazette Notice 2508/50, three of which were:—

(*i*) To carry out inspections of the Native Courts.
(*ii*) To supervise the drafting of amendments to the N.C.O.
(*iii*) To examine the development of native customary law.

Law to be Administered

(9) General law.—A number of ordinances contained provisions empowering Native Courts to apply them in whole or in part, e.g., the Native Authority (Colony) Ordinance, 1944, and the Moneylenders Ordinance (cap. 176). Orders were also made empowering Native Courts in one or more territories to enforce specific provisions of the following: the Criminal Code, Book 2, excluding Title 12; the Mosquitoes Ordinance (cap. 75).

(10) Customary law.—"Subject to the provisions of this Ordinance a Native Court shall administer the native customary law prevailing within the jurisdiction of the Native Court so far as it is not repugnant to natural justice, equity and good conscience nor incompatible either directly or by necessary implication with any Ordinance for the time being in force " [N.C.(C.)O., s. 15]. Similar provisions are enacted for the other territories.

(11) Islamic or other law.—The general impression gained after reading Anderson, J. N. D., *Islamic Law in Africa*, pp. 249–286, is that Native Courts rarely administered Islamic law as such. However, the Native Courts administered " Islamic law " particularly in marriage and succession causes, since in some areas it is the customary law prevailing among a section of the people.

B. 2 LOCAL COURTS

As a result of the recommendations embodied in the Report of the Commission on Native Courts (1951), the Local Courts Act was passed in 1958 to provide for the establishment of Local Courts in place of Native Courts [No. 23 of 1958].

" We consider the name ' Native Courts ' should be discarded for the main reason that the term is misleading when applied to the new Courts. The expression may have been an appropriate description of the customary tribunals both before and after 1883, but . . . the present Native Courts have already got past this state, and the term is quite inappropriate for the new Courts . . . " [*Report of the Commission on Native Courts*, p. 24].

The Local Courts Act, 1958, has since been repealed and replaced by the Courts Act, 1960, ss. 91–149 of which deal more specifically with Local Courts. The pre-1960 law has been retained basically unaltered, and details of it are given at II. Republic of Ghana, p. 31, *post*.

II. REPUBLIC OF GHANA

By art. 4 of the Constitution of the Republic of Ghana, Ghana became a sovereign unitary republic on July 1, 1960. In accordance with the provisions of art. 41 of the Constitution, the Courts Act, 1960, C.A.9 was enacted to operate from July 1, 1960.[1]

The courts system consists of:—

A. Courts primarily administering the general law, viz.:—

    (1) The Supreme Court (Final Court of Appeal).
    (2) The High Court.
    (3) Circuit Courts.
    (4) District Courts.
    (5) Juvenile Courts;

B. Courts primarily administering African customary law, viz.:—

    (6) Local Courts.

A. 1 THE SUPREME COURT

CONSTITUTION AND POWERS

(1) Establishment.—Established by art. 41 of the Constitution.

(2) Composition.—When sitting, it comprises three or five Judges of the Supreme Court, including the Chief Justice, provided that the Supreme Court shall be deemed to be duly constituted notwithstanding that it includes a Judge of the High Court or temporary Judge, or that a vacancy occurs in the office of the Chief Justice [C.A., s. 7(1)]. There are five Supreme Court Judges altogether, including the Chief Justice.

(3) Jurisdiction—original.—Constitutional questions as to whether legislation is *ultra vires* [Constitution, art. 42(2)].

(4) Jurisdiction—appellate.—The appellate jurisdiction of the Supreme Court consists of:—

    " (a) The hearing of appeals from any judgment of the High Court in any civil cause; or
    (b) the hearing of appeals from any decision of a High or Circuit Court in a criminal matter exercised in accordance with the provisions of this Act or any other enactment.
    (c) the hearing of appeals from any decision given by the High Court in any other matter whatsoever; and
    (d) any other jurisdiction conferred by this Act or any other enactment:—

Provided that:—

    (a) an appeal shall lie to the Supreme Court from a judgment of the High Court in the exercise of its appellate jurisdiction on any matter except a matter arising out of a criminal case:—

        (*i*) where the High Court has affirmed the decision of the Court from which the appeal is made to the High Court, by special leave of the High Court, and

---

[1] " C.A.9 " is used to denote 9th Act of the Constituent Assembly.

(*ii*) where the High Court has reversed or materially altered the decision of the Court from which the appeal is made to the High Court upon the High Court giving leave to appeal from its judgment upon like terms and subject to the like conditions as if the judgment had been given in a suit or matter originating in the High Court; and

(b) no appeal shall lie except by special leave of the High Court or of the Supreme Court from an order made *ex parte* or by consent or as to costs only.

Any judgment of the Supreme Court shall be executed and enforced as if it were an original judgment of the Court from which the appeal is made to the Supreme Court " [C.A., s. 8(1)(2)].

" A person convicted by the High Court or a Circuit Court or a person whose conviction by any other Court is affirmed by such Court may appeal to the Supreme Court:—

(a) against his conviction on any ground of appeal which involves a question of law alone;

(b) with the leave of the Supreme Court or upon a certificate of the judge who tried him that it is a fit case for appeal against his conviction on any ground of appeal which involves a question of fact alone or a question of mixed law and fact or any other ground which appears to the Supreme Court to be a sufficient ground of appeal and

(c) with leave of the Supreme Court against the sentence passed on his conviction unless the sentence is one fixed by law " [C.A., s. 14].

' Notwithstanding anything to the contrary in any other provision of this Act, the Supreme Court may entertain any appeal from any Court on any terms which it may think just " [C.A., s.13].

LAW TO BE ADMINISTERED

(9) General law

(10) Customary law } As High Court, *infra*.

(11) Islamic or other law

A. 2 THE HIGH COURT

CONSTITUTION AND POWERS

(1) Establishment.—Established by the Constitution, art. 41.

(2) Composition.—When sitting, it consists of the Chief Justice, or any judge of the Supreme Court or temporary judge or Circuit Judge requested to do so by the Chief Justice [C.A., s. 28(1)(2)]. Subject to the foregoing, the High Court is duly constituted when it consists of one or three Judges [C.A., s. 30]. Judges of the High Court have equal powers [C.A., s. 32]. The total number of High Court Judges is nine.

(3) Jurisdiction—original.—The High Court has jurisdiction in all matters except where an enactment is alleged to be *ultra vires* [C.A., s. 29(a)].

" Notwithstanding the repeal of the enactments referred to in section 156[1] of this Act, every statutory instrument made under those enactments and in force on the day immediately before the commencement of this Act shall, until such instrument is altered, revoked or otherwise modified under this Act, continue in force as if such instrument had been made under this Act.

Notwithstanding the repeal by this Act of section 15 of the Courts Ordinance (Cap. 4), the Admiralty jurisdiction referred to in that section shall continue to apply in Ghana until other provision in that behalf is made by law, and in so far as section 85 of that Ordinance applie heretofore in relation to the said section 15 in respect of such jurisdicti it shall continue so to apply notwithstanding its repeal by this Act

Notwithstanding the repeal by this Act of sections 16 and 17 Courts Ordinance (Cap. 4) [which relate to infants and person sound mind and to probate and matrimonial causes respective   se sections shall continue to apply in Ghana until other provis   made by law, and in so far as section 85 of that Ordinance appli   retofore in relation to those sections, it shall continue so to a y notwithstanding its repeal by this Act " [C.A., s. 154(1), (2), (3)].

The High Court has no jurisdiction to entertain any civil cause or matter instituted for:—

    (a) the trial of any question relating to the election, installation, deposition or abdication of any Chief whatsoever;

    (b) the recovery or delivery of stool or skin property in connection with any such election, installation, deposition or abdication; or

    (c) the trial of any question touching the political or constitutional relations subsisting according to customary law between such Chiefs [C.A., s. 41(a)–(c)].

(4) Jurisdiction—appellate.—The High Court has appellate jurisdiction from any decision, other than a decision in a criminal case, of a Circuit Court; and any other jurisdiction conferred by the Courts Act or any other enactment for the time being in force [C.A., s. 29(b), (c)].

CONTROL OF COURTS

(5) Appeals from.—Appeals from the High Court in both civil and criminal causes lie to the Supreme Court [C.A., ss. 8(1), (14)].

(6) Review/revision.—Nil.

(7) Transfer.—The Chief Justice may by order at any time or stage and either with or without application from any of the parties, transfer any cause or matter from a Judge of a Court to any other Judge of such Court [C.A., s. 42(1)].

Any Judge of the High Court may himself or on application of any person concerned, report to the Chief Justice any case, civil or

---

[1] Enactments repealed include the Courts Ordinance 1951, the Court of Appeal Ordinance, No. 35 of 1957, and the Local Courts Act, No. 23 of 1958.

criminal, pending before him for transfer to any other Court or Judge [C.A., s. 43]. A Judge of the High Court is empowered to remit any civil cause pending before him to a Circuit or District Court if he thinks fit [C.A., s. 45(1)].

(8) Inspection, supervision, etc.—Nil.

LAW TO BE ADMINISTERED

(9) General law.—See under (10), below.

(10) Customary law.—" (1) Subject to the provisions of any enactment other than this subsection, in deciding whether an issue arising in civil proceedings is to be determined according to the common law or customary law and, if the issue is to be determined according to customary law, in deciding which system of customary law is applicable, the court shall be guided by the following rules in which references to the personal law of a person are references to the system of customary law to which he is subject or, if he is not shown to be subject to customary law, are references to the common law:—

Rule 1. Where two persons have the same personal law one of them cannot, by dealing in a manner regulated by some other law with property in which the other has a present or expectant interest, alter or affect that interest to an extent which would not in the circumstances be open to him under his personal law.

Rule 2. Subject to Rule 1, where an issue arises out of a transaction the parties to which have agreed, or may from the form or nature of the transaction be taken to have agreed, that such an issue should be determined according to the common law or any system of customary law effect should be given to the agreement.

In this rule " transaction " includes a marriage and an agreement or arrangement to marry.

Rule 3. Subject to Rule 1, where an issue arises out of any unilateral disposition and it appears from the form or nature of the disposition or otherwise that the person effecting the disposition intended that such an issue should be determined according to the common law or any system of customary law effect should be given to the intention.

Rule 4. Subject to the foregoing rules, where an issue relates to entitlement to land on the death of the owner or otherwise relates to title to land:—

    (a) if all the parties to the proceedings who claim to be entitled to the land or a right relating thereto trace their claims from one person who is subject to customary law, or from one family or other group of persons all subject to the same customary law, the issue should be determined according to that law;

    (b) if the said parties trace their claims from different persons, or families or other groups of persons, who are all subject to the same customary law, the issue should be determined according to that law;

    (c) in any other case, the issue should be determined according to the law of the place in which the land is situated.

Rule 5. Subject to Rules 1 and 3, where an issue relates to the devolution of the property (other than land) of a person on his death it should be determined according to his personal law.

Rule 6. Subject to the foregoing rules, an issue should be determined according to the common law unless the plaintiff is subject to any system of customary law and claims to have the issue determined according to that system, when it should be so determined.

(2) Where under this section customary law is applicable in any proceedings but a relevant rule of customary law has been assimilated by the common law under any enactment such as is mentioned in section 18(1) of the Interpretation Act, 1960, that rule shall nevertheless apply in those proceedings, but in the form in which it has been so assimilated.

(3) Notwithstanding anything contained in the foregoing provisions of this section, but subject to the provisions of any other enactment:—

    (a) the rules of the common law relating to private international law shall apply in any proceedings in which an issue concerning the application of law prevailing in any country outside Ghana is raised;

    (b) the rules of estoppel and such other of the rules generally known as the common law and the rules generally known as the doctrines of equity as have heretofore been treated as applicable in all proceedings in Ghana shall continue to be so treated." [C.A., s. 66 (1), (2), (3)].

" (1) Any question as to the existence or content of a rule of customary law is a question of law for the Court and not a question of fact.

(2) If the Court entertains any doubt as to the existence or content of a rule of customary law relevant in any proceedings after considering such submissions thereon as may be made by or on behalf of the parties and consulting such reported cases, text-books and other sources as may be appropriate, the Court shall adjourn the proceedings to enable an inquiry to take place under the next subsection.

(3) The inquiry shall be held as part of the proceedings in such manner as the Court considers expedient, and the provisions of this Act relating to the attendance and testimony of witnesses shall apply for the purpose of the tendering of opinions to the Court at the inquiry, but shall apply subject to such modifications as may appear to the Court to be necessary:—

Provided that:—

    (a) The decision as to the persons who are to be heard at the inquiry shall be one for the Court, after hearing such submissions thereon as may be made by or on behalf of the parties;

    (b) the Court may request a House of Chiefs, State Council or other body possessing knowledge of the customary law in question to state its opinion, which may be laid before the inquiry in written form " [C.A., s. 67(1), (2), (3)].

" The repeal by this Act of section 83 of the Courts Ordinance (Cap. 4) shall not be taken to affect the continued application of such of the statutes of general application which were in force in England on

24th July, 1874 as applied in Ghana immediately before the commencement of this Act:

Provided that the said statutes shall be subject to such modifications as may be requisite to enable them to be conveniently applied in Ghana " [C.A., s. 154(4)].

" The common law, as comprised in the laws of Ghana, consists, in addition to the rules of law generally known as the common law, of the rules generally known as the doctrines of equity and of rules of customary law included in the common law under any enactment[1] providing for the assimilation of such rules of customary law as are suitable for general application.

In the case of inconsistency, an assimilated rule shall prevail over any other rule, and a rule of equity shall prevail over any rule other than an assimilated rule.

While any of the statutes of general application continue to apply by virtue of the Courts Act, 1960 [see 9th Act of Constituent Assembly] they shall be treated as if they formed part of the common law, as defined in subsection (1), prevailing over any rule thereof other than an assimilated rule.

In deciding upon the existence or content of a rule of the common law, as so defined, the Court may have regard to any exposition of that rule by a court exercising jurisdiction in any country.

A reference in an enactment to the common law shall be construed as a reference to it as affected by any enactment for the time being in force [Interpretation Act, 1960, s. 17].

" Customary law, as comprised in the laws of Ghana, consists of rules of law which by custom are applicable to particular communities in Ghana, not being rules included in the common law under any enactment providing for the assimilation of such rules of customary law as are suitable for general application.

A reference in an enactment to a customary law shall be construed as a reference to it as affected by any enactment for the time being in force " [The Interpretation Act, 1960, s. 18(1), (2)].

(11) Islamic or other law.—See under I. Before July 1, 1960, A. 2(11), p. 25, *ante*. Note that, under the above definition of customary law, Islamic law would be treated as customary law if a particular community in Ghana were shown to practise it.

A. 3 CIRCUIT COURTS

Constitution and Powers

(1) Establishment.—Established by the Courts Act, 1960 [C.A.9., ss. 36–41]. The Chief Justice may by legislative instrument order the division of the Republic into Circuits with such limits as may be specified therein [C.A., s. 36].

(2) Composition.—There shall be in respect of each circuit a Circuit Court to which shall be assigned by the Chief Justice a Circuit Judge appointed under any other enactment for the time being in force (i.e., the Judicial Service Act, 1960 (C.A.10)) [C.A., s. 36].

---

[1] No such enactment yet exists.

(3) Jurisdiction—original.—" The jurisdiction of a Circuit Court shall consist of:—

(a) an original jurisdiction in civil matters:—

    (*i*) in all personal suits, arising under contract or tort, or for the recovery of any liquidated sum, where the amount claimed is not more than £G500,

    (*ii*) in all suits between landlord and tenant for the possession of land claimed under lease and refused to be delivered up, where the annual value or rent does not exceed £G500,

    (*iii*) to appoint guardians of infants and to make orders for the custody of infants,

    (*iv*) to grant in any suit instituted in the Court injunctions or orders to stay waste or alienation, or for the detention and preservation of any property the subject of that suit, or to restrain breaches of contracts or torts, and

    (*v*) in all claims for relief by way of interpleader in respect of land or other property attached in execution of a decree made by a Circuit Court provided that the jurisdiction conferred by this paragraph shall not, unless the parties consent, be exercisable in respect of land or other property exceeding £G500;

(b) an original jurisdiction in criminal matters in the case of offences, other than offences where the maximum punishment

(c) . . . is death or life imprisonment;

(d) any other jurisdiction conferred by this Act or any other enactment " [C.A., s. 39(1)(a), (b), (d)].

A Circuit Court has no jurisdiction in any civil cause instituted for:—

(a) the trial of any question relating to the election, installation, deposition or abdication of any Chief whatsoever;

(b) the recovery or delivery of stool or skin property in connection with any such election, installation, deposition or abdication; or

(c) the trial of any question touching the political or constitutional relations subsisting according to customary law between such Chiefs.

(4) Jurisdiction—appellate.—A Circuit Court has appellate jurisdiction from decisions of any District Court situated within its circuit [C.A., s. 39(1)(c)].

CONTROL OF COURTS

(5) Appeals from.—Appeals from a Circuit Court in civil causes lie to the High Court [C.A., s. 40]. Appeals from a Circuit Court in criminal matters lie to the Supreme Court [C.A., s.8(1)(b)].

(6) Review/revision.—The High Court has full powers of supervision and revision in respect of all proceedings in Circuit Courts, except proceedings in Circuit Courts in criminal cases [C.A., s. 31].

(7) Transfer.—The Chief Justice may by order at any time or stage and either with or without the application of any of the parties, transfer any cause or matter from a Judge of a Court to any other Judge of such Court [C.A.9, s. 42(1)].

(8) Inspection, supervision, etc.—See A. 3(6), above.

LAW TO BE ADMINISTERED

(9) General law
(10) Customary law   } As High Court (see A. 2(9)–(11),
(11) Islamic or other law   pp. 34–36, *ante*).

A. 4 DISTRICT COURTS

CONSTITUTION AND POWERS

(1) Establishment.—Established by the Courts Act, 1960 [ss.47– 64]. The Chief Justice may by legislative instrument order the division of the Republic into Districts with such limits as may be specified therein [C.A., s. 47].

(2) Composition.—There shall be in respect of each district a District Court to which shall be assigned by the Chief Justice a District Magistrate [C.A., s. 48].

(3) Jurisdiction—original.—(*i*) *Civil.*—" (a) in all personal suits, arising under contract or tort, or for the recovery of any liquidated sum, where the amount claimed is not more than £G150;

(b) in all suits between landlord and tenant for the possession of land claimed under lease and refused to be delivered up, where the annual value or rent does not exceed £G150;

(c) to appoint guardians of infants and to make orders for the custody of infants;

(d) to grant in any suit instituted in the Court injunctions or orders to stay waste or alienation, or for the detention and preservation of any property the subject of that suit, or to restrain breaches of contracts or torts;

(e) in all claims for relief by way of interpleader in respect of land or other property attached in execution of a decree made by a District Court provided that the jurisdiction conferred by this paragraph shall not, unless the parties consent, be exercisable in respect of land or other property exceeding £G150 in value " [C.A., s. 52(a)–(e)].

A District Court has no jurisdiction to entertain any civil cause or matter instituted for:—

  (*i*) the trial of any question relating to the election, installation, deposition or abdication of any Chief;
  (*ii*) the recovery or delivery of stool or skin property in connection with any such election, installation, deposition, or abdication;
  (*iii*) the trial of any question touching the political or constitutional relations subsisting according to customary law between such Chiefs [C.A., s. 50(1)–(3)].

(*ii*) *Criminal*—(a)—Jurisdiction to try summarily:—

(*i*) " an offence punishable by fine not exceeding £G100 or imprisonment for a term not exceeding 12 months or both; "

(*ii*) " an indictable offence other than an offence punishable by death or punishable on first conviction by imprisonment for a term of not more than seven years if the Court having regard to the nature of the offence, the absence of circumstances which would render the offence of a grave or serious character and all other circumstances of the case is of opinion that the case is suitable to be tried summarily; "

(*iii*) an attempt to commit an offence to which paragraph (*i*) or (*ii*) applies;

(*iv*) abetment of or conspiracy in respect of any such offence.

(b) Subject to subsection (3) (which deals with previous convictions) a District Court cannot impose imprisonment for a term exceeding twelve months or a fine exceeding £G100 [C.A., s. 52(1), (2)].

(4) Jurisdiction—appellate.—A District Court has jurisdiction to hear appeals from any Local Court within the district, except in land cases [C.A., s. 51].

CONTROL OF COURTS

(5) Appeals from.—Appeals from any decision of a District Court lie to the Circuit Court of the circuit in which such District Court is situated [C.A., s. 63].

(6) Review/revision.—Every District Magistrate must forward a monthly list of all criminal cases decided by him to the Circuit Court in which the court of such Magistrate is situated [C.A., s. 59]. A Circuit Judge, upon receipt of that list, has power to revise the decisions of such District Magistrate [C.A., s. 60(1)–(3)].

(7) Transfer.—The Chief Justice may by order at any time or stage and either with or without application from any of the parties, transfer any cause or matter from a Judge of a Court to any other Judge of such Court [C.A., s. 42(1)].

" Nothing in this section [s. 42(1)] shall authorise the transfer of a cause or matter which is before a District Magistrate, sitting in an appellate capacity from a decision of a Local Court or validate any transfer made by telegraphic communication and not confirmed forthwith by order signed and sealed in a manner specified by the Chief Justice or any other person authorised in that behalf by him " [C.A., s. 42(2)].

" Subject to the provisions of subsection (2) (which saves the Chief Justice's powers of transfer) a Judge of the High Court shall have and may exercise all the powers of the Chief Justice with respect to the transfer of any cause or matter from one District Court to another or from a District Court to a Circuit Court " [C.A., s. 44(1)].

(8) Inspection, supervision, etc.—(*i*) " Every District Magistrate shall, in respect of any civil matter, be subject to the orders and directions of the High Court as fully as any other officer of the Court."

(*ii*) " Every District Magistrate shall, in respect of any criminal matter, be subject to the orders and directions of the Circuit Judge of the circuit, in which such District Magistrate's Court is situated, as fully as any other officer of the Court."

(*iii*) " The High Court may, whenever it so thinks fit, require any District Magistrate to render to the Court in such form as the Court directs a report of any civil case which may be brought before him."

(*iv*) " The Circuit Judge of the circuit, in which a District Magistrate's Court is situated, may require such Magistrate to render to him in such form as he directs a report of any criminal case which be brought before him " [C.A., ss. 61, 62; see also s. 64].

LAW TO BE ADMINISTERED

(9) General law

(10) Customary law ⎫ As High Court.

(11) Islamic or other law ⎭

A. 5 JUVENILE COURTS

CONSTITUTION AND POWERS

(1) Establishment.—Established by the Courts Act, 1960 [C.A., s. 65]. The President may by legislative instrument order the constitution of Juvenile Courts in any area of the Republic [C.A., s. 65(1)].

(2) Composition.—" Every Juvenile Court shall consist of:—

   (a) Not less than three members of the panel of Juvenile Court Magistrates, who shall select one of their number to be chairman, or
   (b) the District Magistrate for the district within which the Juvenile Court is situate as chairman, sitting with not less than two members of the panel " [C.A., s. 65(4)].

(3) Jurisdiction—original.—" Juvenile Courts shall exercise such summary jurisdiction as the President confers on them in relation to the hearing of charges against, or the disposal of other matters affecting juveniles, (i.e., persons under the age of sixteen), but so that such jurisdiction shall not exceed that of a District Court " [C.A., s. 65(1)].

" The President may, by legislative instrument apply by order to Juvenile Courts all or any of the provisions of any enactment relating to criminal courts or criminal procedure " [C.A., s. 65(2)].

(4) Jurisdiction—appellate.—Nil.

B. LOCAL COURTS

By the Local Courts (Establishment) Instrument, 1960 (E.I. 118), Local Courts were established for every part of Ghana and all Native Courts were abolished. The Native Courts (Repeal) Proclamation 1960 (L.I. 37) repealed all the Native Courts Ordinances. Both instruments were made under the old Local Courts Act and came into force on July 1, 1960

CONSTITUTION AND POWERS

(1) Establishment.—The Minister responsible for local government may by instrument establish Local Courts which exercise jurisdiction in accordance with the Act within a defined area [C.A., s. 92(1)].

(2) Composition.—Local Courts are presided over by magistrates known as Local Court Magistrates. They are appointed by the Minister, responsible for Local Government assisted by an Advisory Committee. The Minister may, as he thinks necessary or expedient, make provision that either one Local Court Magistrate sitting alone, or three Local Court Magistrates sitting together, shall constitute the Local Court. One of such three Local Court Magistrates shall be appointed as the President of the Local Court [C.A., s. 93(1), (2)].

(3) Jurisdiction—original.—Local Courts have unrestricted jurisdiction as to persons [C.A., s. 96(1)]. No Local Court has jurisdiction in any cause or matter affecting chieftaincy or in which the Republic or any public officer acting *virtute officii* is a party [C.A., ss. 96(2), 101].

(*i*) *Civil.*—Local Courts have jurisdiction in suits relating to ownership, occupation, etc., of land, paternity, custody of children, marriage and divorce, succession, where the applicable law is customary law; and personal suits where the debt, damage or demand does not exceed £G100 [C.A., s. 98(1)].

Where it appears that the subject matter of a land cause exceeds £G200 the Court shall not exercise jurisdiction, except with the consent of the parties [C.A., s. 98(2)].

(*ii*) *Criminal.*—" A Local Court shall have jurisdiction in criminal causes to the extent set forth in sections 146 and 147 of the Courts Act, but no such Court shall impose a penalty exceeding a fine of £G25 or a sentence of three months imprisonment or both " [C.A., s. 99].

" In every case in which imprisonment is ordered in default of payment of the fine inflicted such imprisonment shall be according to the following scale, i.e. :—

	Where the fine	*The period of imprisonment shall not exceed*
Does not exceed SG10	..	Ten days
Exceeds SG10 but does not exceed £G1	..	One month
Exceeds £G1 but does not exceed £G10	..	Two months
Exceeds £G10 but does not exceed £G25	..	Three months "

[C.A., s. 110(2)].

" Every Local Court shall have the same jurisdiction " [C.A., s. 97].

(4) Jurisdiction—appellate.—Nil.

CONTROL OF COURTS

(5) Appeals from.—" Except in land and succession causes, any party aggrieved by the decision of a Local Court :—

(a) in any cause in which the subject matter of the cause is of the value of £G10 or upwards; or

(b) in any criminal cause whatsoever; or

(c) in any cause in which the costs exceed £G10; or

(d) in a cause in which a point of law is involved, may appeal to the District Court.

When an appeal is brought from a Local Court to a District Court under subsection (1), no further appeal shall lie unless the District Court or a Circuit Court grants special leave for such further appeal upon a point of law " [C.A., s. 125(1), (2)].

" Any party aggrieved by the decision of a Local Court in land and succession causes in which the subject matter of the cause does not exceed the value of £G100 may appeal to a Circuit Court.

Any party aggrieved by the decision of a Local Court in land and succession causes in which the subject matter of the cause exceeds the value of £G100 may appeal to the High Court and thereafter to the Supreme Court " [C.A., s. 126(1), (2)].

(6) Review/revision.—Every month, an officer of a Local Court designated for the purpose by such Court must forward a complete list of all the causes decided by such Local Court to the District Magistrate of that area, who has powers of review and revision [C.A., s. 133].

(7) Transfer.—" The District Court may either of its own motion or on the application of either party to a cause by order stop the hearing of any cause, matter or question before a Local Court on such terms as it may consider just and upon any such order being made the District Court in its discretion may, provided that neither party nor the trial Court objects and if the cause or matter appears to the District Court to be within the jurisdiction of some other Local Court, by the same or another order direct that the same enquired into or tried and determined by such Local Court as shall appear to it to have jurisdiction over the same.

A District Magistrate shall not transfer any cause, matter or question before any Local Court to his own Court.

Whenever it shall appear to any Court that any civil cause or matter brought before it is one properly cognisable by a Local Court, the Court shall stop the further progress of such civil cause or matter before it and refer the parties to a competent Local Court " [C.A., ss. 131, 132].

(8) Inspection, supervision, etc.—The Minister may by legislative instrument make such regulations as he considers necessary for the practice and procedure of Local Courts [C.A., s. 143(1), (2)].

" Regulations made under section 72 of the Local Courts Act, 1958 (No. 23), and in force immediately before the commencement of this Act shall continue in force and be deemed to have been made under this section.

For the purposes of this Act the Minister may appoint an officer to be known as " Senior Local Courts Adviser " who shall be a legal practitioner of not less than three years' standing, and may further, from time to time, appoint not less than four Local Courts Advisers who shall be persons with knowledge of law and judicial process who shall assist the Senior Local Courts Adviser in the performance of his duties.

The duties of the Senior Local Courts Adviser shall include:—

(a) the provision of courses of instruction for Local Court Magistrates and the training of the officers and servants of Local Courts;

(b) the administrative arrangements for the appointment, conditions of service and salaries of Local Court Magistrates;

(c) the supervision of the arrangements to be made by the local authority under this Part of this Act;

(d) the arrangements for the sittings of a Local Court in different places in the area; and

(e) the inspection of Local Court record books and accounts and the submission of reports on any irregularities discovered therein to the District Magistrate.

The Local Court Advisers shall at all times have access to all Local Courts and the records, accounts and proceedings thereof and the like right shall be enjoyed by the District Magistrate of the district in which the Local Court is exercising jurisdiction " [C.A. s. 144].

LAW TO BE ADMINISTERED

(9) General law.—Local Courts are empowered to administer the provisions of certain Acts or Ordinances, e.g., the provisions of Book 2 of the Criminal Code, which is based on English law [C.A., s. 146].

(10) Customary law.—As High Court [C.A., ss. 66, 67] (see under A. 2(10), p 34, *ante*). " The criminal jurisdiction of Local Courts under customary law shall be to hear and determine charges against persons for the following offences:—

(a) putting any person into fetish;

(b) recklessly, unlawfully or frivously swearing an oath;

(c) possessing any poisonous, noxious or offensive thing with intent to use such thing to endanger or destroy human life or to hurt aggrieve or annoy any person " [C.A., s. 147].

(11) Islamic or other law.—See under A. 2(11), p. 36, *ante*.

FEDERATION OF NIGERIA

The Federation consists of a Federal Territory of Lagos and three Regions—Eastern, Northern and Western [Nigeria (Constitution) Order in Council, 1960, Second Schedule, arts. 2, 3].

The legal and judicial system of Nigeria is a complicated one. The constitutional provisions for the establishment of the Federation are to be found in the Nigeria (Const.) O-in-C, 1960. This O-in-C contains provisions constituting the Federal Supreme Court and the High Courts.

Before 1954 Nigeria was a unitary state with the accent on regionalisation. The pre-1954 Nigerian legislation has generally continued in force and forms the basis of the law of each Region, except in so far as statutorily amended by the Federal or Regional legislatures. In order to ascertain the law of any Region, therefore, it is necessary to have regard to (a) the pre-1954 Nigerian legislation, (b) post-1954 Regional legislation amending the foregoing, and (c) Federal legislation in so far as it applies in any Region.

THE FEDERATION[1]

A. 1(a) THE PRIVY COUNCIL

On the same day as the Federal Supreme Court assumed its functions (see A. 1(b), *infra*) the West Africa (Appeals to the Privy Council) Order in Council, 1949, ceased to apply in Nigeria. It was replaced by the Nigeria (Appeals to Privy Council) Order in Council, 1955, which made provision for appeals from the decisions of the Federal Supreme Court to be heard and determined by the Privy Council.

A. 1(b) THE FEDERAL SUPREME COURT

CONSTITUTION AND POWERS

(1) **Establishment.**—Established by the N.(C.) O-in-C, 1960, Second Schedule (hereinafter called " Federal Constitution, 1960 "), s. 104 (consolidating the Nigeria (Constitution) Order in Council, 1954, s. 138). In pursuance of that Order, the Federal Supreme Court Ordinance, No. 12 of 1960, has been passed to amend and consolidate the law relating to the Federal Supreme Court. This Ordinance—*inter alia*—repeals the Federal Supreme Court (Appeals) Ordinance and the Federal Supreme Court (General Provisions) Ordinance, 1955 [F.S.C.O., No. 12 of 1960, s. 38(1)]. This Court exercises jurisdiction throughout the whole Federation.

---

[1] For diagram of courts system, see p. 211, *post.*

(2) Composition.—It consists of:—

    (a) the Chief Justice of the Federation as President;

    (b) not less than three Federal Justices;

    (c) the Chief Justices of each Region and the Chief Justice of Lagos; and

    (d) such acting Federal Justices as may be appointed [Federal Constitution, 1960, ss. 104, 105]. The number of Federal Justices may be increased at any time by the Governor-General [F.S.C.O., 1960, s. 3(1)]. The Supreme Court is duly constituted if it consists of three judges [F.S.C.O., 1960, s. 9].

(3) Jurisdiction—original.—The Federal Supreme Court has exclusive jurisdiction " in any dispute between the Federation and a Region or between Regions if and in so far as that dispute involves any question (whether of law or fact) on which the existence or extent of a legal right depends " [Federal Constitution, 1960, s. 107(1)].

Parliament may confer additional original jurisdiction on the Court by Act (but not in criminal matters) [Federal Constitution, 1960, s. 107(2)], and an advisory jurisdiction [*ibid.*, s. 109]. If a substantial question as to the interpretation of the Federal or a regional constitution arises in any proceedings in any court in Nigeria the Federal Supreme Court has a special jurisdiction (subject to certain restrictions) to dispose of the question on a reference from the court in which proceedings are being taken [*ibid.*, s. 108].

" In addition to any other powers conferred upon the Federal Supreme Court and subject to the Constitution Order, the Court shall have and may exercise any powers and authorities which are vested in or capable of being exercised by Her Majesty's High Court of Justice in England, so far as the same may be appropriate to the exercise of the said jurisdiction " [F.S.C.O., s. 16(3)].

(4) Jurisdiction—appellate.—By virtue of s. 110 of the Federal Constitution, 1960, the Federal Supreme Court has jurisdiction to the exclusion of any other court in Nigeria to hear and determine appeals from the High Court of a territory (i.e., a Region or the Federal territory).

" An appeal shall lie from decisions of the High Court of a territory to the Federal Supreme Court as of right in the following cases:—

    (a) final decisions in any civil proceedings before the High Court sitting at first instance;

    (b) where the ground of appeal involves questions of law alone, decisions in any criminal proceedings before the High Court sitting at first instance;

    (c) decisions in any civil or criminal proceedings on questions as to the interpretation of this Constitution or the constitution of a Region;

    (d) decisions in any civil or criminal proceedings on questions as to whether any of the provisions of Chapter III of this Constitution has been contravened in relation to any person;

    (e) decisions in any criminal proceedings in which any person has been sentenced to death by the High Court or in which the High Court has affirmed a sentence of death imposed by some other court; and

(f) such other cases as may be prescribed by any law in force in the territory " [Federal Constitution, 1960, s. 110(2)].

Appeals by leave of the High Court or Federal Supreme Court lie in the following cases:—

(a) where the ground of appeal involves questions of fact, mixed law and fact or *quantum* of sentence, decisions in any criminal proceedings before the High Court sitting at first instance;

(b) decisions in any civil or criminal proceedings in which an appeal has been brought to the High Court from some other court;

(c) such other cases as may be prescribed by any law in force in the territory.

Appeals from *ex parte* orders, consent orders, orders as to costs, lie only by leave and not of right [Federal Constitution, s. 110(2), (4)].

The Federal Supreme Court also has jurisdiction to hear appeals from the Sharia Court of Appeal and Court of Resolution of the Northern Region [Federal Constitution, s. 112], and from any other court or tribunal as prescribed by Parliament [Federal Constitution, s. 111].

On the hearing of an appeal in a criminal case from a High Court sitting in its appellate jurisdiction, the Federal Supreme Court may exercise any power that could have been exercised by the High Court or may order the case to be retried by a court of competent jurisdiction [F.S.C.O., s. 30]. Where right of appeal, with or without leave, from decisions of the High Court of a Region given in the exercise of its appellate jurisdiction in respect of regional matters are prescribed by a law of a Region, the Federal Supreme Court must, except in so far as other provision is made by any law enacted by, or having effect as if enacted by, the legislature of the Federation, have the like jurisdiction to hear and determine appeals from decisions of that High Court given in the exercise of its appellate jurisdiction in respect of matters included in the Exclusive Legislative List or in the Concurrent Legislative List [F.S.C.O., s. 15(1)]. The section does not apply to Lagos [s. 15(2)].

CONTROL OF COURT

(5) Appeals from.—Appeals from the decisions of the Federal Supreme Court lie to the Privy Council [Federal Constitution, 1960, s. 114].

(7) Transfer.—The exclusive jurisdiction is subject to a power of transfer [s. 19(1)] in the Federal Supreme Court Ordinance, 1960, which states that the Federal Supreme Court may order any cause or matter before it to be transferred to a High Court or a magistrate's court having jurisdiction in respect thereof, for hearing and determination.

LAW TO BE ADMINISTERED

(9) General law.—In the exercise of the original jurisdiction of the Federal Supreme Court " . . . law and equity shall be administered concurrently and in the same manner as they are administered by Her Majesty's High Court of Justice in England ", and in the case of any " conflict or variance between the rules of equity and the rules of the common law with reference to the same matter, the rules of equity shall prevail " [F.S.C.O., s. 16(a), (c)].

(10) Customary law.—" The Supreme Court shall observe and enforce the observance of native law and custom to the same extent as such law and custom is observed and enforced in the High Court of Lagos " [F.S.C.O., s. 16(e)].

(11) Islamic or other law.—[See s. 3(2A) of the F.S.C. (Appeals) (Amendment) Ordinance, No. 28 of 1955, which states:—" In the hearing and determining of an appeal by the Court of Appeal, the law to be applied shall be the law applicable in the Region from the High Court of which the appeal is brought."]

FEDERAL TERRITORY OF LAGOS[1]

Laws for the Federal Territory are made by the Federal Legislature. Although not a Region, Lagos is defined as a " territory " (which expression includes a Region) by the Nigeria Constitution, and many statutory provisions apply equally to Regions and the Federal Territory.

The courts consist of a High Court and a Magistrate's Court. There are no customary courts.

A. 2 THE HIGH COURT

CONSTITUTION AND POWERS

(1) Establishment.—Established by the Nigeria (Constitution) Order in Council, 1960, Federal Constitution, s. 115; and by the High Court of Lagos Ordinance, No. 25 of 1955, (Laws of the Federation of Nigeria and Lagos 1958 Revision, cap. 80) since amended by the H.C.L.(A.)O., No. 11 of 1960.

(2) Composition.—It consists of a Chief Justice and six or more judges appointed by the Governor-General [Federal Constitution, s. 116].

(3) Jurisdiction—original.—(*i*) General jurisdiction as conferred by the Federal Constitution, s. 115(3);

(*ii*) that of the High Court in England, other than Admiralty jurisdiction [H.C.L.O., s. 9];

(*iii*) any Federal Act or Ordinance, etc.;

(*iv*)—" (a) all Her Majesty's civil jurisdiction which immediately before the coming into operation of this Ordinance, was, or at any time afterwards may be, exercisable in the Federal Territory of Lagos, for the administration or control of property and persons; and (b) all Her Majesty's criminal jurisdiction which immediately before . . . in such Territory, for the repression or punishment of crimes or offences or for the maintenance of order " [H.C.L.O., s. 11].

(4) Jurisdiction—appellate.—The High Court has appellate jurisdiction to hear and determine appeals from the decisions of the

---

1 For diagram of courts system see p. 213, *post.*

Magistrate's court in civil and criminal causes [Federal Constitution, s. 118].

CONTROL OF COURT

(5) Appeals from.—To the Federal Supreme Court [Federal Constitution, s. 110; H.C.L.O., s. 50].

LAW TO BE ADMINISTERED

(9) General law.—Her Majesty's civil and criminal jurisdiction exercisable in the Federal Territory: (a) immediately before the coming into operation of the H.C.L.O.; or (b) " at any time afterwards " [H.C.L.O., s. 11]; in other words:—

> (a) the Nigerian law in force in Lagos at December 31, 1955, consisting of (*i*) the common law, equity, and statutes of general application in force in England on January 1, 1900, as varied by (*ii*) U.K. legislation specifically extended to Nigeria, and Imperial Orders and (*iii*) Nigerian Ordinances.
>
> (b) Federal legislation since December 31, 1955, applying to Lagos.

(10) Customary law.—" The High Court shall observe and enforce the observance of every native law and custom which is applicable and is not repugnant to natural justice, equity and good conscience, nor incompatible either directly or by implication with any law for the time being in force, and nothing in this Ordinance shall deprive any person of the benefit of any such native law or custom.

Any such law or custom shall be deemed applicable in causes and matters where the parties thereto are natives and also in causes and matters between natives and non-natives, where it may appear to the court that substantial injustice would be done to either party by a strict adherence to any rules of law which would otherwise be applicable.

No party shall be entitled to claim the benefit of any native law or custom if it shall appear either from express contract or from the nature of the transactions out of which any suit or question may have arisen, that such party agreed that his obligations in connection with such transactions should be exclusively regulated otherwise than by native law and custom or that such transactions are transactions unknown to native law and custom." [H.C.L.O., 5, 27 (1), (2), (3)].

A. 3 THE MAGISTRATE'S COURT

CONSTITUTION AND POWERS

(1) Establishment.—The Federal Legislature may establish courts of justice for Nigeria in addition to the Federal Supreme Court and the High Courts [Federal Constitution, s. 119]. A magistrate's court has been established by the Magistrate's Court (Lagos) Ordinance, 1955, (cap. 113).

(2) Composition.—The Governor-General may appoint magistrates to the Court in the following grades: Chief Magistrate, Magistrates of grades I, II and III.

(3) Jurisdiction—original.—Every magistrate has jurisdiction throughout Lagos [M.C.(L.)O., s. 5]. The civil and criminal jurisdiction of the magistrates varies according to their grades [M.C.(L.)O., ss. 14–20].

Thus in civil causes or matters, a Chief Magistrate has jurisdiction in the following cases:—

(a) in all personal matters to the suit value of £500;

(b) in all actions between landlord and tenant;

(c) in all actions for the recovery of any penalty, rates, etc. if:—

(*i*) it is not expressly provided by that or any other Ordinance that the demand shall be recoverable in some other court; (*ii*) the amount claimed does not exceed £500;

(d) to appoint guardians;

(e) to grant injunctions [M.C.(L.)O., s. 14(1)].

The Chief Magistrate has no jurisdiction in any cause or matter which raises any issue as to the title to land or any issue as to the validity of any devise, bequest or limitation under any will or settlement [M.C.(L.)O., s. 14(2)].

Magistrates grades I, II and III have similar jurisdiction, except that the maximum suit value is reduced to £200 in relation to a magistrate grade I; £100 in relation to a magistrate grade II; and £25 in relation to a magistrate grade III [M.C.(L.)O., s. 14(3)].

In criminal causes magistrates have jurisdiction to hear and determine summary offences. The extent of their jurisdiction is as follows:—

Chief Magistrate—£500 fine or 5 years imprisonment;
Magistrate grade I—£200 fine or 2 years imprisonment;
Magistrate grade II—£100 fine or 1 year imprisonment;
Magistrate grade III—£25 fine or 3 months imprisonment

[M.C.(L.)O., s. 15].

(4) Jurisdiction—appellate.—Nil.

CONTROL OF COURT

(5) Appeals from.—Appeals from the decisions of the Magistrate's Court lie to the High Court [M.C.(L.)O., ss. 54–69; see also A. 2(4), p. 47 *ante*].

(6) Review/revision.—The High Court has power to revise the proceedings in the Magistrate's Court in petty civil cases and in criminal cases [H.C.L.O., ss. 34, 35].

(7) Transfer.—A Judge of the High Court may transfer any cause or matter before him to the Magistrate's Court [H.C.L.O., s. 53]. The Chief Justice may transfer a case from one Magistrate to another, or to the High Court [M.C.(L.)O., ss. 30, 31]. A Magistrate may transfer a case before him to any other Magistrate with the consent of such Magistrate [M.C.(L.)O., s. 29].

LAW TO BE ADMINISTERED

(9) General law.—As High Court (see A. 2(9), p. 48, *ante*).

(10) Customary law.—See A. 2(10), p. 48, *ante* [M.C.(L.)O., s. 22].

C

WESTERN REGION[1]

A. 2 THE HIGH COURT

CONSTITUTION AND POWERS

(1) Establishment.—Established by the Nigeria (Constitution) Order in Council, 1960, Fourth Schedule, Constitution of Western Nigeria, s. 48.

Under s. 42 of the Nigeria (Constitution) O-in-C, 1954, each Regional Legislature was authorised to establish courts of justice for that Region. In pursuance of this Order, the Western Region High Court Law, No. 3 of 1955 was passed. (It is now cap. 44 of the Laws of the Western Region of Nigeria, 1959 Revision.)

(2) Composition.—Subject to the provisions of the Constitution of Western Nigeria, 1960, ss. 48 and 49, the number of judges of the Court, in addition to the Chief Justice, is to be such as may be prescribed by the Governor in Council from time to time [W.R.H.C.L., s. 3].

(3) Jurisdiction—original.—The High Court is a superior court of record and possesses all the jurisdiction, civil and criminal, powers and authorities which are vested in or capable of being exercised by Her Majesty's High Court of Justice in England [W.R.H.C.L., ss. 8 and 9]. The Court is invested with all the powers and authorities of the Lord High Chancellor of England in relation to, e.g., the appointment and control of guardians of infants and their estates, (W.R.H.C.L., s. 10]. The jurisdiction of the High Court includes such jurisdiction as may be vested in it by Federal law [W.R.H.C.L., s. 9(2)].

" Where by the law of a Region jurisdiction is conferred upon a High Court . . . for the hearing and determination of civil causes relating to matters with respect to which the Legislature of the Region may make laws, and of appeals arising out of such causes, the Court shall, except in so far as other provision is made by any law in force in the Region, have the like jurisdiction with respect to the hearing and determination of civil cases relating to matters within the exclusive legislative competence of the Federal Legislature, and of appeals arising out of such cases " [Regional Courts (Federal Jurisdiction) Ordinance, Laws of the Federation, 1958 Revision, cap. 177, s. 3].

The jurisdiction of the High Court of a Region in relation to probate, divorce and matrimonial causes, is, in so far as the practice and procedure are concerned, to be exercised by the Court in conformity with the law and practice for the time being in force in England. The High Court also has jurisdiction to hear and determine causes concerning questions of fundamental rights [Federal Constitution, 1960, s. 31]. Except in so far as the Governor may by order in council otherwise direct, the High Court does not exercise original jurisdiction in any matter which is subject to the jurisdiction of a customary court relating to marriage, family status, guardianship of children and inheritance or disposition of property on death [W.R.H.C.L., s. 9].

---

1 For diagram of courts system, see p. 212, *post.*

(4) Jurisdiction—appellate.—(*i*) *As of right.*—An appeal lies from decisions of a subordinate court to the High Court of the Region as of right or, if it is provided by any law in force in the Region that an appeal as of right lies, from that subordinate court to another subordinate court, an appeal thereafter lies to the High Court as of right in the following cases:

    (a) in civil proceedings, where the matter in dispute is of the value of £50 or upwards;

    (b) on questions of law in criminal proceedings, where sentence passed exceeded three months or six strokes or a fine of £25;

    (c) in proceedings on the interpretation of the Federal or a regional constitution;

    (d) where breaches of Chapter III of the Federal Constitution (fundamental rights) are alleged;

    (e) in any criminal proceeding where the accused has been sentenced to death;

    (f) in any other criminal proceedings before a subordinate court sitting at first instance from which no appeal lies as of right to another subordinate court;

    (g) in such other cases as prescribed by any law in force in the Region.

(*ii*) *By leave of court.*—Appeal lies:—

    (a) in any criminal proceedings from which no appeal lies, as of right to the High Court; or

    (b) in such other cases in which no appeal lies as of right to the High Court as may be prescribed by any law in force in the Region [Constitution (Western Nigeria), s. 51].

The foregoing should be read in conjunction with ss. 17 and 18 of the W.R.H.C.L., cap. 44, which confer appellate jurisdiction on the High Court—(a) to hear and determine appeals from the decisions of Magistrates' Courts in civil and criminal matters; and (b) to hear and determine appeals from customary courts and appeals from the decisions of Magistrates on appeal from customary courts.

Under s. 48 of the Customary Courts Law, 1957, cap. 31, the High Court has jurisdiction to hear and determine appeals from:—

    (a) a Grade A customary court;

    (b) a customary court of appeal;

    (c) a magistrate's court made or given on appeal from a customary court.

CONTROL OF COURT

(5) Appeals from.—Appeals from the decisions of the High Court lie to the Federal Supreme Court (see A. 1(b), p. 45, *ante*).

(7) Transfer.—A judge may at any time or at any stage of the proceedings before final judgment, transfer any cause or matter before him to a magistrate's court having jurisdiction to hear such cause or matter, or to a judge in the same or any other jurisdictional division [W.R.H.C.L., cap. 44, s. 31(1)]. The Chief Justice may at any time and at any stage of the proceedings before judgment similarly, transfer any cause or matter before a judge to any other judge [W.R.H.C.L., s. 31(2)].

The Court may at any stage of the proceedings by order direct that any cause or matter pending before it be transferred to a customary court having jurisdiction in such cause or matter [W.R.H.C.L., s. 34].

Law to be Administered

(9) General law.—" From and after the commencement of this Law and subject to the provisions of any written law, the common law of England and the doctrines of equity observed by Her Majesty's High Court of Justice in England shall be in force throughout the Region " [Law of England (Application) Law, 1959, cap. 60, s. 3].

" Subject to the provisions of this Law no Imperial Act hitherto in force within the Region shall have any force or effect therein; provided that, subject to the express provisions of any written law, this section shall not—

(a) revive anything not in force or existing at the commencement of this Law; or

(b) affect the previous operation of any Imperial Act to which this section applies or anything duly done or suffered under such Act; or

(c) affect any right, privilege, obligation and or liability accrued or incurred under any such Act; or

(d) affect any penalty, forfeiture or punishment incurred in respect of any offence committed against any such Act; or

(e) affect any investigation, legal proceeding or remedy in respect of any such right, privilege, obligation, liability, penalty, forfeiture or punishment as aforesaid; and any such investigation, legal proceeding or remedy may be instituted, continued or enforced and any such penalty, forfeiture or punishment may be imposed as if this Law had not been passed:

Provided that where the penalty, forfeiture or punishment imposed by any written law in force upon or after the commencement of this Law is heavier than that imposed by any such Act as aforesaid, the provisions of such Act whereby the lighter penalty, forfeiture or punishment is imposed shall, unless such written law as aforesaid otherwise provides, be applied if the Court decides to inflict any punishment " [Law of England (Application) Law, 1959, cap. 60, s. 4].

(10) Customary law.—By the W.R.H.C.L., cap. 44, s. 12:—

" (1) The High Court shall observe and enforce the observance of every customary law which is applicable and is not repugnant to natural justice, equity and good conscience, nor incompatible either directly or by implication with any written law for the time being in force, and nothing in this Law shall deprive any person of the benefit of any such customary law.

(2) Any such customary law shall be deemed applicable in causes and matters where the parties thereto are Nigerians and also in causes and matters between Nigerians and non-Nigerians where it may appear to the court that substantial injustice would be done to either party by a strict adherence to any rules of law which would otherwise be applicable.

(3) No party shall be entitled to claim the benefit of any customary law if it shall appear either from express contract or from the nature of the transactions out of which any suit or question may have arisen, that such party agreed that his obligations in connection with such transactions should be exclusively regulated otherwise than by customary law or that such transactions are transactions unknown to customary law.

(4) Where the High Court determines that customary law is applicable in any cause or matter, it shall apply the particular customary law which is appropriate in that cause or matter having regard to the provisions of section 20 of the Customary Courts Law, 1957.''

(11) Islamic or other law.—Islamic law is applied (where it is applied at all) under the extensive and elastic umbrella of '' native law and custom ''. And it is as such, alone, that it is applied in Western Nigeria; see Anderson, J. N. D., '' Customary law and Islamic law in British African Territories '' in *The Future of Customary Law in Africa*, 1955, p. 77.

A. 3 MAGISTRATES' COURTS

Constitution and Powers

(1) Establishment.—Established by the Magistrates Courts (W.R.) Law, 1954 (Laws of the Western Region of Nigeria, 1959, cap. 74). The Western Region is divided into magisterial districts in each of which there is established a magistrate's court [M.C.(W.R.) L., ss. 3, 5].

(2) Composition.—A court is duly constituted when presided over by a magistrate, who is then described as a presiding officer [s. 6(1)(a)]. Magistrates are graded into Chief Magistrates, Senior Magistrates and Magistrates [s. 7(1)]. Every magistrate is *ex officio* a justice of the peace for the Western Region of Nigeria [s. 9].

(3) Jurisdiction—original.—Every magistrate has jurisdiction throughout the Western Region, but may be assigned to any specific district, e.g., transferred from one district to another, by the Chief Justice. Subject to the provisions of this or any other law, a Chief Magistrate has jurisdiction in civil causes, e.g.:—

(a) in all personal suits to the suit value of £500;
(b) in all suits between landlord and tenant;
(c) to appoint guardians;
(d) to grant injunctions;

(e) in any appeal from the decision of an Assessment Committee constituted under the provisions of the W.R. Local Government Law, 1952. [M.C.(W.R.) L., s. 19(1)].

Senior Magistrates and Magistrates have and exercise jurisdiction in civil causes similar in all respects to that set out above, except that the suit value is £200 in the case of a Senior Magistrate, and £100 in the case of a Magistrate. Nothing in s. 19 is to be construed to confer upon any Chief Magistrate, Senior Magistrate or Magistrate original jurisdiction in any matter specified in paragraphs (a) to (e) above [M.C.(W.R.) L., s. 19(4)].

However, the Governor in Council may by order direct that a magistrate's court may exercise original jurisdiction in all or any of the following matters:—

(a) Suits which raise an issue as to title to land or any interest in land.

(b) Suits in which the validity of a devise, bequest or limitation under will or settlement is disputed.

(c) Suits relating to the custody of children, under customary law.

(d) Causes relating to inheritance upon intestacy under customary law and the administration of intestate estates under customary law.

(e) Matrimonial causes and matters between persons married under customary law [M.C.(W.R.) L., s. 20].

On the criminal side magistrates have power to try summary offences. But their powers of punishment vary. A Chief Magistrate can impose the following punishments:—

(i) Imprisonment for not more than five years.

(ii) A fine not exceeding £500.

In the case of Senior Magistrates, the maximum period of imprisonment is two years, and the maximum fine is £200.

In the case of Magistrates, the maximum period of imprisonment is one year, and the maximum fine is £100 [M.C.(W.R.) L., ss. 21 and 22].

(4) Jurisdiction—appellate.—A magistrate's court has power to hear and determine appeals from customary courts [M.C.(W.R.) L., s. 25].

CONTROL OF COURTS

(5) Appeals from.—Appeals from the decisions, both civil and criminal, of magistrates' courts lie to the High Court [M.C.(W.R.) L., s. 41].

(6) Review/Revision.—The High Court has power to revise decisions of the magistrates' courts [W.R.H.C.L., s. 19].

(7) Transfer.—When the Chief Justice assigns two or more magistrates to any district the one magistrate can transfer a cause to the other magistrate [M.C.(W.R.) L., s. 37].

A magistrate may, of his own motion, report to a judge any cause or matter, which in his opinion ought to be transferred from his court to any other magistrate's court, or to the High Court [M.C.(W.R.) L., s. 38].

The Chief Justice or a judge may at any time and at any stage before judgment transfer any cause or matter before a magistrate's court to any other magistrate's court, or to a customary court or to the High Court [M.C.(W.R.) L., s. 39].

(8) Inspection, supervision, etc.—The Chief Justice may require specified magistrates to forward to the Chief Justice or to another judge, a monthly list containing all criminal cases decided by such magistrates [M.C.(W.R.) L., s. 42].

LAW TO BE ADMINISTERED

(9) General law.—As High Court (see A. 2(9), p. 52, *ante*).

(10) Customary law.—The provisions are substantially the same as those for the High Court [M.C.(W.R.)L., s. 32] (see A. 2(10), p. 52, *ante*).

(11) Islamic or other law.—As High Court (see A. 2(11), p. 53, *ante*).

B. CUSTOMARY COURTS

CONSTITUTION AND POWERS

(1) Establishment.—Established under the Customary Courts Law, 1957, cap. 31. By s. 3 the responsible Minister may by warrant establish such customary courts as he may think fit.

(2) Composition.—The Minister may delegate the power of appointment and of dismissal of members to the Local Government Service Board. The number of the members is fixed in the warrant [C.C.L., ss. 3 and 4]. No person is qualified to be appointed as President of a customary court grade A, unless he is a legal practitioner. Further, no person shall be qualified to be appointed as the president or vice-president of a customary court grade B, or a customary court of appeal unless he is literate in the English language [s. 6(2)].

(3) Jurisdiction—original.—Customary courts have jurisdiction over all Nigerians [C.C.L., s. 17]. There are 4 grades of customary courts, namely: grades A, B, C and D, and the jurisdiction and powers of each grade of customary court are set out in the Schedule [C.C.L., s. 18].

(a) *Civil Jurisdiction.*—(i) *Grade A Courts.*—Unlimited jurisdiction in all civil causes arising under the law to be administered by the Court.

(ii) *Grade B Courts.*—Unlimited jurisdiction in matrimonial causes arising out of customary law; in land matters; in causes relating to the custody of children under customary law; in causes relating to inheritance. Jurisdiction in other causes and matters which are capable of being administered by the court, where the debt, demand or damages do not exceed £100.

(iii) *Grade C Courts.*—Unlimited jurisdiction in matrimonial causes and suits relating to the custody of children under customary law.

Jurisdiction in causes and matters relating to inheritance to the value of £50, jurisdiction in land matters to the value of £50; jurisdiction in personal suits to the value of £50.

(*iv*) *Grade D Courts.*—Unlimited jurisdiction in matrimonial causes and suits relating to the custody of children under customary law. Jurisdiction in suits relating to land and inheritance to the value of £25. Jurisdiction in personal suits to the value of £25 [2nd Schedule to C.C.L.].

(b) *Criminal jurisdiction.*—The Governor in Council may empower any customary courts to administer within the local limits of the jurisdiction of such courts, any law of the Region, except jurisdiction in the following: homicide; treason; sedition; rape; procuration; defilement of girls; offences other than against official secrets laws; any other capital offences.

The maximum fine and the maximum imprisonment which may be imposed by a customary court, other than a customary court grade A, are as follows:—

> Grade B: £100 fine and 1 year imprisonment;
> Grade C: £50 fine and 6 months imprisonment;
> Grade D: £25 fine and 3 months imprisonment

[s. 9 of the C.C.(A.) L., 1959, which replaces s. 24 of the C.C.L., 1957].

(4) Jurisdiction—appellate.—Where a customary court of appeal has been established, any party aggrieved by the decision of a grade B, C or D court having jurisdiction in that area, may appeal to the customary court grade A [C.C.L., s. 46]. Otherwise the right of appeal lies to a magistrate's court [s. 47].

CONTROL OF COURTS

(5) Appeals from.—Appeals from the decisions of a grade A customary court lie to the High Court [C.C.L., s. 48(1)]. Appeals from the decisions of a magistrate's court made on an appeal from a customary court in both civil and criminal cases lie to the High Court [C.C.L., s. 48(2)].

(6) Review/revision.—Any magistrate, president or member of any customary court may be appointed by the Minister to act as a " supervising authority ". Such a person may of his own motion, or on the application of any person concerned, review any of the proceedings, whether civil or criminal. Wide powers are conferred on the supervising authority, but a person aggrieved by a decision or order of the supervising authority in a criminal cause in which a term of imprisonment or a fine exceeding £5 is imposed, may appeal to the High Court. In a civil cause an appeal lies when the subject matter is valued at £50 or more [C.C.L., s. 44(a)–(e), inserted by s. 13 of the C.C.(A.) L., 1959].

(7) Transfer.—The High Court may at any time or at any stage of the proceedings:—

> (a) on the application of the Director of Public Prosecutions transfer any criminal case which is before a customary court

to the High Court, or to a Magistrate's Court having jurisdiction in that matter;

(b) of its own motion, or on the application of any party to the
cause or matter, transfer any cause or matter relating to the
administration of an intestate estate which is before a
customary court to the High Court [C.C.L., s. 29A, inserted
by C.C.(A.) L., 1959, s. 11].

A customary court may, either of its own motion, or upon the application of either party to a cause, transfer to a lower grade customary
court, any cause before it, which in its opinion can be more appro-
priately dealt with by such lower court [C.C.L., s. 30].

(8) Inspection, supervision, etc.—See (6), *supra.*

LAW TO BE ADMINISTERED

(9) General law.—Under s. 19 of the C.C.L., customary courts
are empowered to administer: (a) any written law, if so authorised
by an order made under s. 24; (b) any enactment in respect of which
jurisdiction is conferred on the court by that enactment; and (c) all
rules and bylaws made by a Local Government Council.

(10) Customary law.—" Subject to the provisions of this Law,
a customary court shall administer the appropriate customary law
specified in section 20 in so far as it is not repugnant to natural justice,
equity and good conscience, nor incompatible either directly or by
necessary implication with any written law for the time being in force "
[C.C.L., s. 19].

" (1) In land matters the appropriate customary law shall be the
customary law of the place where the land is situated.

(2) In causes and matters arising from inheritance the appropriate
customary law shall, subject to sub-sections (1) and (4) of this section,
be the customary law applying to the deceased.

(3) Subject to the provisions of sub-sections (1) and (2) of this section:—

(a) in civil causes or matters where:—

(*i*) both parties are not natives of the area of jurisdiction
of the court; or

(*ii*) the transaction, the subject of the cause or matter, was
not entered into the area of the jurisdiction of the court;
or

(*iii*) one of the parties is a non-native of the area of jurisdiction of the court, and the parties agreed or may be
presumed to have agreed that their obligations should
be regulated, wholly or partly, by the customary law
applying to that party, the appropriate customary law
shall be the customary law binding between the parties;

(b) In all other civil causes and matters the appropriate customary law shall be the law of the area of jurisdiction of the
court.

57

(4) Where the customary law applying to land prohibits, restricts or regulates the devolution on death to any particular class of persons of the right to occupy such land, it shall not operate to deprive any person of any beneficial interest in such land (other than the right to occupy the same) or in the proceeds of sale thereof to which he may be entitled under the rules of inheritance of any other customary law.

(5) [*This sub-section, which dealt with the appropriate customary law in criminal matters, was repealed by s. 7 of the C.C.(A.) L., 1959*].

(6) In this section ' native ', in relation to the area of jurisdiction of a court, means a person who is a member of a community indigenous to that area " [C.C. L., 1957, s. 20].

(11) Islamic or other law.—As High Court (see A. 2(11), p. 53, *ante*).

EASTERN REGION[1]

A. 2 THE HIGH COURT

Constitution and Powers

(1) Establishment.—Established by the Nigeria (Constitution) O-in-C, 1960, Fifth Schedule, Constitution of Eastern Nigeria, s. 48, replacing Nigeria (Constitution) O-in-C, 1954 (as amended), under which the High Court of the Eastern Region was established by the High Court Law, 1955, E.R. No. 27 of 1955 (since amended by the High Court (Amendment) Laws, E.R., Nos. 129 of 1955, 4 of 1956, and 14 of 1960; and by s. 69 of the Customary Courts Law, 1956).

(2) Composition.—By s. 48(2) of the Constitution, the Judges of the High Court are:—

- (a) the Chief Justice of the Region; and
- (b) such number of other judges (not being less than six) as may be prescribed by the Legislature of the Region.

(3) Jurisdiction—original.—The High Court is a superior court of record. Subject to the provisions of ss. 11, 12 and 13 of the High Court Law, 1955, the jurisdiction vested in the Court includes " the judicial hearing and determination of matters in difference, the administration or control of property or persons, and the power to appoint or control guardians of infants and their estates . . ." [*ibid.*, s. 10(2); see also s. 24]. The jurisdiction of the Court also includes " all Her Majesty's criminal jurisdiction which at the commencement of this Law was, or at any time afterwards may be, exercisable within the jurisdiction of the Court for the repression or punishment of crimes or offences or for the maintenance of order " [s. 10(3)]. " The jurisdiction of the Court in probate, divorce and matrimonial causes and matters shall, subject to this Law . . . be exercised by the Court in conformity with the law and practice for the time being in force in England " [s. 16]. Law and equity are administered concurrently [s. 21(1)]. The High Court has concurrent jurisdiction with that of the magistrates' courts [s. 19].

---

[1] For diagram of courts system, see p. 212, *post.*

However, the jurisdiction of the Court is excluded in certain cases, for example:—

(a) in any dispute between the Federation and the Region, or between the Region and another Region, or the Southern Cameroons;

(b) in any matter arising under any treaty, or

(c) in any matter affecting consular officers [s. 11];

(d) jurisdiction as to the interpretation of the Nigeria (Constitution) O-in-C, 1954 [s. 12, as amended by the H.C.(A.) L. E.R. No. 29 of 1955].

(e) jurisdiction in any cause or matter which is subject to the jurisdiction of a native court and customary court relating to marriage, family status, guardianship of children, or the inheritance or disposition of property on death [s. 13].

The High Court also has jurisdiction to hear and determine causes concerning questions of fundamental rights [the Nigeria (Constitution) (Amendment) No. 3. O-in-C, 1959, S.I. 1959/1772, Schedule].

(4) Jurisdiction—appellate.—(*i*) *As of right.*—" An appeal shall lie from the decisions of a subordinate court to the High Court of the Region as of right or, if it is provided by any law in force in the Region that an appeal as of right shall lie from that subordinate court to another subordinate court an appeal shall thereafter lie to the High Court as of right in the following cases:—

(a) where the matter in dispute on the appeal to the High Court is of the value of £50 or upwards or where the appeal involves directly or indirectly a claim to or question respecting property or a right of the value of £50 or upwards, final decisions in any civil proceedings;

(b) where the ground of appeal to the High Court involves questions of law alone, decisions in any criminal proceedings in which any person has been sentenced to imprisonment for a term exceeding three months or corporal punishment exceeding six strokes or a fine or forfeiture exceeding £25 . . . ;

(c) decisions in any civil or criminal proceedings on questions as to the interpretation of this Constitution, the Constitution of the Federation or the Constitution of another Region;

(d) decisions in any civil or criminal proceedings on questions as to whether any of the provisions of Chapter III of the Constitution of the Federation has been contravened in relation to any person;

(e) [where a person has been sentenced to death];

(f) decisions in any other criminal proceedings before a subordinate court sitting at first instance from which no appeal lies as of right to another subordinate court; and

(g) such other cases as may be prescribed by any law in force in the Region . . . "

(*ii*) *By leave of court.*—" (a) decisions in any criminal proceedings from which no appeal lies as of right to the High Court; or

(b) such other cases in which no appeal lies as of right to the High

Court as may be prescribed by any law in force in the Region " [Constitution, Eastern Nigeria, s. 51].

The foregoing should be read in conjunction with the other provisions embodied in the Eastern Region High Court Law (E.R. No. 27 of 1955). By s. 34 the Court has appellate jurisdiction to hear and determine all appeals from the decisions of magistrates' courts in civil and criminal causes. The Court has appellate jurisdiction to hear and determine appeals from native courts or customary courts [Customary Courts Law, 1956, s. 60(a), (c)], and appeals from decisions of magistrates on appeal from native courts or customary courts [High Court Law E.R. No. 27 of 1955, s. 35, Customary Courts Law E.R. No. 21 of 1956, s. 69].

CONTROL OF COURTS

(5) Appeals from.—Any person aggrieved by a decision of the High Court in a civil appeal in respect of a regional matter, may appeal further to the Federal Supreme Court (E.R. No. 27 of 1955, s. 37]. " Any person who, having the right to appeal under . . . section 57 and 59 of the Magistrates' Courts Law, 1955, in respect of a Regional matter and having so appealed, is aggrieved by the decision of the High Court upon his appeal, may appeal further to the Federal Supreme Court on a matter of law, but not on a matter of fact or against sentence without the leave of the Federal Supreme Court " [H.C.L., 1955, E.R. No. 27 of 1955]. " Subject to the provisions of section 110 of the Federal Constitution, an appeal shall, in accordance with the provisions of the High Court Law, 1955, and the Federal Supreme Court (Appeals) Ordinance [now repealed], lie to the Federal Supreme Court from the order or decision of the High Court given in the exercise of its appellate jurisdiction " [C.C.L., s. 60(d), (1)].

(7) Transfer.—A judge may by order under his hand and either with or without application from any of the parties thereto, transfer any cause or matter before him to a magistrate's court or to a judge in the same Judicial Division [H.C. L., s. 48(1)].

A Chief Justice has power to transfer any cause or matter before a judge to any other judge [*ibid.*, s. 49(1)]. The Court has power to transfer any civil cause or matter pending before it to a native court or customary court having jurisdiction in such cause or matter [H.C. L., s. 50(1)].

LAW TO BE ADMINISTERED

(9) General law.—" Subject to the provisions of this section and except in so far as other provision is made by any law in force in the Region, the common law of England, the doctrines of equity and the statutes of general application that were in force in England on the first day of January, 1900, shall, in so far as they relate to any matter for which the Legislature of the Region is for the time being competent to make laws, be in force within the jurisdiction of the Court " [H.C. L., s. 14].

" All statutes of general application or other Acts of Parliament which apply within the jurisdiction of the Court by reason of this Law or any other written law shall be in force so far only as the limits of the local jurisdiction and local circumstances permit.

It shall be lawful for the Court to construe such statutes or Acts with such verbal alterations, not affecting the substance, as may be necessary to make the same applicable to the proceedings before the Court.

Every Judge, or officer of the Court, having or exercising functions of the like kind or analogous to the functions of any Judge or officer referred to in any such Statute or Act, shall be deemed to be within the meaning of the enactments thereof relating to such last-mentioned Judge or officer " [H.C. L., s. 20].

(10) Customary law.—" The Court shall observe and enforce the observance of every local custom and shall not deprive any person of the benefit thereof except when any such custom is repugnant to natural justice, equity and good conscience or incompatible, either directly or by its implication, with any law for the time being in force.

Such local custom shall be deemed applicable in any civil cause or matter where the parties thereto are persons of Nigerian descent, also in any civil cause or matter between persons of Nigerian descent and persons who are not of Nigerian descent where it may appear to the Court that substantial injustice would be done to either party by a strict adherence to the rules of any law or laws other than local custom.

No party shall be entitled to claim the benefit of any local custom if it shall appear either from express contract or from the nature of the transaction out of which any civil cause or matter shall have arisen, that such party agreed or must be taken to have agreed that his obligations in connection with any such transaction should be regulated exclusively by some law or laws other than local custom, or that such transaction is one which is unknown to local custom " [H.C. L., s. 22].

(11) Islamic or other law.—" Islamic law is applied (where it is applied at all) under the extensive and elastic umbrella of ' native law and custom '. It is as such, alone, that it is applied in Nigeria " [*sc.* Eastern Region]: Anderson, J. N. D., " Customary law and Islamic law in British African Territories " in *The Future of Customary Law in Africa*, 1955, p. 77.

A. 3 MAGISTRATES' COURTS

CONSTITUTION AND POWERS

(1) Establishment.—Established by the Magistrates' Courts Law, 1955, E.R. No. 10 of 1955, since amended by the Magistrates' Courts (Amendment) Laws E.R., Nos. 30 of 1955, 2 of 1956, 8 of 1958, 13 of 1960; the C.C. Law No. 21 of 1956, s. 69, and the Eastern Region Local Government Law, No. 17 of 1960 (5th Schedule). The Eastern Region has been divided into Magisterial Districts for the purpose of this Law [M.C.L. (E.R.) No. 10 of 1955, s. 6(1), and M.C.(A.) L., (E.R.) No. 13 of 1960, s. 3].

(2) Composition.—A court is duly constituted when presided over by a Chief Magistrate or Magistrates. Every magistrate is *ex officio* a Justice of the Peace for the Region [M.C.L., s. 8].

(3) Jurisdiction—original—A Chief Magistrate has jurisdiction in civil causes or matters:—

- (a) in all personal suits;
- (b) in suits between landlord and tenant;
- (c) in all actions for the recovery of any penalty, rates, expenses, contribution or other like demand, where the amount claimed does not exceed £500;
- (d) to appoint guardians;
- (e) to grant injunctions [E.R. No. 10 of 1955, s. 17];
- (f) in an appeal from a decision of an Assessment Committee [E.R. Local Government Law, E.R. No. 17 of 1960, 5th Schedule].

A magistrate has civil jurisdiction similar to that set out above, except that the amount claimed must not exceed £200 [E.R.L.G.L., E.R. No. 17 of 1960, s. 18].

On the criminal side, magistrates have power to try and determine summary offences, but their powers of punishment vary, as follows:—

Chief Magistrate—a maximum fine not exceeding £500, or imprisonment not exceeding 5 years, or both [M.C.L., s. 20, amended by M.C.(A.)L., E.R. No. 30 of 1955].

Magistrate—a maximum fine not exceeding £200, or imprisonment not exceeding 2 years, or both [s. 22, replaced by M.C.(A.)L., E.R. No. 30 of 1955, s. 5].

For other jurisdictions of the Court see M.C. L., E.R. No. 10 of 1955, ss. 23 and 24, as amended by M.C.(A.)L., No. 30 of 1955, s. 6. Note also that every magistrate has jurisdiction throughout the Region, but may be assigned to a specified District [E.R. No. 10 of 1955, s. 7(1)].

(4) Jurisdiction—appellate.—A magistrate, within the limits of his jurisdiction, hears and determines:—

- (a) appeals from native courts or customary courts in accordance with the provisions of the N.C.O., and
- (b) appeals from the decision of an Assessment Committee [M.C.L., s. 28(a), (b)].

CONTROL OF COURTS

(5) Appeals from.—Appeals lie to the High Court from the decisions of the magistrates' courts in both civil and criminal matters [M.C. L., ss. 54–60].

(6) Review/revision.—The High Court has revisional jurisdiction over magistrates' courts in respect of criminal proceedings before any magistrate. The purpose of this power is to enable the High Court to satisfy itself as to the correctness, legality or propriety of any finding, sentence or order recorded by a magistrate [M.C.(A.) L., E.R. No. 8 of 1958, s. 2].

(7) Transfer.—Any magistrate may, at any stage of the proceedings before final judgment, transfer any cause or matter before him to another magistrate of competent jurisdiction in the same District [M.C. Law, s. 47].

" Where, in respect of any civil proceedings before him, a magistrate shall be of the opinion that the same ought to be transferred to the court of a magistrate assigned to another District, or to the High Court, the magistrate may report their pendency to a judge " [M.C. Law, s. 48].

A magistrate has power to transfer cases before him to a native court or customary court having jurisdiction in that matter [M.C.L., s. 48].

A judge has power to transfer any civil cause or matter pending before a magistrate's court to another magistrate's court, or to the High Court [M.C.L., s. 51].

(8) Inspection, supervision, etc.—See (6), *supra*.

Law to be Administered

(9) General law ⎫ As High Court (see A. 2(9), (10), pp. 60–61,
(10) Customary law ⎭   *ante*) [M.C. Law, ss. 40–43].

(11) Islamic or other law.—As High Court (see A. 2(11), p. 61, *ante*).

B. CUSTOMARY COURTS

The old native courts are being replaced by customary courts of varying grades according to their jurisdiction. The Customary Courts Law, enacted in 1956 (C.C.L., 1956, E.R. No. 21 of 1956), came into force on November 29, 1957 [E.R. No. 31 of 1958]. By s. 9 of the C.C.(A.)L., E.R. No. 12 of 1957, native courts are deemed to cease, and have effect within the area of jurisdiction of any customary court established by the responsible Minister. (Note that the expression " customary court " means a County Court and a District Court. A " District Court " means a District Court Grade A and a District Court Grade B.) The Customary Courts Law, 1956, has been amended by the following:—C.C.(A.) Law, E.R. Nos. 12 of 1957, No. 31 of 1958; Native Courts (Interim Provisions) E.R. No. 12 of 1960; the Eastern Region Local Government Law, E.R. No. 17 of 1960.

Constitution and Powers

(1) Establishment.—Customary courts are established by the Minister [C.C.L., E.R. No. 21 of 1956, s. 3(1), 2()].

(2) Composition.—Appointed by the Minister and such members who are to be *ex-officio* or otherwise members of such court [C.C.L., s. 4(1)]. The President or Vice- President of the Court must be literate in the English language [C.C.L., s. 6]. The members of the Court may be assisted by assessors [C.C.L., s. 6(1)].

(3) Jurisdiction—original.—The jurisdiction of a customary court is set out in the warrant establishing it [C.C.L., s. 3(4)]. The extent of the criminal and civil jurisdiction of the two grades of District Courts is set out in the 1st Schedule to the Law.

The criminal jurisdiction of District Court Grade A is as follows:— criminal causes, including theft of farm produce or livestock, which can be adequately punished by six months' imprisonment, twelve strokes (in the case of juvenile offenders) or a fine not exceeding £50 or the equivalent by customary law [C.C.(A.)L., E.R. No. 31 of 1958, s. 4].

In the case of District Court Grade B, the maximum fine is £25, otherwise its jurisdiction is the same as that of the District Court Grade A.

The jurisdiction of the District Court Grade A in civil causes is as follows:—

(*i*) Civil actions which do not exceed the suit value of £50;

(*ii*) unlimited jurisdiction in matters concerning ownership, possession and occupation of land;

(*iii*) causes relating to the succession to property and administration of estates under customary law where the value of the property does not exceed £50;

(*iv*) unlimited jurisdiction in matrimonial causes and matters between persons married under customary law, and suits relating to the custody of children under customary law [C.C.L., First Schedule].

In the case of District Court Grade B, the maximum suit value is £25.

Note that the following persons or classes of persons are those subject to the jurisdiction of customary courts:—

(a) Persons of African descent, provided that the mode of life of such persons is that of the general community;

(b) persons whether of African or non-African descent whom the Governor in Council may direct to be subject to the jurisdiction of the customary courts;

(c) any persons who have at any time instituted proceedings in any customary court [C.C.(A.)L., E.R. No. 12 of 1957, s. 3, which replaces s. 19 of the principal Law].

(4) Jurisdiction—appellate.—The Minister by warrant may appoint a County Court to be the Court of Appeal for all or any of the District Courts [C.C.L., ss. 59 and 60, which has been replaced by s. 7 of the C.C.(A.)L., E.R. No. 12 of 1957]. Any party aggrieved by the decision of a Grade A or B District Court may appeal to the County Court (if one has been established) or to the Magistrate's Court.

CONTROL OF COURTS

(5) Appeals from.—Appeals from the decisions of Grade A or Grade B Courts lie to the County Court, if one is established. Appeals from the decisions of County Courts lie to the Magistrate's Court, thence to the High Court [C.C.L., s. 60(a), (c)].

(6) Review/revision.—At the end of each month, every customary court must forward to the Customary Courts Adviser a list of all causes or matters decided by that customary court during the month [C.C.L., s. 56(1)].

(7) Transfer.—The Customary Courts Adviser may, at any stage of the proceedings before the final judgment transfer a cause or matter before a customary court to a magistrate's court or to the High Court [C.C.L., s. 35].

A customary court has power to transfer any cause or matter to any other customary court of competent jurisdiction [C.C.L., s. 38]. " Whenever it shall appear to the High Court or to a Magistrate's Court that any cause or matter brought before it is one properly cognisable by a customary court, the High Court or the Magistrate's Court may stop the [case] . . . and refer the parties to a competent customary court . . . " [C.C.L., s. 39].

(8) Inspection, supervision, etc.—The Customary Courts Adviser has at all times access to District and County Courts and to their records [C.C.L., s. 58].

Law to be Administered

(9) General law.—This is " the provisions of any Ordinance or law which the Court may be authorised to enforce by an Order under s. 26 " [C.C.L., s. 23(1), (b)] and the provisions of all rules and orders made under the Native Authority Ordinance, bylaws, etc. [C.C.L., s. 23(1) (c)].

(10) Customary law.—This is " the customary law prevailing in the area of the jurisdiction of the Court or binding between the parties, so far as it is not repugnant to natural justice, equity and good conscience, not incompatible either directly or by necessary implication with any Ordinance or Law for the time being in force " [C.C.L., s. 23(1), (a)].

(11) Islamic or other law.—" Islamic law is applied—where it is applied at all—under the extensive and elastic umbrella of ' native law and custom ' " (Anderson, J. N. D., " Customary law and Islamic law in British African Territories ", in *The Future of Customary Law in Africa* (1955), p. 77).

NORTHERN REGION[1]
A. 2 THE HIGH COURT
Constitution and Powers

(1) Establishment.—Established by the Nigeria (Constitution) Order in Council, 1960, Third Schedule, Constitution of Northern Nigeria, s. 49, replacing the Nigeria (Constitution) O-in-C, 1954, s. 142, in pursuance of which the High Court of Justice of the Northern Region of Nigeria was established by the Northern Region High Court Law, N.R. No. 8 of 1955, since amended by N.R.H.C. (Amendment) Law, No. 13 of 1955, and the Native Courts Law, N.R. No. 6 of 1956, ss. 87 and 88.

(2) Composition.—" The judges of the High Court of the Region shall be:—

    (a) the Chief Justice of the Region; and
    (b) such number of other judges (not being less than six) as may be prescribed by the Legislature of the Region " [Constitution, N.N., s. 49(2)].[2]

---

[1] For diagram of courts system see p. 213, *post*.

[2] Note that " judge " also includes a judge of the Sharia Court of Appeal sitting as a member of the High Court [N.R. H.C. (Amdt. No. 2) L., 1961, s. 2].

(3) Jurisdiction—original.—" The High Court is a superior court of record, and in addition to any other jurisdiction conferred by the Order in Council, this Law or any other written law shall, within the limits . . . possess and exercise all the jurisdiction, powers and authorities which are vested in Her Majesty's High Court of Justice in England " [N.R.H.C.L., s. 11(1)]. The jurisdiction vested in the Court also includes all Her Majesty's criminal jurisdiction which at the commencement of this Law was, or at any time afterwards may be exerciseable within the Region [N.R.H.C.L., s. 12(c)].

The High Court has no jurisdiction in the following cases:—

    (*i*) original jurisdiction in any suit which raises any issue as to title to land which is subject to the jurisdiction of a native court [N.R.H.C.L., s. 16(1), (a)].

    (*ii*) in any dispute in respect of any question in relation to which its jurisdiction is excluded by the provisions of the O-in-C [N.R.H.C.(A.)L., N.R. No. 12 of 1956, s. 5, which replaces s. 13 of the Principal Law].

(4) Jurisdiction—appellate.—The High Court has appellate jurisdiction to hear and determine all appeals from decision at first instance of District Courts and magistrates' courts [N.R.H.C.L., s. 37, as amended by N.R.H.C.(A.)L., 1960, s. 8; see also Constitution, N.N., s. 52(1)]. In addition:—

" Nothing in paragraph (a) of sub-section (1) of this section shall confer any right of appeal:—

    (a) from any decision of a subordinate court on a question relating to Moslem matters in any case in which it is provided by any Regional law that an appeal shall lie as of right to the Sharia Court of Appeal;

    (b) from any decision of the Sharia Court of Appeal on any such question; or

    (c) from any decision of the Court of Resolution on any question relating to the respective jurisdictions of the High Court of the Region and the Sharia Court of Appeal " [Constitution, N.N., s. 52(2)].

The High Court has jurisdiction to hear appeals from Grade A, A limited, native courts, and provincial courts [N.R.H.C.(Amdt. No. 2)L., 1961, s. 3].

CONTROL OF COURT

(5) Appeals from.—" A decision of the High Court shall be subject to appeal to the Court of Resolution on the ground that the Sharia Court of Appeal and not the High Court had jurisdiction in any particular cause or matter " [N.R.H.C.L., s. 35A, *inserted* by N.R.H.C. (Amendment)L., 1960, N.R. No. 14 of 1960, s. 7].

    (a) Any person aggrieved by a decision of the High Court in a civil appeal; and

    (b) the prosecutor and any person aggrieved by the decision of the High Court in a criminal appeal from a native court, may appeal against such decision to the Federal Supreme Court with the leave of the High Court only [s. 4 of the N.R.H.C.L., No. 2 of 1957, replacing s. 65 of the N.R.H.C.L., 1955].

(7) Transfer.—The Chief Justice may transfer a cause or matter from one judge to another judge [N.R.H.C.L., s. 73(1)].

LAW TO BE ADMINISTERED

(9) General law.—" Subject to the provisions of any written law and in particular of this section and of sections 26, 32 and 35 of this Law:—

(a) the common law;
(b) the doctrines of equity; and
(c) the statutes of general application which were in force in England on the 1st day of January, 1900,

shall, in so far as they relate to any matter with respect to which the Legislature of the Region is for the time being competent to make laws, be in force within the jurisdiction of the Court " [N.R.H.C.L., s. 28]. Law and equity are to be concurrently administered and in case of any conflict the rules of equity shall prevail [N.R.H.C.L., ss. 29 and 30].

The jurisdiction of the High Court in probate, divorce and matrimonial causes and proceedings is to be exercised by the Court in conformity with the law and practice for the time being in force in England.

(10) Customary law.—" The High Court shall observe, and enforce the observance of, every native law and custom which is not repugnant to natural justice, equity and good conscience, nor incompatible either directly or by inplication with any law for the time being in force, and nothing in this Law shall deprive any person of the benefit of any such native law or custom.

Such laws and customs shall be deemed applicable in causes and matters where the parties thereto are natives and also in causes and matters between natives and non-natives, where it may appear to the Court that substantial injustice would be done to either party by a strict adherence to the rules of English law.

No party shall be entitled to claim the benefit of any native law or custom, if it shall appear either from express contract or from the nature of the transactions out of which any suit or question may have arisen, that such party agreed that his obligations in connection with such transactions should be regulated exclusively by English law or that such transactions are transactions unknown to native law or custom.

In cases where no express rule is applicable to any matter in controversy, the Court shall be governed by the principles of justice, equity and good conscience " [N.R.H.C.L., s. 34].

(11) Islamic or other law.—Special provision is made for the application of " Moslem law " in the Northern Region, which is defined as follows:—

" ' Moslem law ' means such system of Moslem law as may be prescribed in any Regional law . . . as applied subject to the provisions of any such law;
' question relating to Moslem matters ' means:—

(a) any question of Moslem law regarding a marriage concluded in accordance with that law, including a question relating to the dissolution of such marriage or a question that depends on such a marriage relating to family relationship or the guardianship of an infant;
(b) where all the parties to the proceedings are Moslems, any question regarding a marriage, including the dissolution of

that marriage, or regarding family relationship, a foundling or the guardianship of an infant;

(c) any question regarding a wakf, gift, will or succession where the endower, donor, testator or deceased person is a Moslem;

(d) any question regarding an infant, prodigal or person of unsound mind who is a Moslem or the maintenance or guardianship of a Moslem who is physically or mentally infirm; or

(e) where all the parties to the proceedings (whether or not they are Moslems) have by writing under their hand requested the court that hears the case in the first instance to determine that case in accordance with Moslem law, any other question " [Constitution, N.N., s. 52(5)].

A. 3 MAGISTRATES' COURTS

CONSTITUTION AND POWERS

(1) Establishment.—By the Criminal Procedure Code Law, 1960, N.R. No. 11 of 1960, s. 4, the Northern Region is divided into magisterial districts for the purposes of this Law; in each of the districts there is established a magistrate's court [Crim. P.C.L., s. 5].

(2) Composition.—The Governor has power to appoint magistrates who are styled Chief Magistrates, and first, second and third grade magistrates [Crim. P.C.L., s. 6].

(3) Jurisdiction—original.—Every magistrate has jurisdiction throughout the Region unless his appointment is specifically limited to the area of any district [Crim. P.C.L., ss. 5, 16–19].

Unless otherwise provided for in the order of appointment, a Chief Magistrate has the powers prescribed in s. 16 of the Criminal Procedure Code [N.R. No. 11 of 1960], i.e., imprisonment for a term not exceeding five years; a fine not exceeding £500, caning; detention under s. 71 of the Penal Code. A magistrate of the first grade may pass the following sentences:—imprisonment for a term not exceeding two years; a fine not exceeding £200; caning; detention under s. 71 of the Penal Code [Crim. P.C.L., s. 16]. A magistrate of the second grade may pass a sentence of imprisonment not exceeding one year; a fine not exceeding £100; caning and detention. A magistrate of the third grade may pass a sentence of imprisonment not exceeding three months and a fine not exceeding £25. Additionally, the Governor may by order authorise an increased jurisdiction in criminal matters to be exercised by any magistrate, to such an extent as the Chief Justice may specify [Crim. P.C.L., s. 19]. No magistrate's court has jurisdiction to dispose of civil cases since the repeal of the Magistrates Court (Northern Region) Law, N.R. No. 7 of 1955. Jurisdiction in civil cases is vested in District Courts.

A. 4 DISTRICT COURTS

CONSTITUTION AND POWERS

(1) Establishment.—By the District Courts Law (N.R. No. 15 of 1960), the Northern Region is divided into districts; in each district there is established a District Court for the disposal of civil causes and matters.

(2) Composition.—The Governor has power to appoint District Judges, who are styled Senior District Judges and District Judges of the first, second or third grade [D.C.L., s. 7].

(3) Jurisdiction—original.—A District Judge has jurisdiction throughout the Region unless his appointment is specifically limited to the area of any district [D.C.L., s. 5]. A Senior District Judge has jurisdiction similar to that of a Chief Magistrate acting in his civil jurisdiction in the Western Region. £500 is the limit of his suit value. The civil jurisdiction of other grades of District Judges is the same as that of the Senior District Judge, except that the suit value is scaled down [D.C.L., ss. 13–17].

(4) Jurisdiction—appellate.—Nil.

CONTROL OF COURTS

(5) Appeals from.—Appeals lie from the decisions of the District Court to the High Court, in criminal matters, by virtue of s. 279 of the Crim. P.C., and in civil matters by virtue of s. 70 of the D.C.L.

(6) Review/revision.—The High Court has powers of revision in respect of all proceedings in Magistrates' Courts and District Courts [N.R.H.C.L., s. 39]. The Chief Justice may require specified magistrates to forward a monthly list to him, or to another judge (by rule made under Crim.P.C., s. 373(1), (c)). The Chief Justice may call for and examine the record of the proceedings in any criminal case before any court for the purpose of satisfying himself as to the correctness, legality or propriety of any finding, sentence or order recorded or passed and as to the regularity of the proceedings of the court [Crim. P.C., s. 285].

(7) Transfer.—The Chief Justice may, in respect of criminal matters, wherever it appears to him that the transfer of a case will promote the ends of justice or will be in the interests of public tranquillity, transfer any case from one court to another at any stage of the proceedings [Crim. P.C., s. 138]. A judge may transfer any cause or matter before him to a magistrate's court [N.R.H.C.L., s. 72(1)]. A magistrate may transfer any cause or matter from his court to another court. In civil matters the powers of a District Judge to transfer are limited to: (a) power to report for transfer [D.C.L., s. 30]; (b) a power to transfer to another District Court in the same district [D.C.L., s. 29(1)]; and (c) a power to transfer to a native court [D.C.L., ss. 31, 32].

(8) Inspection, supervison, etc.—Nil.

LAW TO BE ADMINISTERED

(9) General law.—Magistrates' courts exercise jurisdiction in conformity with the Penal Code Law, 1959, No. 19 of 1959, and the Criminal Procedure Code. District Courts are bound, in the exercise of their civil jurisdiction, to follow the provisions of the District Courts Law, 1960, but, as this Law is not a comprehensive code of civil procedure, a District Court enjoys a greater degree of elasticity in the disposing of a case before it than does a Magistrate's Court operating under the Criminal Procedure Code.

(10) Customary law.—See (9), *supra.*

(11) Islamic or other law.—As High Court (see A. 2(11), p. 67, *ante*).

B. 1 SHARIA COURT OF APPEAL

Constitution and powers

(1) Establishment.—Established by the Sharia Court of Appeal Law, 1960, N.R. No. 16 of 1960.

(2) Composition.—" The Court shall consist of a Grand Kadi, a Deputy Grand Kadi and two other Judges learned in the Sharia " [S.C.A.L., s. 4(1)].
  " A person shall be qualified to be a Judge if he is:—
     (a) a Moslem;
     (b) not less than thirty-five years of age; and
     (c)—(*i*) a person who has been an alkali or adviser on Moslem law in the service of a native authority for not less than ten years; or (*ii*) the holder of a certificate that he has satisfactorily completed a recognised course of study in Sharia law at a university college or school approved by the Governor in Council " [S.C.A.L., s. 5].

(3) Jurisdiction—original.—Nil.

(4) Jurisdiction—appellate.—" (1) Subject as otherwise provided in this Law the Court shall have jurisdiction to hear and determine appeals in respect of Regional matters in cases governed by Moslem personal law from any decision of:—
     (a) a Grade " A " native court;
     (b) a Grade " A limited " native court;
     (c) a Provincial Court.

(2) For all the purposes of and incidental to the hearing and determination of any appeal, and the amendment, execution and enforcement of any judgment, order or decision made therein, the Court shall have all the powers, authority and jurisdiction of every native court of which the judgment, order or decision is the subject of an appeal to the Court, and, without prejudice to the generality of the foregoing, shall have all the powers conferred upon native courts exercising appellate jurisdiction by the provisions of sections 69, 70A and 70B of the Native Courts Law, 1956.

(3) Except as provided in sub-section (2), the Court shall have no original jurisdiction in any cause or matter " [S.C.A.L., s. 11(1), (2), (3)].

(5) Appeals from.—A limited right of appeal to the Federal Supreme Court.

Law to be Administered

(9) General law
(10) Customary law } Nil.

(11) Islamic or other law.—" The Court, in the exercise of the jurisdiction vested in it by this Law as regards both substantive law and practice and procedure, shall administer, observe and enforce the observance of, the principles and provisions of:—

(a) Moslem law of the Maliki school as customarily interpreted at the place where the trial at first instance took place;

(b) this Law;

(c) the Native Courts Law, 1956, and any other law affecting native courts in so far as it appertains to a cause or matter within section 12 of this Law; and

(d) natural justice, equity and good conscience" [S.C.A.L., s.15].

B. 2 NATIVE COURTS

CONSTITUTION AND POWERS

(1) Establishment.—Native courts, except Provincial Courts, are established by the Resident of a Province by warrant under his hand, subject to the confirmation of the Governor [Native Courts Law, 1956, N.R. No. 6 of 1956, s. 34, since amended by the Native Courts (Amendment) Law, N.R. Nos. 12 of 1957 and 22 of 1958].

A Provincial Court is established in each Province in accordance with the provisions of s. 3 of the Native Courts Law, 1956, N.R. No. 6 of 1956, (as amended by the Native Courts (Amendment) Law of 1960, N.R. No. 10 of 1960).

(2) Composition.—The Resident appoints members of a native court, other than the court of an Alkali [N.C.L., s. 4(1)]. Where the court of an Alkali is established under the provisions of s. 3 the native authority in whose area the court is established must, subject to the approval of the Resident, appoint an Alkali to such court [N.C.L., s. 4(3)]. Members of Provincial Courts are appointed by the Governor acting on the advice of the Judicial Service Commissioner [s. 3 of the N.C.L. 1956 (as amended by the N.C.(A.)L., 1960, N.R. No. 10 of 1960]. The Sharia Court of Appeal is not a native court, being separately established by statute.

A native court consists of (a) head chiefs or chiefs, or any other persons (who may include non-natives) sitting with or without assessors, or (b) an alkali sitting with or without assessors [N.C.L., s. 5(1)].

(3) Jurisdiction—original.—Every native court, in addition to having jurisdiction within such territorial limits as may be defined by its warrant, has jurisdiction over, e.g., the following classes of persons:—

(a) all persons who (*i*) permanently reside on the land within the area of jurisdiction of a native authority, and (*ii*) " whose general mode of life is that of the general native community ";

(b) all persons who are temporarily resident within the area of jurisdiction of a native authority, and whose mode of life is similar to that of the general community;

(c) persons whether of African or non-African descent, who have at any time instituted proceedings in any native court;

(d) all natives of Nigeria and all native foreigners in cases in which they consent to the exercise of the jurisdiction of the native court [N.C.L., s. 15(1)]. (Native foreigner means any person, not being a native of Nigeria, whose parents were members of a tribe or tribes indigenous to some part of Africa, and the descendants of such persons [Interpretation Ordinance, cap. 94, Laws of Nigeria, 1948].)

Criminal and civil.—There are 5 grades of native courts:—grades A, A limited, B, C and D, and the jurisdiction and power of any native courts of these grades must not exceed those prescribed in the 1st Schedule, e.g. Grade A has virtually unlimited jurisdiction in criminal causes, but no sentence of death is to be carried out until it has been confirmed by the Governor [Crim. P.C., 1960, s. 394]. Grade D courts can impose a maximum fine of £15 or a sentence of 9 months' imprisonment.

The jurisdiction of a native court is set out in the warrant of its establishment [N.C.L., s. 18(1)]. The jurisdiction of all native courts is subject to the limitation imposed by the provisions of s. 15(a) of the N.C.L., [added by the Native Courts (A.) Law, 1958, No. 22 of 1958], which gives a non-Moslem or accused person or defendant the right to opt out of trial by a Moslem court, and vice-versa. A Moslem court is defined in s. 2 of that law as a court which customarily administers the principles of Moslem law.

Under the Penal Code Law, 1959, (N.R. No. 18 of 1959) and by virtue of the Native Courts (A.) Law, 1960, in criminal matters native courts are guided by the provisions of the Criminal Procedure Code Law, 1960, and bound by the provisions of Cap. XXIII thereof, which *inter alia* provide that all convictions in native courts must be by way of reference to a section of the Penal Code or other ordinance or law. The effect of these amendments is that no person may be convicted of a criminal offence under any native law or custom. " Guidance " means that although the native courts must apply the new codified criminal law to every case which is before them, they are allowed latitude to err (subject to being bound strictly to observe certain essential provisions). In the event of such errors becoming apparent on appeal, the appeal court may not quash the proceedings of the lower court solely on account of the errors in procedure, or because the court has not been guided or properly guided by the codes [Crim. P.C., s. 386].

(4) Jurisdiction—appellate.—A case originating in a grade B, C or D native court goes on appeal to a Provincial Court. Provincial Courts, set up by the N.C.(A.)L., 1960, with jurisdiction to hear all appeals arising within a Province from native courts of grades B, C and D, consist of a single Alkali sitting in each province with the exception of the provinces of Benin, Kabba and Plateau, where the court is constituted by a President and two members, one of whom must be an Alkali learned in Moslem law. The staff of these courts are all appointed by the Governor on the advice of the Judicial Service Commissioner, and are therefore servants of the Regional Government. Provision is made for Provincial Courts to use assessors [N.C.(A.)L., 1960, N.R. No. 10 of 1960]. At the order of the Resident of the Province, the Provincial Court may exercise first instance powers in a particular cause or matter, and in such cases has the jurisdiction of a native court of grade A limited.

CONTROL OF COURTS

(5) Appeals from.—Appeals from native courts of grades A and A limited go to the Native Courts Appellate Division of the High Court, unless the matter is one properly governed by Moslem personal law when the appeal goes to the Sharia Court of Appeal. Appeals from grade B, C and D native courts lie to the Provincial Courts, and thereafter to the Native Courts Appellate Division of the High Court or the Sharia Court of Appeal (as is appropriate to the particular cause or matter) [N.C.L., 1956 (No. 6 of 1956) as amended by the N.C.(A.)L., 1960, N.R. (No. 10 of 1960)].

(6) Review/revision.—Every Resident may of his own motion, or in his absolute discretion, on the application of any person concerned, review any of the proceedings, whether civil or criminal, (save and except a sentence of death) of any native court in his province [N.C.L., s. 55(2)]. A Native Courts Adviser may of his own motion review any cause or matter determined by a grade C or D native court [N.C.L., s. 55(5)]. The proceedings of a Provincial Court are not subject to review by a Resident or Native Courts Adviser.

(7) Transfer.—Every Resident and District Officer has power at any time, or at any stage of the proceedings before final judgment, to stay the hearing of any cause or matter and transfer the cause to a magistrate's court or to the High Court [N.C.L., s. 32]. A native court may transfer any cause or matter before it to any other native court of competent jurisdiction [N.C.L., s. 34; see also ss. 35–37]. A Resident may transfer a cause or matter at any stage before judgment from a native court within his Province to the Provincial Court for trial by that court at first instance [N.C.L., 1956, ss. 32–37, (N.R. No. 6 of 1956]. In any criminal cause or matter, the Chief Justice may call for and examine the proceedings and may direct that the case be transferred to the court to which appeal will ordinarily lie, and that court must then treat the matter as if it was before it on appeal [s. 285 of the Crim. P.C., 1960].

(8) Inspection, supervision, etc.—Every Resident, District Officer and Native Courts Adviser shall at all times have access to native courts of first instance in his province or division, and to the records of and proceedings of such courts [N.C.L., s. 55].

LAW TO BE ADMINISTERED

(9) General law.—Native courts are now empowered to administer the Penal Code Law, 1961, the Criminal Procedure Code Law, 1960, as well as any written law which they may be authorised to enforce [N.C.L., s. 22, as replaced by Native Courts (Amendment) Law, 1960, s. 8]. In addition they are entitled to administer; the provisions of all rules and orders made under the Native Authority Law, 1954 and orders and bylaws made by a native authority under any other written law and in force in the area of the jurisdiction of the court.

(10) Customary law.—In the civil jurisdiction only, the native law and custom prevailing in the area of the jurisdiction of the court, or binding between the parties, so far as it is not repugnant to natural justice, equity and good conscience, nor incompatible either directly or by necessary implication with any written law for the time being in force [N.C.L., s. 20(1), (a)].

" In mixed civil causes, other than land causes, the native law and custom to be applied by a native court shall be:—

(a) the particular native law and custom which the parties agreed or intended, or may be presumed to have agreed or intended, should regulate their obligations in connection with the transactions which are in controversy before the court; or

(b) that combination of any two or more native laws or customs which the parties agreed or intended, or may be presumed to have agreed or intended, should regulate their obligations as aforesaid; or

(c) in the absence of any such agreement or intention or presumption thereof:—

(*i*) the particular native law and custom; or
(*ii*) such combination of any two or more native laws or customs,
which it appears to the court, ought, having regard to the nature of the transaction and to all the circumstances of the case, to regulate the obligations of the parties aforesaid,

but if, in the opinion of the court, none of the paragraphs of this sub-section is applicable to any particular matter in controversy, the court shall be governed by the principles of natural justice, equity and good conscience " [N.C.L., s. 21(2)].

" In mixed land causes the native law and custom to be applied by a native court shall be the native law and custom in force in relation to land in the place where the land is situate;

Provided that no native law or custom prohibiting, restricting or regulating the devolution on death to any particular class of persons of the right to occupy any land shall operate to deprive any person of any beneficial interest in such land (other than the right to occupy the same) or in the proceeds of sale thereof to which he may be entitled under the rules of inheritance of any other native law and custom " [N.C.L., s. 21(3)].

(11) Islamic or other law.—By definition native law and custom includes Muslim law [N.C.L., s. 2].

C. 1 MOSLEM COURTS

Distinction is now made for several purposes between " Moslem " and " non-Moslem " native courts. The Moslem native courts are those constituted by alkalai (see B. 2(2), p. 71, *ante*); in addition there is the Sharia Court of Appeal (see B. 1, p. 70, *ante*).

A Moslem Court is defined in s. 2 of the Native Courts Law, 1956 (No. 6 of 1956) as a court which customarily applies the principles of Moslem law. Under the Penal Code and the Criminal Procedure Code the distinction between Moslem and non-Moslem native courts is of no meaning in criminal cases, because both sets of courts will be administering the same laws; the distinction is therefore only of importance in *civil* matters.

C. 2 COURT OF RESOLUTION

CONSTITUTION AND POWERS

(1) Establishment.—By the Court of Resolution Law, 1960, N.R. No. 17 of 1960, s. 2(1): " There shall be a court for the resolution of any conflict of jurisdiction arising between the High Court of Justice of the Northern Region (hereinafter referred to as the High Court) and the Sharia Court of Appeal."

(2) Composition.—" (1) The Court of Resolution shall consist of:—

(a) the Chief Justice of the High Court, who shall be President of the Court;
(b) the Grand Kadi;
(c) one judge of the High Court to be nominated by the Chief Justice;
(d) one judge of the Sharia Court of Appeal to be nominated by the Grand Kadi.

(2) In the event of the opinions of the members of the Court of Resolution being evenly divided on any matter before it, then the court shall by order make a declaration in accordance with the opinion supported by the Chief Justice of the High Court " [*ibid.*, s. 3].

LAW TO BE ADMINISTERED

" The Court of Resolution, in the exercise of the powers vested in it by this Law as regards both substantive law and practice and procedure, shall administer, observe, and enforce the observance of, the principles and provisions of:—

(a) this Law,
(b) the Northern Region High Court Law, 1955;
(c) the Native Courts Law, 1956; and
(d) the Sharia Court of Appeal Law, 1960 " [*ibid.*, s. 8].

NORTHERN CAMEROONS

By the Northern Cameroons Administration Order in Council, 1960 (S.I. 1960 No. 1656), a separate High Court was set up for the Northern Cameroons. Appeals lie from the High Court to the Nigerian Federal Supreme Court. Appeals lie from decisions of Northern Cameroons subordinate courts to the Sharia Court of Appeal [arts. 14 and 15]. (See also the Nigeria Constitution, first Amendment, 1961, s. 3(1) and the Constitution of Northern Nigeria Amendment Law, No. 26 of 1961, which provide that all the laws applicable in Northern Nigeria on May 31, 1961, shall, as from June 1, 1961 apply to the former trust territory of the Northern Cameroons.)

SOUTHERN CAMEROONS[1]

The British Cameroons consisted of the Northern Cameroons, formerly administered integrally with the Northern Region of Nigeria, and the Southern Cameroons. From October 1, 1960 the Cameroons ceased to be administered with the Federation of Nigeria. Recently the Southern Cameroons has by plebiscite opted to federate with Cameroun (formerly under French administration), whilst the Northern Cameroons has opted for union with Nigeria. Consequently the Northern Cameroons has adopted the judicial and legal system of the Northern Region of Nigeria (of which it forms part: *q.v.*).

The courts system in the Southern Cameroons consists of :—

A. courts primarily administering " English " law, viz., the High Court and the Magistrates' Courts.

B. courts primarily administering customary law.

A. 1(a) THE PRIVY COUNCIL

Appeals lie from the Federal Supreme Court of Nigeria, when hearing appeals from the S. Cameroons High Court, to the Privy Council [the Southern Cameroons (Constitution) O-inC, 1960 (S.I. 1960, No. 1654), s. 57].

A. 1(b) THE FEDERAL SUPREME COURT

" The Federal Supreme Court of Nigeria shall have jurisdiction to hear and determine appeals from the High Court " [*ibid.*, s. 55]. " The Federal Supreme Court of Nigeria shall be a superior court of record in the Southern Cameroons ", and its decisions are enforceable by S. Cameroons courts [*ibid.*, s. 56].

A. 2 THE HIGH COURT

(1) Establishment.—Established by S. Cameroons O-in-C, 1960, s. 50(1), and S. Cameroons High Court Law, 1955, S.C. No. 7 of 1955, as amended by the S.C.H.C.(A.)L., S.C. Nos. 9 of 1955 and 3 of 1958, and the Customary Courts Law, 1956, S.C. No. 9 of 1956 (2nd Schedule).

(2) Composition.—The High Court consists of a single judge appointed by the Commissioner by instrument [S. Cameroons O-in-C, ss. 50(2), 51(1)].

(3) Jurisdiction—original.—The High Court possesses and exercises " all the jurisdiction, powers and authorities other than Admiralty jurisdiction, which are vested in or are capable of being exercised by Her Majesty's High Court of Justice in England " [S.C.H.C.L., s. 7]. " This includes all Her Majesty's civil and criminal jurisdiction which immediately before the coming into operation of this Law was, or at any time afterwards may be exercisable in the Southern Cameroons " [S.C.H.C.L., s. 8].

---

[1] For diagram of courts system see p. 210, *post.*

" The High Court shall not, unless otherwise directed, exercise original jurisdiction in any suit or matter which:—

(a) concerns title to land which is subject to the jurisdiction of a native court;

(b) relates to marriage, family status, guardianship of children, inheritance or the disposition of property on death, and is subject to the jurisdiction of a native court " [S.C.H.C.L., s. 9(1)(a), (b)].

The High Court, however, has jurisdiction in suits referred to above on transfer to the High Court under the provisions of the Native Courts Ordinance, or any law replacing the same [S.C.H.C.L., s. 9(2)(a), (b)]. The High Court is empowered to administer law and equity concurrently [S.C.H.C.L., s. 12].

The jurisdiction of the High Court in probate, divorce and matrimonial causes and proceedings may, subject to the provisions of the High Court Law, be exercised by the court in conformity with the law and practice for the time being in force in England [S.C.H.C.L., s. 15].

(4) Jurisdiction—appellate.—This is regulated by S. Cameroons O-in-C, 1960, s. 54, and S.C.H.C.L., 1955.

The High Court has appellate jurisdiction to hear and determine all appeals from the decisions of magistrates' courts [S.C.H.C.L., s. 30(1)]. Further, the High Court has power to hear and determine appeals from the decisions of magistrates' courts and district officers on appeal from customary courts [C.C.L.(S.C.), No. 9 of 1956, 2nd Schedule].

CONTROL OF COURT

(5) Appeals from.—Appeals from the decisions of the High Court in civil and criminal causes in respect of a regional matter lie to the Federal Supreme Court [S.C.H.C.L., s. 52].

(6) Review/revision.—Nil.

(7) Transfer.—The Chief Justice may at any time or at any stage before judgment transfer any cause or matter before a judge to any other judge [S.C.H.C.L., s. 57(1)]. A judge may transfer any cause or matter before him to a magistrate's court which has jurisdiction in such cause or matter [S.C.H.C.L., s. 56(1)]. A judge may transfer any matter before him to a native court [S.C.H.C.L., s. 61].

(8) Inspection, supervision, etc.—Nil.

LAW TO BE ADMINISTERED

(9) General law.—All offices, courts of law, authorities, etc., constituted under the Orders in Council revoked by the S. Cameroons O-in-C, 1960, continue in existence after the commencement of that Order as if they were offices, etc., under the Order [*ibid.*, s. 93].

The general law applied by the High Court consists of:—

(a) the common law;

(b) the doctrines of equity; and

(c) the statutes of general application which were in force in England on January 1, 1900, so far as these relate to any matter with respect to which the Legislature of the S. Cameroons is for the time being competent to make laws [S.C.H.C.L., s. 11].

(10) Customary law.—" (1) The High Court shall observe, and enforce the observance of, every native law and custom which is not repugnant to natural justice, equity and good conscience, nor incompatible either directly or by implication, with any law for the time being in force, and nothing in this Law shall deprive any person of the benefit of any such native law or custom.

(2) Such laws and customs shall be deemed applicable in causes and matters where the parties thereto are natives and also in causes and matters between natives and non-natives where it may appear to the court that substantial injustice would be done to either party by a strict adherence to the rules of English law.

(3) No party shall be entitled to claim the benefit of any native law or custom, if it shall appear either from express contract, or from the nature of the transactions out of which any suit or question may have arisen, that such party agreed that his obligations in connection with such transactions should be regulated exclusively by English law or that such transactions are transactions unknown to native law and custom.

(4) In cases where no express rule is applicable to a matter in controversy, the court shall be governed by the principles of justice, equity and good conscience " [S.C.H.C.L., s. 27].

(11) Islamic or other law.—According to the interpretation section, the phrase " native law and custom " includes Moslem law [S.C.H.C.L., s. 2].

A. 3 MAGISTRATES' COURTS

CONSTITUTION AND POWERS

(1) Establishment.—Established by the Magistrates' Courts (S.C.) Law, 1955 [S.C. No. 6 of 1955, since amended by the M.C.(S.C.) (A.)L. Nos. 8 of 1955, 4 of 1956; and the Customary Courts Law, 1956, S.C. No. 9 of 1956 (the Schedule)].

(2) Composition.—The Commissioner appoints magistrates who are styled Chief Magistrates and first, second and third grade magistrates [M.C.L., s. 6].

(3) Jurisdiction—original.—Every magistrate has jurisdiction (civil and criminal) throughout the S. Cameroons. The extent of the jurisdiction of a magistrate varies according to his grade. Thus the civil jurisdiction of a Chief Magistrate is as follows:—

    (a) Personal suits to the value of £500;
    (b) landlord and tenant cases to the suit value of £500;
    (c) actions for the recovery of any penalty, rates, expenses, contribution or other like demands, to the value of £500;
    (d) proceedings in respect of which jurisdiction has been conferred upon a magistrate's court by the Land and Native Rights Ordinance, e.g., to appoint guardians.

A Chief Magistrate is not to exercise jurisdiction in causes and matters subject to the jurisdiction of native courts or customary courts.

On the criminal side, a Chief Magistrate has full jurisdiction for the trial and determination of summary offences. The maximum fine to be imposed is £500, and the maximum sentence should not exceed a term of 5 years' imprisonment.

Magistrates of the first, second and third grades have similar jurisdiction, except that the money value is scaled down [M.C.(S.C.)L., ss. 18 and 19].

(4) Jurisdiction—appellate.—" A party aggrieved by the decision or order of an Appeal Officer given on appeal from a customary court may . . . appeal to a Magistrate's Court, which Court shall have jurisdiction to hear and determine such appeal " [C.C.L., 1956, S.C. No. 9 of 1956, s. 53].

CONTROL OF COURTS

(5) Appeals from.—Appeals from the decisions of magistrates' courts in both civil and criminal causes lie to the High Court [M.C.(S.C.)L., ss. 82–87].

(6) Review/revision.—The Chief Justice may require specified magistrates to forward a monthly list to the Chief Justice or to another judge for review [M.C.(S.C.)L., s. 43]. The High Court has powers of revision in respect of all proceedings in magistrates' courts [S.C.H.C.L., s. 32].

(7) Transfer.—A magistrate may transfer a cause or matter before him to another magistrate in the same district [M.C.(S.C.)L., s. 36]. A magistrate may of his own motion report certain causes to a judge for transfer either to any other magistrate's court or to the High Court [M.C.(S.C.)L., s. 37]. A magistrate may transfer any case pending before him to a native court having jurisdiction in that matter, except, e.g., matrimonial causes arising out of or in connection with a marriage under the Marriage Ordinance; or a cause or matter which has been transferred to his court by the High Court [M.C.(S.C.)L., ss. 38, 39].

(8) Inspection, supervision, etc.—See (6), *supra*.

(9) General law.—As High Court (see A. 2(9). p. 77, *ante*) [M.C. (S.C.)L., ss. 29 and 30].

(10) Customary law.—As High Court (see A. 2(10), p. 78, *ante*) [M.C.(S.C.)L., s. 31].

(11) Islamic or other law.—See A. 2(11), p. 78, *ante*.

B. CUSTOMARY COURTS

CONSTITUTION AND POWERS

(1) Establishment.—Established by the Customary Courts Law, 1956, S.C. No. 9 of 1956, since amended by the C.C.(A.)L., No. 5 of 1959. A customary court is established by warrant by the Commissioner [C.C.L., s. 3(1)].

(2) Composition.—Members are appointed by the Commissioner, [C.C.L., s. 4(1), replaced by C.C.(A.)L., 1959, s. 3]. A customary court consists of five members sitting with or without assessors. The Commissioner may from time to time designate any person as the president or vice president of a customary court [C.C.L., s. 5(1) and (2)].

(3) Jurisdiction—original.—" Every customary court shall have full jurisdiction and power, to the extent set forth in the warrant establishing it, and, subject to the provisions of this law, in all civil and criminal cases in which all the parties belong to a class of persons who have ordinarily been subject to the jurisdiction of customary tribunals " [C.C.L., s. 14(1)]. There are three grades of customary courts, namely, grades A, B, and C; the extent of their jurisdiction varies according to their grade [C.C.L., s. 16(2)], as follows:—

(*i*) *Grade A courts.*—(a) *Civil.*—Causes and matters concerning marriage, land and succession under customary law. The limit of the suit in personal actions is £200.

(b) *Criminal.*—Causes which can be adequately punished by imprisonment for one year, six strokes, or a fine of £50, or the equivalent by native law and custom.

(*ii*) *Grade B courts.*—(a) *Civil.*—The suit value limit is £100.

(b) *Criminal.*—Punishment by six months' imprisonment or by a fine of £30.

(*iii*) *Grade C courts.*—(a) *Civil.*—The suit value limit is £50.

(b) *Criminal.*—Punishment by three months' imprisonment or by a fine of £15 [C.C.L., 1st Schedule].

(4) Jurisdiction—appellate.—The Commissioner may appoint such persons as he thinks fit to be Appeal Officers having appellate jurisdiction to hear and determine appeals from the decisions of a customary court in any matter other than a land cause [C.C.L., ss. 50, 52(1)]. Appeals in land causes lie to the District Officer [C.C.L., s. 52(2)].

CONTROL OF COURTS

(5) Appeals from.—Appeals from the decisions of Appeal Officers lie to the Magistrates' Courts [C.C.L., s. 53(1)]. Appeals from the decisions of District Officers in land causes lie to the High Court [C.C.L., s. 53(2)].

(6) Review/revision.—See (8) *infra*.

(7) Transfer.—A District Officer may transfer a cause or matter from one customary court to another customary court, or to a magistrate's court, or to the High Court [C.C.L., s. 29]. A customary court may transfer a cause or matter before it to any other customary court of competent jurisdiction [C.C.L., s. 31].

(8) Inspection, supervision, etc.—Every District Officer has at all times access to customary courts in his division and to the records and proceedings of such courts [C.C.L., s. 28(1)].

LAW TO BE ADMINISTERED

(9) General law.—This comprises the provisions of any written law which the court may be authorised to enforce by an order made under s. 21 [C.C.L., s. 18(1), (b)], and the provisions of all rules and orders made under the Native Authority Ordinance, bylaws, etc. [C.C.L., s. 18(1), (c)].

(10) Customary law.—This is " the native law and custom prevailing in the area of the jurisdiction of the court so far as it is not repugnant to natural justice, equity and good conscience, nor incompatible either directly or by natural implication with any written law for the time being in force " [C.C.L., s. 18(1), (a)].

(11) Islamic or other law.—See under High Court (A. 2(11), p. 78, *ante*).

D

LIBERIA[1]

By MILTON R. KONVITZ, *Professor, Cornell University;*
Director, Liberian Codification Project; Member of New
Jersey Bar.

The judicial system of Liberia and the law administered by it clearly
reflect the dual origin of its inhabitants. On the one hand, the influence
of the American founders of Liberia is evidenced in its court structure
and procedure, its system of substantive law, and above all, in its
adoption of the fundamental principles of civil liberties. On the other
hand, the tribal population is the source of the vast body of native
laws and customs administered by the government and is the reason
for the special parallel system of courts established for its benefit.

The Anglo-American legal heritage of Liberia is clearly apparent in its
Constitution. In this document is found a " Declaration of Rights "
containing safeguards against the suppression of civil liberties similar
to those stated in the first Ten Amendments to the United States
Constitution. The tripartite structure of government created by the
Liberian Constitution has its prototype in the executive, legislative, and
judicial branches of government in the United States.

The background and traditions of the founders of Liberia are mani-
fest also in the adoption of the common law as the foundation of its
legal system. The infant colony was committed to this system of law
soon after its establishment. The Constitution of 1820 proclaimed " the
common law as in force and modified in the United States, and applicable to the situation of the people " to be the law of Liberia [art. VI].
Subsequent statutes restated this principle with some variations concerning the authorities to be used in determining the rules of the common law, but the basic doctrine has always remained the one expressed
by the first Constitution [Liberian Code of Laws of 1956, tit. 16, s. 40].
English statutes passed before the emigration of the American colonists,
if not in derogation of the common law, constitute part of the law of
Liberia. The Statute of Wills and Statute of Uses have been cited
by the Liberian Supreme Court as examples of the ancient Acts thus
adopted (*Roberts* v. *Roberts*, (1878), 1 Lib. L.R. 107, 112).

The common law of Liberia may be, and frequently is, superseded
by legislative enactments. Indeed, many of the fundamental principles
of the common law, which in most jurisdictions form part of the *lex
non scripta*, were adopted by the Legislature in 1841 and still appear in
statutory form in various parts of the present Code. (See, e.g., Liberian
Code of Laws of 1956, tit. 17.) Common law crimes, long recognised in
Liberia, were abolished by the Criminal Code of 1914, which contained
definitions and specific penalties for major offences.

In the history of Liberia, several codifications of its statutes have
been made, the most recent of which is the Liberian Code of Laws of
1956. This Code is a compilation of all general public statutes in force

---

[1] For diagram of courts system, see p. 214, *post.*

at the time of its adoption, and, by virtue of its repeal of all statutes codified, the only authority for the law which it contains.

The judicial system of Liberia bears the imprint of American influence as deeply as the laws it administers. The Constitution [art. IV, s. 1] vests the judicial power in a Supreme Court and "such subordinate courts as the Legislature may from time to time establish ". The Supreme Court is at present composed of five Justices, any three of whom constitute a quorum. The original jurisdiction of the Court is limited by the Constitution to cases affecting ambassadors, public ministers, and consuls, and to cases to which a county (the main political subdivision of the country) is a party [art. IV, s. 2]. It hears appeals from courts of record and from rulings of individual Justices of the Court on motions for writs [Liberian Code of Laws of 1956, tit. 18, s. 501].

The Circuit Court is the principal court of original jurisdiction. The country is divided into six judicial circuits, one of which is located in each of four counties. The fifth county, Montserrado County, where most of the legal business is transacted, is the seat of the Circuit Courts of the First and Sixth Judicial Circuits [Liberian Code of Laws, 1956, tit. 18, s. 30]. The First Judicial Circuit has jurisdiction only of criminal cases, and the Sixth only of civil cases [*ibid.*, s. 510]. Each Circuit has a resident judge, who is also assigned to hear cases in the other circuits. A seventh judge is appointed to be assigned where the need for his services is most urgent [*ibid.*, ss. 31, 33]. In the language of the statute, the Circuit Court may " exercise original jurisdiction over all cases as to which another court or government agency or official is not expressly given original jurisdiction by Constitutional or statutory provision " [*ibid.*, s. 510]. It may decide even those cases involving small amounts of damages over which stipendiary magistrates and justices of the peace have concurrent jurisdiction, although a plaintiff bringing such an action in the Circuit Court forfeits his right to costs [*ibid.*, s. 510(a)]. Original criminal jurisdiction in the Circuit Court extends in general to those cases in which the fine is more than one hundred dollars or in which imprisonment is mandatory [*ibid.*, ss. 510, 556(d), 557(h)]. The Circuit Court also handles probate and estate matters in its Probate Divisions, except that in Montserrado County and three other smaller territorial divisions, special Monthly and Probate Courts have been established for that purpose [*ibid.*, ss. 512, 530, 531]. The appellate jurisdiction of the Circuit Court is exercised in appeals from administrative decisions of government agencies and officials and from decisions of courts not of record [*ibid.*, s. 511].

The lowest division of the Liberian judicial system in this line of courts consists of the courts of the stipendiary magistrates and justices of the peace. These are courts not of record and are conducted without juries. Stipendiary magistrates are qualified lawyers [*ibid.*, tit. 18, s. 94] and in general exercise a broader jurisdiction in civil cases than is permitted to justices of the peace. Both courts are confined to determination of civil cases in which the damages claimed are comparatively small and of criminal cases in which the penalties are limited [*ibid.*, ss. 556, 557].

Side by side with the Anglo-American system of jurisprudence exists a second system of an entirely different nature and derivation. This is composed of the laws and customs of the many tribes inhabiting

Liberia and the courts established to hear cases involving aborigines or persons residing in the Hinterland. It is the announced policy of the government to administer tribal affairs according to tribal law and custom to the extent that they do not conflict with statutes or administrative regulations [Liberian Code of Laws of 1956, tit. 1, s. 350]. Accordingly, in suits to which aborigines are parties, the native laws, some based on enactment by tribal governing bodies and some only on established custom, may be the controlling authority. Such laws will be invoked in the appropriate cases not only in the special system of courts to which reference was just made, but also in the Supreme Court, Circuit Court, and other courts usually engaged in applying the common and statutory law of Liberia (*Karpeh* v. *Manning* (1936), 5 Lib. L.R. 162, 167). President Tubman himself has on occasion attended native convocations in the Hinterland and participated in a judicial capacity in meting out justice to litigants in accordance with the native laws.

The special system of courts established by the government for the native population is complicated by the fact that the officials administering it and the names of the courts in the Hinterland differ to a large extent from those in the County Area. (The County Area is the forty-mile wide strip of territory along the seacoast divided into counties.) In both the Hinterland and the County Area, the Courts of the Clan Chiefs and Courts of the Paramount Chiefs form the lowest rungs of the judicial ladder. Above them are courts presided over by the administrative officials of the Department of the Interior—the District Commissioners and Provincial Commissioners in the Hinterland and the County Commissioners and County Superintendents in the County Area. Appeals may be taken from the decisions of the Provincial Commissioners and County Superintendents to the Provincial Circuit Court of Assize and the Department of the Interior, respectively [*ibid.*, ss. 121, 130]. Cases arising in a Court of the Clan Chief may go through five different stages of appeal. The jurisdiction of the courts in this system is graded from the smallest civil and criminal cases to cases involving major felonies and capital punishment. It is to be noted also that the jurisdiction of the Court of the District Commissioner extends to disputes between persons not aborigines and to any suit by a person residing in the County Area against a person residing in the Hinterland [*ibid.*, s. 123(a), (d)]. The two systems of Liberian courts cannot be distinguished from one another, therefore, by any hard and fast rule concerning the system of law administered by them. Neither the common law nor native law is administered exclusively by one judicial organisation or the other.

Whether in any particular case tribal law applies as opposed to common law or non-conflicting statutory law is often doubtful, since the answer to this question may depend on the degree of affiliation which a party to the suit, if an aborigine by birth, preserves toward his tribe. In many cases, the extent to which such a party follows tribal customs or has renounced tribal loyalty will be difficult to ascertain. Not only the applicable system of law, but also the court having jurisdiction may have to be determined according to these considerations. The rules concerning the systems of law and the jurisdiction of the systems of courts which have been noted, while apparently definite and easy of application, are, therefore, to some extent based on a foundation as inexact and shifting as the nature of the population itself. This uncertain state of the law cannot be improved, however, until, as the government plans and as will occur almost inevitably in the course of industrialisation of the country, the old tribal lines are broken and the aboriginal population becomes fully integrated into a more modern society. As such a change is brought about, tribal laws and the special courts created because of the tribal population will gradually give way to Anglo-American legal traditions and the influence of the common law.

Finally, mention may be made of recent developments. In 1952 the Liberian government authorised, by agreement, the establishment of the Liberian Codification Project at Cornell University. The Project thus far has prepared the Liberian Code of Laws, in four volumes, now the official body of legislative enactments. It has begun to edit and publish the opinions of the Liberian Supreme Court, of which four volumes have thus far been published. It has prepared the first Supplement to the Code of Laws, which is now in press. It has trained personnel to administer the court work in Liberia, and one of the trained men has become Court Administrator and another has become Clerk of the Supreme Court. It is now training four Liberian lawyers in the work of statutory drafting. It is also working on new laws, especially on a new code of civil procedure, which is intended to modernise the court work.

PART II

EAST AFRICA

By

E. COTRAN, LL.B., Dipl. I.L.

of Lincoln's Inn, Barrister-at-Law; Research Officer, Restatement of African Law Project, School of Oriental and African Studies.

SUMMARY

		PAGE
KENYA	. . . .	89
TANGANYIKA	. . . .	98
UGANDA	. . . .	106
ZANZIBAR	. . . .	118
SUDAN	. . . .	125
SOMALI REPUBLIC	. . . .	136

KENYA[1]

The Courts comprise;—

A. Courts primarily administering the general law (viz.: the Supreme Court and Subordinate Courts); and

B. Courts primarily administering African customary law (viz.: the African Courts).

A. 1(a) THE PRIVY COUNCIL

Appeals lie from the Court of Appeal for Eastern Africa (*q.v.*, *infra*) to the Judicial Committee of the Privy Council, normally upon the following terms:—

    (*i*) in civil cases, as of right, where the matter in dispute is of £500 value or more;

    (*ii*) in criminal cases, at the discretion of the Court of Appeal for Eastern Africa, when the question involved in the appeal is considered to be of great general public importance.

A. 1(b) THE COURT OF APPEAL FOR EASTERN AFRICA

The system of appeals from each of the superior courts of Kenya, Uganda, Tanganyika and Zanzibar is the same and is regulated by the Eastern African Court of Appeal Order in Council, 1950. This Order in Council makes provision for the continuance of His Majesty's Court of Appeal for Eastern Africa (which was constituted under the Eastern African Court of Appeal Orders in Council, 1921–1947).

The Court consists of a President, a Vice-President, one or more Justices of Appeal and the Judges of the Superior Courts of these territories [O-in-C, 1950, art. 6].

The conditions upon which an Appeal lies to the Court are usually as follows:—

    (*i*) without leave, against conviction on a question of law;

    (*ii*) with leave of the Court of Appeal or upon a certificate of the Judge or Magistrate who originally tried the case that it is a fit case for appeal, on any ground of appeal which involves a question of fact alone, or a question of mixed law and fact or any other ground which appears to the court to be a sufficient ground of appeal;

    (*iii*) with leave of the Court of Appeal against sentence, unless such sentence is one fixed by law.

A. 2 THE SUPREME COURT

CONSTITUTION AND POWERS

(1) Establishment.—Established by art. 59(1) of the Kenya (Constitution) O-in-C, 1958. The Court was first established by the Kenya Colony O-in-C, 1921, s. 4(1).

---

[1] For diagram of courts system see p. 215, *post*.

(2) Composition.—It consists of the Chief Justice, who is President of the Court, and such number of puisne judges as may from time to time be appointed [K.(Const.) O-in-C, art. 59(1)]. In the Supreme Court all criminal trials are with the aid of assessors [Criminal Procedure Code, cap. 27, s. 258], except that Europeans are tried by a jury composed of Europeans [*ibid.*, s. 222].

(3) Jurisdiction—original.—Unlimited original jurisdiction in civil and criminal matters within Kenya [K.(Const.) O-in-C, art. 59(2)]. The Supreme Court is a Court of Admiralty.

(4) Jurisdiction—appellate.—Appeals lie to the Supreme Court from subordinate courts in all civil matters [Civil Procedure Code, cap. 27, s. 65] and criminal matters [Crim. P.C., s. 347].

LAW TO BE ADMINISTERED

(9) General law.—The K.(Const.) O-in-C, 1958 (which revokes the Kenya Colony Order in Council, 1921) provides in art. 74:—

" Notwithstanding the revocation of the Kenya Colony Order in Council, 1921, the jurisdiction of the Supreme Court and courts subordinate to the Supreme Court shall, subject to the provisions of this Order and until any law made under this Order otherwise provides, be exercised in accordance with the provisions of paragraph (2) of article 4 and article 7 of that Order as if those provisions extended to the Protectorate as well as to the Colony and references therein to the Colony were references to Kenya."

In other words, the law to be administered by the Supreme Court is still to be found in arts. 4(2) and 7 of the 1921 O-in-C, and this law now applies to the whole of Kenya (Colony and Protectorate), and not merely to the Colony. Article 4(2) of the 1921 O-in-C provides:—

" Subject to the other provisions of this Order, such civil and criminal jurisdiction shall, so far as circumstances admit, be exercised in conformity with the Civil Procedure and Penal Codes of India and the other Indian Acts[1] which are in force in the Colony at the date of the commencement of this Order and subject thereto and so far as the same shall not extend or apply shall be exercised in conformity with the substance of the common law, the doctrines of equity and the statutes of general application in force in England on the twelfth day of August, 1897, and with the powers vested in and according to the procedure and practice observed by and before courts of Justice and Justices of the Peace in England according to their respective jurisdiction and authorities at that date, save in so far as the Civil Procedure and Penal Codes of India and other Indian Acts in force as aforesaid and the said common law doctrines of equity and the statutes of general application and the said powers, procedure and practice may at any time before the commencement of this Order have been or hereafter may be modified, amended or replaced by other provision in lieu thereof by or under the authority of any Order of Her Majesty in Council, or by any Ordinance or Ordinances for the time being in force in the Colony:

---

[1] Many of these Indian Acts have now been replaced by local Ordinances.

Provided always that the said common law doctrines of equity and the statutes of general application shall be in force in the Colony so far only as the circumstances of the Colony and its inhabitants permit and subject to such qualifications as local circumstances render necessary."

(10) Customary law.—Article 4(2), *supra* was qualified by art. 7 of the same Order, which provides:—

" In all cases civil and criminal to which natives are parties, every Court

(a) shall be guided by native law so far as it is applicable and is not repugnant to justice and morality or inconsistent with any Order in Council or Ordinance, or any regulation or rules made under any Order in Council or Ordinance; and

(b) shall decide all such cases according to substantial justice without undue regard to technicalities or procedure and without undue delay."

(11) Islamic or other law.—The Supreme Court applies Islamic law both in its original and appellate jurisdiction. The principal application of Islamic law is under the Muhammedan Marriage, Divorce and Succession Ordinancem cap. 148, s. 3(2), which gives the Supreme Court jurisdiction in connection with all matrimonial cases arising out of Muhammedan marriages. It also has jurisdiction in Islamic law under certain other ordinances. The Supreme Court also hears appeals from the Muhammedan Subordinate Courts, i.e., the Liwalis', Cadis' and Mudirs' courts which administer Islamic law (see A. 3, *infra*). When hearing appeals from Cadis' courts, the Chief Cadi sits as assessor: [Civil P.C., cap. 5, s. 65].

A. 3 SUBORDINATE COURTS

Constitution and Powers

(1) Establishment.—By s. 2 of the Courts Ordinance, cap. 3, the following classes of subordinate courts were established:—

(a) Subordinate Courts of the First Class;
(b) Subordinate Courts of the Second Class;
(c) Subordinate Courts of the Third Class;
(d) Liwalis' Courts ⎫
(e) Cadis' Courts ⎬ known as " Muslim Subordinate Courts ".
(f) Mudirs' Courts ⎭

(2) Composition.—The following persons by virtue of their office are empowered to hold courts [C.O., s. 3 (as amended in 1959)]:—

class (a): Provincial Commissioner; Senior Resident Magistrate; Resident Magistrate; District Commissioner; District Officer, subject to specified conditions;
class (b): District Officer, subject to specified conditions;
class (c): District Officer; District Officer Cadet;
class (d): Liwalis;
class (e): Cadis;
class (f): Mudirs.

(3) Jurisdiction—original.—Jurisdiction extends as follows [C.O., s. 6(1) (as amended in 1959)]:—

a subordinate court of the first class held by a Senior R.M. or an R.M.—within the Colony.

a subordinate court of the first class held by a P.C.—within the limits of the province in which it is situated.

any other subordinate court of whatever class—within the limits of the district in which it is situated.

(*i*) *Civil.*—Jurisdiction over all persons where matter in dispute does not exceed:—

class (a):—

(*i*) courts of the first class held by a Senior R.M.—shs. 5000;

(*ii*) courts of the first class held by any magistrate other than a Senior R.M.—shs. 1500;

class (b):—shs. 1000;

class (c):—shs. 500;

but in all three classes, where the defendant is an Arab, a Baluchi or an African (including a Somali, a Malagasy and a Comoro Islander), the amounts are doubled, except in the case of a court of the first class held by a Senior R.M.;

class (d): jurisdiction over Arabs, Baluchis and Africans (including a Somali, a Malagasy and a Comoro Islander), where matter in dispute does not exceed shs. 1500;

class (e): jurisdiction over Muhammedan Arabs, Baluchis and Africans (including a Somali, a Malagasy and a Comoro Islander) in matters relating to personal status, marriage, maintenance and divorce, and within the Coast Districts over all Arabs, Baluchis and Africans (including a Somali, a Malagasy and a Comoro Islander) where matter in dispute does not exceed shs. 1000;

class (f): jurisdiction over Arabs, Baluchis and Africans (including a Somali, a Malagasy and a Comoro Islander), where matter in dispute does not exceed shs. 500 [C.O., s. 17, as amended in 1959].

(*ii*) *Criminal.*—Jurisdiction as follows:—

class (a):—

(*i*) a subordinate court of the first class presided over by a Senior R.M. or by any R.M. upon whom the Governor has conferred power—maximum penalty: 7 years' imprisonment; or shs. 10,000 fine; or 24 strokes;

(*ii*) other subordinate courts of the first class—maximum penalty 3 years' imprisonment; or shs. 10,000 fine; or 24 strokes [Crim. P.C., s. 7 (as amended)];

class (b): maximum penalty 12 months' imprisonment; or shs. 5000 fine; or 12 strokes [Crim. P.C., s. 8];

class (c): maximum penalty 3 months' imprisonment; or shs. 1500; or 8 strokes (juveniles only) [Crim. P.C., s. 9];

class (d): jurisdiction over Arabs, Baluchis and Africans (including a Somali, a Malagasy and a Comoro Islander)—as in class (b): [Crim. P.C., s. 10(1)];

class (e): as in class (d): [s. 10(2)];

    class (f): jurisdiction over Arabs, Baluchis and Africans (including a Somali, a Malagasy and a Comoro Islander) as in class (c): [Crim. P.C., s. 10(3)].

(4) Jurisdiction—appellate.—Subordinate courts have no appellate jurisdiction except that a D.O. in certain cases hears appeals from the decisions of either an African Court of Appeal or, where there is no such court, from an African court of first instance (see B. 1(5), p. 95, *post*).

CONTROL OF COURTS

(5) Appeals from.—Appeals from decisions of all subordinate courts go to the Supreme Court (see A. 2(4), p. 90, *ante*).

(6) Review/revision.—(*i*) *Civil cases.*—Any person aggrieved by a decree or order of the court may apply for a review of the judgment to the court which passed the order or decree [Civ. P.C., s. 80].

(*ii*) *Criminal cases.*—The Supreme Court has power to call for records of any criminal proceedings before any subordinate court, for the purpose of satisfying itself as to the correctness, legality or propriety of any finding, sentence or order [Crim. P.C., ss. 361 and 363].

(7) Transfer.—(*i*) *Civil cases.*—The Supreme Court has power to transfer from one subordinate court to another suits which may be initiated in more than one subordinate court [Civ. P.C., s. 17]; to transfer any suit before it to any subordinate court [Civ. P.C., s. 18(1), (a)]; or withdraw any suit from a subordinate court and try it itself [Civ. P.C. s. 18(1), (b)].

(*ii*) *Criminal cases.*—(a) Any court, upon finding that the cause of complaint arose outside the limits of its jurisdiction, may transfer the case to a court having jurisdiction [Crim. P.C., s. 78(1)].

(b) Any magistrate holding a subordinate court of the first class may transfer a case to any other subordinate court, or have transferred to himself a case being heard by any lower subordinate court [Crim. P.C., s. 79].

(c) Any subordinate court lower than a first class subordinate court may transfer a case for hearing by a first class subordinate court [Crim. P.C., s. 80].

(d) In certain circumstances the Supreme Court has power to transfer any criminal case from any subordinate court to itself, or from one subordinate court to another [Crim. P.C., s. 81].

(8) Inspection, supervision, etc.—The Supreme Court exercises general powers of supervision over all subordinate courts [C.O., cap. 3, s. 16].

LAW TO BE ADMINISTERED

(9) General law.—As Supreme Court (see A. 2(9), p. 90, *ante*).

(10) Customary law.—As Supreme Court (see A. 2(10), p. 91, *ante*).

(11) Islamic or other law.—Islamic law is administered by the Muslim subordinate courts (the Liwalis', Kadis' and Mudirs' courts); for details see Anderson, *Islamic Law in Africa*, pp. 11–12.

B. 1 AFRICAN COURTS OF FIRST INSTANCE

CONSTITUTION AND POWERS

(1) Establishment.—By s. 5(1) of the African Courts Ordinance, 1951, a Provincial Commissioner may, with the approval of the Governor, by warrant under his hand, establish within his province such African courts as he may think fit.

(2) Composition.—The constitution of the court is defined by the warrant establishing it [A.C.O., s. 6(1)]. It usually consists of elders appointed having regard to tradition and merit, and who are not chiefs or members of the executive.

(3) Jurisdiction—original.—African courts have jurisdiction over all causes and matters where, in civil cases, the parties are Africans and where, in criminal cases, the accused is an African, and where a party or the accused is an Arab or a Somali, with the consent of that person. The limits of jurisdiction may be prescribed in the P.C.'s warrant. Subject thereto, the jurisdiction of an African court extends:—

    (a) to the trial of civil cases in which the cause of action arose within the limits of the jurisdiction of the court and of civil cases in which the cause of action arose elsewhere when the defendant is ordinarily resident within such limits; and

    (b) to the trial of criminal cases in which the accused is charged with having committed any breach of law either wholly or partly within the limits of the jurisdiction of the court [A.C.O., s. 10, as amended in 1959].

(*i*) *Civil.*—(a) Civil proceedings relating to immovable property *must*, unless the D.O. within whose district the African court has jurisdiction otherwise directs, be taken in the African court within the limits of the jurisdiction of which such property is situate.

(b) Civil proceedings relating to the following matters also *must* be taken in an African court by Africans unless the D.O. otherwise directs, namely:—

    native customary marriage or inheritance; or immovable property situate within the native lands; or any debt arising in connection with immovable property situate within the area of native lands (as defined).

(c) Except as provided by s. 79 of the Native Lands Registration Ordinance, 1959, the civil jurisdiction of an African court does not extend to the trial of any civil case relating to the title to land registered under that Ordinance or to any registered interest in such land.

(d) Proceedings in respect of a partnership in which the sum involved does not exceed shs. 5000 and all parties are Africans *may* be commenced in an African court [A.C.O., s. 12, as amended].

(*ii*) *Criminal.*—This extends to the trial of all criminal matters in which any African is charged with having committed, or with being an accessory to the commission of, any offence, either wholly or partly within the area of the jurisdiction of the African court [A.C.O., s. 11].

(*iii*) *Cases excluded from jurisdiction.*—The following cases are excluded from the jurisdiction of African courts [A.C.O., s. 13]:—

(a) where a person is charged with an offence in consequence of which death is alleged to have occurred, or which is punishable under any law with death or imprisonment for life;

(b) cases in connection with marriage, other than a marriage contracted in accordance with native law, except where the claim is one for bride-price or adultery only, and is founded on native law;

(c) any other case which may be declared by the Governor or his delegate not to be within the jurisdiction of African courts.

(4) Jurisdiction—appellate.—Nil.

CONTROL OF COURTS

(5) Appeals from.—Appeals from African courts lie to an African Court of Appeal; or, if there is no African Court of Appeal, to the D.O. [A.C.O., s. 42(1)]. However, the P.C. of the Coast Province may order that an appeal is to lie to a specified Liwali or Mudir instead of to an African Court of Appeal or D.O. [A.C.O., s. 42(4)].

(6) Review/revision.—The following may revise any of the proceedings of an African court, whether civil or criminal: a Provincial African Courts Officer, a D.O., and where the P.C. so directs, a Liwali or Mudir in the Coast Provinces [A.C.O., s. 39(1), (a)].

(7) Transfer.—The officers mentioned in (6), *supra* may also:—

(a) order any case to be reheard either before the same African court, or some other African court of competent jurisdiction [A.C.O., s. 39(1)];

(b) transfer any case whether before trial or at any stage of the proceedings to any subordinate court of the first or second class, or to another African court [A.C.O., s. 39(1), (c)].

(8) Inspection, supervision, etc.—(*i*) The following, within their province or district, as the case may be, have access at all reasonable times to any African courts, and to the records thereof: P.C., Provincial African Courts Office, D.O., and, where the P.C. so directs, a Liwali or Mudir in the Coast Provinces [A.C.O., s. 39(1)].

(*ii*) The African Courts Officer and all Provincial African Courts Officers have a general supervision over the exercise by African courts of their jurisdiction and powers, and must advise these courts upon matters connected therewith [A.C.O., s. 3(2)].

LAW TO BE ADMINISTERED

(9) General law.—African courts may administer provisions of certain ordinances (e.g., the African District Councils Ordinance, 1950, and certain provisions of the Penal Code) [A.C.O., s. 17].

(10) Customary law.—An African court administers and enforces
" the native law prevailing in the area of the jurisdiction of the court
so far as it is not repugnant to justice or morality or inconsistent with the
provisions of any Order of His Majesty in Council or with any Ordinance
in force in the Colony " [A.C.O., s. 17(a)].

(11) Islamic or other law.—None.

B. 2 AFRICAN COURTS OF APPEAL

CONSTITUTION AND POWERS

(1) Establishment.—By the A.C.O., 1951, s. 5(2), a P.C. may, with
the approval of the Governor, by warrant under his hand confer upon
an African court such appellate jurisdiction as may be specified in such
warrant, and where an African court is to exercise any such appellate
jurisdiction it is to be known as an African Court of Appeal.

(2) Composition.—Defined by warrant. The Court is usually composed of three elders.

(3) Jurisdiction—original.—As African courts of first instance
(see B. 1(3), p. 94, *ante*).

(4) Jurisdiction—appellate.—Appeals are heard from African
courts of first instance [A.C.O., s. 42(1)].

CONTROL OF COURTS

(5) Appeals from.—Appeals from an African Court of Appeal lie,
under certain circumstances, to the D.O. [A.C.O., s. 42(2)].

(6) Review/revision

(7) Transfer   } As African courts of first
instance (see B. 1(6)–(8),
p. 95, *ante*).

(8) Inspection, supervision, etc.

LAW TO BE ADMINISTERED

As African courts of first instance (see B. 1(9)–(11), p. 95, *ante*).

B. 3 DISTRICT OFFICER

POWERS

Note.—The jurisdiction and powers of District Officers in regard to
proceedings originating in African courts are alone stated here. A D.O.
may also exercise jurisdiction as a magistrate (for which see A. 3, p. 91,
ante).

(3) Jurisdiction—original.—Nil.

(4) Jurisdiction—appellate.—In certain circumstances appeals are
heard from decisions of African Court of Appeal and, where there is no
such court, from African courts of first instance [A.C.O., s. 42(1)].

CONTROL

(5) Appeals from.—A party aggrieved by the decision of a D.O.
may apply to the P.C. for a certificate that his case be submitted to the

Court of Review [A.C.O., s. 43(1)]. The P.C. will only grant such a certificate if (*i*) he is of the opinion that an important point of law is involved in the case, and (*ii*) the D.O. has on appeal varied or set aside the order of the African Court of Appeal or, where there is no such court, the African court of first instance [A.C.O., s. 43(2), (b)].

(6) Review/revision.—Notwithstanding s. 43(2), (b) (see (5), *supra*), the P.C. may refer any case to the Court of Review if he is of the opinion that the order or judgment thereunder has resulted, or is likely to result, in grave injustice [A.C.O., s. 43(4)].

(7) Transfer.—Nil.

(8) Inspection, supervision, etc.—Nil.

Law to be Administered

As African courts (see B. 1 and B. 2, *ante*).

B. 4 COURT OF REVIEW

Constitution and Powers

(1) Establishment.—Established by s. 4(1) of the A.C.O.

(2) Composition.—The Court of Review consists of:—
- (a) a Chairman, appointed by the Governor on the advice of the Chief Justice; he must have held high judicial office;
- (b) the Chief Native Commissioner;
- (c) the African Courts Officer;
- (d) an African to be appointed by the Governor [A.C.O., s. 4(2)].

Assessors may sit if their assistance is required [A.C.O., s. 45].

(3) Jurisdiction—original.—Nil.

(4) Jurisdiction—appellate.—By A.C.O., s. 43(1), appeals are heard from decisions of D.O's. The section also applies to the courts of Liwalis and Mudirs, so that the Court of Review also hears appeals from their decisions. The Court of Review may also order any case to be reheard whether before the same African court, or before a subordinate court of competent jurisdiction [A.C.O., s. 45(b)].

Law to be Administered

As African courts (see B. 1 and B. 2, *ante*).

TANGANYIKA[1]

The Courts comprise:—

A. Courts primarily administering the general law, viz., the High Court and Subordinate Courts; and

B. Courts primarily administering customary law, viz., the local courts.

A. 1(a) THE PRIVY COUNCIL

As for KENYA, *q.v.*, p. 89, *ante*.

A. 1(b) THE COURT OF APPEAL FOR EASTERN AFRICA

As for KENYA, *q.v.*, p. 89, *ante*.

A. 2 THE HIGH COURT

CONSTITUTION AND POWERS

(1) Establishment.—Established by art. 17(1) of the Tanganyika Order in Council, 1920. as amended.

(2) Composition.—It consists of the Chief Justice and such number of Puisne Judges, not being less than six, as may be appointed by the Governor [Tang. O-in-C, 1920, art. 19, as amended by Tang. (No. 2) O-in-C, 1961]. Criminal trials are with the aid of two or more assessors [Criminal Procedure Code, cap. 20, s. 248].

(3) Jurisdiction—original.—Full jurisdiction, civil and criminal, over all persons and over all matters in the territory [Tang. O-in-C, art. 17(1)]. The High Court is a Court of Admiralty [Tang. O-in-C, art. 18(1)].

(4) Jurisdiction—appellate.—Appeals lie to it from subordinate courts in all civil [Subordinate Courts Ordinance, cap. 3, s. 17] and criminal [Crim. P.C., s. 312(1)] matters.

LAW TO BE ADMINISTERED

(9) General law.—" Subject to the other provisions of this Order, such civil and criminal jurisdiction, shall, so far as circumstances admit, be exercised in conformity with the Civil Procedure, Criminal Procedure and Penal Codes of India and other Indian Acts[2] and other laws which are in force in the territory at the date of the commencement of this Order or may hereafter be applied or enacted and subject thereto and so far as the same shall not extend or apply shall be exercised in conformity with the substance of the common law, the doctrines of

---

[1] For diagram of courts system see p. 216, *post*.
[2] Many of these Indian Acts have now been replaced by local ordinances.

equity, and the statutes of general application in force in England at the date of this Order,[1] and with the powers vested in and according to the procedure and practice observed by and before courts of justice and Justices of the Peace in England according to their respective jurisdiction and authorities at that date, save in so far as the said Civil Procedure, Criminal Procedure and Penal Codes of India and other Indian Acts and other laws in force as aforesaid and the said common law, doctrines of equity, and the statutes of general application, and the said powers, procedure and practice may at any time before the commencement of this Order have been, or hereafter may be, modified, amended or replaced by other provision in lieu thereof by or under the authority of any Order of His Majesty in Council or by any Proclamation issued by or by any Ordinance or Ordinances passed in and for the territory;

Provided always that the said common law, doctrines of equity and statutes of general application shall be in force in the territory so far only as the circumstances of the territory, and its inhabitants, and the limit of His Majesty's jurisdiction permit, and subject to such qualifications as local circumstances render necessary " [Tang. O-in-C, art. 17(2)].

(10) Customary law.—" In all cases, civil and criminal, to which natives are parties, every Court shall (a) be guided by native law so far as it is applicable and is not repugnant to justice and morality or inconsistent with any Order in Council or Ordinance or any Regulation or Rule made under any Order in Council or Ordinance; and shall (b) decide all such cases according to substantial justice without undue regard to technicalities of procedure and without undue delay " [Tang. O-in-C, art. 24].

(11) Islamic or other law.—The High Court is empowered to administer Islamic law under the provisions of certain Ordinances, e.g. the Marriage, Divorce and Succession (Non-Christian Asiatics) Ordinance, 1923 (as amended by Ordinance, no. 44 of 1947), empowers the High Court to apply " the law of the religion " of the parties, which may be Hindu law, Islamic law, etc. Other Ordinances which specify the application of Islamic law are the Administration (Small Estates) Ordinance, 1947, and the Mohammedan Estates (Benevolent Payment) Ordinance, 1918.

A. 3 SUBORDINATE COURTS (or District Courts)

CONSTITUTION AND POWERS

(1) Establishment.—Section 3(1) of the Subordinate Courts Ordinance, cap. 3, establishes in every district a court subordinate to the High Court.

(2) Composition.—Presided over by a magistrate [S.C.O., s. 3(1)], who can be a magistrate of the first, second or third class [S.C.O., s. 5(1)].

(a) The following have the powers and jurisdiction of a first class magistrate: Provincial Commissioner, Deputy Provincial Commissioner, Resident Magistrate and District Commissioner [S.C.O., s. 5(3)].

---

[1] *I.e.*, the Tanganyika Order in Council, 1920. The exact date is July 22, 1920.

(b) The following have the powers and jurisdiction of a second class magistrate: every Administrative Officer other than an Assistant District Officer (A.D.O.), and those specified under (a) above and (c) below [S.C.O., s. 5(4)].

(c) The following have the powers and jurisdiction of a third class magistrate: every Administrative Officer of cadet rank [S.C.O., s. 5(5)]

(d) The Governor with the concurrence of the Chief Justice may confer the powers:—of first class magistrate on any administrative officer other than an A.D.O.; of first or second class magistrate on any administrative officer; of first, second or third class magistrate on any A.D.O.; and may appoint any fit and proper person, not being an administrative officer, to be a first, second or third class magistrate [S.C.O., s. 5(4), (5), (6), (7)].

A Subordinate Court may, in any proceedings, call for the assistance of one or more assessors to aid them in deciding matters of native law and custom [S.C.O., s. 11].

(3) Jurisdiction—original.—Every subordinate court exercises jurisdiction within the district in which it is established [S.C.O., s. 3(1)]. The jurisdiction of the courts, civil and criminal, varies according to the class of magistrate presiding over the court [S.C.O., s. 4(2)].

(*i*) *Civil.*—[S.C.O., s. 4(4)]. Subject to the High Court's own limiting jurisdiction:—

District Court (when presided over by a resident magistrate)— jursidiction where matter in dispute does not exceed shs. 15,000.

District Court (when presided over by a first class magistrate, other than a resident magistrate)—jurisdiction where matter in dispute does not exceed shs. 4000.

District Court (when presided over by a second class magistrate)— jurisdiction where matter in dispute does not exceed shs. 2000.

District Court (when presided over by a third class magistrate)— jurisdiction where matter in dispute does not exceed shs. 1000.

(*ii*) *Criminal.*—Subordinate court, presided over by a first class magistrate [Crim. P.C., s. 7]: maximum punishment 2 years' imprisonment (and where presided over by a resident magistrate, 3 years); or shs. 3000 fine; or corporal punishment. But no sentence of more than 12 months' imprisonment, or 12 strokes or shs. 1000 fine can be executed until such sentence is confirmed by the High Court.

Subordinate court presided over by a second class magistrate [Crim. P.C., s. 8]: maximum punishment 12 months' imprisonment; or shs. 1500 fine; or 12 strokes. But no sentence of more than 6 months' imprisonment, or 8 strokes, or shs. 750 fine can be executed until it is confirmed by the High Court.

Subordinate court presided over by third class magistrate [Crim. P.C., s. 9]: maximum punishment 3 months' imprisonment; or shs. 500 fine, or 8 strokes (juveniles only). But no sentence of more than 1 months' imprisonment, or shs. 100 fine can be executed until it is confirmed by a first class magistrate, who may refer it to the High Court if he does not see fit to confirm it.

The Governor, on the recommendation of the Chief Justice, may extend the jurisdiction of a first class magistrate to try cases ordinarily

tried in the High Court [Crim. P.C., s. 13(1)]. In such cases, trial is with the aid of two or more assessors [Crim. P.C., s. 14].

(4) Jurisdiction—appellate.—Nil.

CONTROL OF COURTS

(5) Appeals from.—(*i*) *Civil.*—All appeals, references, revisions and similar proceedings from or in respect of any civil proceedings in a subordinate court lie to the High Court [S.C.O., s. 17].

(*ii*) *Criminal.*—Appeals from decisions of all subordinate courts go to the High Court [Crim. P.C., s. 312(1)].

(6) Review/revision.—(*i*) The High Court may, on the application of any party or by its own motion, revise civil proceedings of subordinate courts [S.C.O., s. 10, and see (5), (*i*), *supra*].

(*ii*) The High Court may call for and examine the record of any criminal proceedings before any subordinate courts, and revise it [Crim. P.C., ss. 327 and 329].

(*iii*) A magistrate may call for and examine the record of any criminal proceedings before a magistrate of a lower class than himself, and can forward such record to the High Court, with such remarks as he thinks fit [Crim. P.C., s. 328].

(7) Transfer.—(*i*) *Civic.*—Where a suit may be instituted in more than one subordinate court, not being the court of a resident magistrate, it may be transferred to the resident magistrate for trial [Indian Acts (Application) Ordinance, 1920, s. 9(1) (replacing s. 22 of the Indian Code of Civil Procedure)].

(*ii*) *Criminal.*—(a) Any court, upon finding that the offence has been committed outside its jurisdiction, may transfer the case to a court having jurisdiction [Crim. P.C., s. 77(1)].

(b) Any first class magistrate may transfer a case to any subordinate court, or may direct a second or third class magistrate to transfer a case for trial by himself [Crim. P.C., s. 78].

(c) A second or third class magistrate may submit a report to a first class magistrate asking him to transfer a case under his powers in s. 78 of the Crim. P.C. [Crim. P.C., s. 79].

(d) The High Court may order any criminal proceedings to be transferred from any magistrate's court to any other magistrate's court of equal or superior jurisdiction; and order that any accused person be committed for trial to itself [Crim. P.C., s. 80].

(*iii*) *Transfer to local courts.*—Any subordinate court in any civil or criminal proceedings, and at any stage of the proceedings, before judgment, may order such proceedings to be transferred for trial to any local court within the area of jurisdiction of the subordinate court [S.C.O., s. 7(1)].

(8) Inspection, supervision, etc.—The High Court exercises general powers of supervision over all subordinate courts, and may at any time call for and inspect or direct the inspection of all or any of the records of such court [S.C.O., s. 15].

101

Law to be Administered

(9) General law } As High Court (see A. 2(9), (10), pp. 98–99,
(10) Customary law } *ante*).

(11) Islamic or other law.—As with the High Court, subordinate courts are empowered by certain Ordinances to administer Islamic law.

B. 1 LOCAL COURTS OF FIRST INSTANCE

Constitution and Powers

(1) Establishment.—By s. 4(1) of the Local Courts Ordinance, 1951, cap. 299, a Provincial Commissioner may, with the approval of the Governor, by warrant under his hand, establish within his province such local courts as he may think fit.

(2) Composition.—The constitution, composition and membership of a local court are prescribed in the warrant establishing it [L.C.O., s. 5(1)]. In their traditional form, they are presided over by a Chief, or sub-Chief, assisted by assessors. There is now, however, a tendency to separate the judiciary from the executive and independent magistrates or ' Hakimus ' are gradually replacing Chiefs as Presidents of local courts.

(3) Jurisdiction—original.—The warrant establishing the court defines the area within which the court may exercise jurisdiction [L.C.O., s. 4(1)], and the matters in respect of which it shall have jurisdiction [L.C.O., s. 5(1)].

(*i*) *Jurisdiction over persons.*—Local courts only have jurisdiction over causes and matters, civil and criminal, in which the accused or parties is or are Africans [L.C.O., s. 10(1)], and Arabs, Somalis, Comorians, Baluchis or Malagasis provided they consent [L.C.O., s. 10(2)].

(*ii*) *Criminal jurisdiction.*—Extends to the trial of all criminal matters in which any African is charged with having committed, or with being an accessory to or after the commission of, any offence either wholly or partly within the area of the jurisdiction of such local court [L.C.O., s. 11].

(*iii*) *Civil jurisdiction.*—Extends to the trail of all civil suits and matters in which the cause of action arose, or the defendant is ordinarily resident, within the area of jurisdiction of such local court, except that suits relating to immovable property shall be taken in a local court within the area of jurisdiction of which the property is situate [L.C.O., s. 12(1)].

Civil proceedings in respect of (a) customary marriage, or inheritance; and (b) immovable property (other than freehold land, leasehold property or land held under a right of occupancy for a term of years) *must* be commenced by Africans in local courts [L.C.O., s. 12(3)].

(*iv*) *Cases excluded from the jurisdiction of local courts.*—The following are excluded [L.C.O., s. 13]:—

> (a) any proceedings in which a person is charged with an offence in consequence of which death is alleged to have occurred, or which is punishable under any law with death;

(b) any proceedings in connection with marriage, other than a marriage contracted in accordance with customary law, except where the claim arises only in regard to bride-price or adultery and is founded only on customary law;

(c) any proceedings affecting the title to, or any interest in, land registered under the Land Registration Ordinance;

(d) any proceedings in relation to witch-craft;

(e) any proceedings removed from the jurisdiction of the court by the terms of any warrant or order, or by order of the Governor.

(4) Jurisdiction—appellate.—(See under **B. 2**, p. 104, *post*).

CONTROL OF COURTS

(5) Appeals from.—Appeals lie to the Local Court of Appeal or, where there is no such court, directly to the District Commissioner [L.C.O., s. 38(3), (a)]. However, the Provincial Commissioner may specify in the warrant establishing the court that no appeal shall lie at all in certain cases [L.C.O., s. 38(1), (b)].

(6) Review/revision.—The Provincial Commissioner and any Provincial Local Courts Officer or District Commissioner may of his own motion, or upon the application of any interested party, revise the proceedings of a local court [L.C.O., s. 34(1)], and the Local Courts Adviser has the same power [L.C.O., s. 42].

(7) Transfer.—(*i*) Where any proceedings, civil or criminal, have been commenced in a local court, such court, or the District Commissioner, or the Provincial Local Courts Officer, may at any time before judgment, transfer the same for hearing by some other local court, or a District (subordinate) Court [L.C.O., s.35]. The Local Court Adviser may also exercise this power of transfer [L.C.O., s. 42].

(*ii*) Any court in the territory other than a local court can transfer a case to a local court, if the proceedings are of such a nature as to be more properly cognizable by a local court [L.C.O., s. 36(1)].

(8) Inspection, supervision, etc.—(*i*) The Local Courts Adviser and the Provincial Local Courts Officer exercise a general supervision over the exercise by local courts of their jurisdiction and powers, and advise such courts upon matters connected therewith [L.C.O., s. 3(2)].

(*ii*) The Provincial Commissioner and any Provincial Local Courts Officer, or District Commissioner, have access at all reasonable times to any local court within the area of their province or district, and any records thereof [L.C.O., s. 34(1)].

LAW TO BE ADMINISTERED

(9) General law.—(*i*) The provisions of all rules or orders made in accordance with the provisions of the Native Authority Ordinance in force in the area within which the court is established [L.C.O., s. 15(b)].

(*ii*) The provisions of certain Ordinances (e.g. the Natives Tax Ordinance), which specifically confer jurisdiction on local courts [L.C.O., s. 15(c)].

(10) Customary law.—A local court administers " the customary law prevailing in the area of the jurisdiction of the Court, so far as it is applicable and is not repugnant to natural justice or morality or is not, in principle, in conflict with the provisions of any law in force in the Territory " [L.C.O., s. 15(a)].

(11) Islamic or other law.—Many of the local courts of first instance—especially in the coastal districts of Tanganyika—are presided over by Liwalis. These Liwalis administer Islamic law extensively with regard to all that concerns personal status and family law, i.e. questions of marriage, divorce, legitimacy, guardianship, maintenance, bequests, inheritance, gifts and waqf. No general provision is made for the application of Islamic law to Africans in the local courts, where it is applied in the guise of " customary law ". (For details see Anderson, J. N. D., *Islamic law in Africa*, pp. 122–147.)

B. 2 LOCAL COURTS OF APPEAL

Constitution and Powers

(1) Establishment.—A Provincial Commissioner may, by the warrant establishing any local court, or by subsequent order, confer upon a local court such appellate jurisdiction as may be specified in such warrant or order, and where any local court sits to exercise any such appellate jurisdiction, it shall be known as a local court of appeal [L.C.O., s. 4(2)].

(2) Composition.—Prescribed by warrant [L.C.O., s. 5(1)].

(3) Jurisdiction—original.—As local courts of first instance.

(4) Jurisdiction—appellate.—Appeals lie to it from local courts of first instance [L.C.O., s. 38(3), (a)].

Control of Courts

(5) Appeals from.—Appeals from its decisions lie to the District Commissioner [L.C.O., s. 38(3), (b)].

(6) Review/revision

(7) Transfer } As local courts of first instance (see B. 1, *ante*).

(8) Inspection, supervision, etc.

Law to be Administered

As local courts of first instance (see B. 1, *ante*).

B. 3 DISTRICT COMMISSIONER

Powers

(3) Jurisdiction—original.—Nil (but see under A. 3, p. 99, *ante*).

(4) Jurisdiction—appellate.—Hears appeals from local courts of appeal or where there is no such court, from local courts of first instance [L.C.O., s. 38(3), (a) and (b)].

CONTROL

(5) Appeals from.—Appeals lie to the Central Court of Appeal, but only with the leave of the Provincial Commissioner [L.C.O., s. 38(3), (c)].

(6) Review/revision.—The Provincial Commissioner may [L.C.O., s. 38(4):—

    (a) instead of granting leave to appeal to the Central Court of Appeal (under (5), *supra*), quash the proceedings in any criminal cause or matter; or

    (b) before granting leave to appeal in any civil case (*i*) order fresh evidence to be recorded either before the court of first instance, or the local court of appeal, or the authority having jurisdiction; or (*ii*) order the case to be reheard *de novo* either before the court of first instance, or some other local court or authority, or any subordinate court having jurisdiction.

(7) Transfer.—An appeal to the District Commissioner may at the discretion of the District Commissioner be transferred to the Provincial Local Courts Officer, and when so transferred it must be heard by him [L.C.O., s. 38(2)]. As with appeals from decisions of District Commissioners, appeals from decisions of the Provincial Local Courts Officer also lie to the Central Court of Appeal with leave of the Provincial Commissioner [L.C.O., s. 38(3), (c)].

LAW TO BE ADMINISTERED

As local courts (see under B. 1, *ante*).

B. 4 CENTRAL COURT OF APPEAL

CONSTITUTION AND POWERS

(1) Establishment.—Established by L.C.O., s. 39(1).

(2) Composition.—A President, who must be a judge of the High Court nominated by the Chief Justice and two other members, being the Minister for Provincial Affairs, and the Local Courts Adviser [L.C.O., s. 39(2)]. The court is empowered to sit with elders or assessors [L.C.O., s. 38(6), (a)].

(3) Jurisdiction—original.—Nil.

(4) Jurisdiction—appellate.—Hears appeals from the decisions of District Commissioners, or Provincial Local Courts Officers, but only with the leave of the Provincial Commissioner [L.C.O., s. 38(3), (c) (see B. 3(7) *supra*)].

LAW TO BE ADMINISTERED

As local courts (see under B. 1, *ante*).

UGANDA[1]

The Protectorate of Uganda consists of four provinces, one of which is the Kingdom of Buganda. The system of Protectorate courts comprising the High Court and subordinate courts is the same for the three provinces and Buganda, but the system of African or native courts is not the same, and is dealt with under separate headings, I and II, pp. 109, 115, *post*).

A. 1(a) THE PRIVY COUNCIL

As for KENYA, *q.v.*, p. 89, *ante*.

A. 1(b) THE COURT OF APPEAL FOR EASTERN AFRICA

As for KENYA, *q.v.*, p. 89, *ante*.

A. 2 THE HIGH COURT

CONSTITUTION AND POWERS

(1) Establishment.—Established by art. 15(1) of the Uganda Order in Council, 1902.

(2) Composition.—The Chief Justice and an unspecified number of puisne judges [O-in-C, art. 15(2), (a)]. In criminal cases, the court sits with the aid of two or more assessors [Criminal Procedure Code, s. 251].

(3) Jurisdiction—original.—Full jurisdiction, civil and criminal, over all persons and over all matters in Uganda [O-in-C, 1902, art. 15(1)].

(4) Jurisdiction—appellate.—Hears appeals from:—

    (a) subordinate courts in civil matters [Civil Procedure Ordinance, s. 67], and criminal matters [Crim. P.C., s. 323(1)];

    (b) Principal Court of Buganda [Buganda Courts Ordinance, s. 26(1)], in criminal cases where a court has passed a sentence of imprisonment exceeding 5 years' or a fine exceeding shs. 2000 and in civil cases where the value of the subject matter exceeds shs. 2000;

    (c) Judicial Adviser, Buganda [Buganda C.O., s. 26(3)], in his appellate jurisdiction on a matter of law only;

    (d) A District African court in its appellate or original jurisdiction (see I.B. 2(5), p. 113, *post*).

LAW TO BE ADMINISTERED

(9) General law.—Art. 15(2) of the O-in-C, 1902, provides:—

" Subject to the other provisions of this Order, such civil and criminal jurisdiction shall, so far as circumstances admit, be exercised in conformity with the Civil Procedure, Criminal Procedure and Penal

---

[1] For diagram of courts system see p. 217, *post*.

Codes of India[1] in force at the date of the commencement of this Order and subject thereto and so far as the same shall not extend or apply shall be exercised in conformity with the substance of the common law, the doctrines of equity and the statutes of general application in force in England on the 11th day of August, 1902, and with the powers vested in and according to the procedure and practice observed by and before Courts of Justice and Justices of the Peace in England according to their respective jurisdiction and authorities at that date, save in so far as the said civil procedure, criminal procedure and penal codes of India and the said common law, doctrines of equity, and statutes of general application, and the said powers, procedure and practice may at any time before the commencement of this Order have been, or hereafter may be, modified, amended or replaced by other provision in lieu thereof by or under the authority of any Order of His Majesty in Council or by any Ordinance, or Ordinances passed in and for the Protectorate:

Provided always that the said common law, doctrines of equity and statutes of general application shall be in force in the Protectorate so far only as the circumstances of the Protectorate and its inhabitants, and the limit of His Majesty's jurisdiction permit, and subject to such qualifications as local circumstances render necessary."

(10) Customary law.—Art. 20 of the O-in-C, 1902 lays down that:—

" In all cases, civil and criminal, to which natives are parties, every court shall (a) be guided by native law so far as it is applicable and is not repugnant to justice and morality or inconsistent with any Order in Council or Ordinance or any Regulation or Rule made under any Order in Council or Ordinance, and shall (b) decide all such cases according to substantial justice without undue regard to technicalities of procedure and without undue delay."

(11) Islamic or other law.—The High Court administers Islamic law under the provisions of certain Ordinances. The main Ordinance concerning Islamic law is the Marriage and Divorce of Mohammedans Ordinance, 1906.

A. 3 SUBORDINATE COURTS

CONSTITUTION AND POWERS

(1) Establishment.—Established by s. 3(1) of the Subordinate Courts Ordinance, 1940.

(2) Composition.—Presided over by a magistrate [S.C.O., s. 3(1)], who may be a magistrate of the first, second or third class [S.C.O., s. 6].

(a) Every resident magistrate and every Provincial or District Commissioner is *ex-officio* a first class magistrate.

(b) Every administrative officer other than a Provincial Commissioner or a District Commissioner is *ex-officio* a third class magistrate.

(c) Any fit and proper person may be appointed a first, second or third class magistrate by the Governor with the concurrence of the Chief Justice.

---

[1] These Indian Acts have now been replaced by the Civil P.O., cap. 6, the Crim. P.C., and the Penal Code, cap. 24.

Subordinate Courts may sit with assessors in criminal cases [Crim. P.C., s. 7].

(3) Jurisdiction—original.—(*i*) *Civil* [Civil P.O., s. 11(2)]:—

    (a) first class magistrate: where value of subject matter in dispute does not exceed shs. 2000;

    (b) second class magistrate: where value of subject matter in dispute does not exceed shs. 1000;

    (c) third class magistrate: where value of subject matter in dispute does not exceed shs. 500.

(*ii*) *Criminal* [Crim. P.C., s. 5]:—

    (a) a Subordinate Court may try any offence under any law other than treason, murder, manslaughter, rape or attempts to commit, or aiding, abetting or inciting the commission of these offences;

    (b) a Subordinate Court of the first or second class may pass any sentence authorised by law;

    (c) a Subordinate Court of the third class may pass a sentence not exceeding 6 months' imprisonment, or shs. 400 fine, or both.

Note.—Subordinate Courts have concurrent jurisdiction with any native court established in accordance with the Native Courts Ordinance [S.C.O., s. 4(1)].

(4) Jurisdiction—appellate.—Subordinate Courts may hear appeals from native courts [Native Courts Ordinance, cap. 76, s. 25(1)].

CONTROL OF COURTS

(5) Appeals from.—Appeals lie to the High Court (see under A. 2(4), (a), p. 106, *ante*).

(6) Review/revision.—(*i*) *Civil matters.*—(a) Any court may review its own judgment [Civ. P.O., s. 83].

(b) The High Court may call for the record of any case determined by a Subordinate Court and revise it [Civ. P.O., s. 84].

(*ii*) *Criminal matters.*—(a) The High Court may call for and examine the record of any criminal proceedings before any Subordinate Court and revise it [Crim. P.C., s. 339].

(b) Any magistrate may call for and examine the record of any criminal proceedings before a Subordinate Court inferior to his, and may report any irregularity to the High Court [Crim. P.C., s. 340].

(7) Transfer.—(*i*) *To Native Courts.*—Any Subordinate Court may, at any stage of a civil or criminal proceeding before judgment, transfer the case to a native court which exercises jurisdiction within the area of jurisdiction of such Subordinate Court [S.C.O., s. 5(1)].

(*ii*) *Civil matters.*—(a) The High Court has power to transfer suits which may be instituted in any one of two or more Subordinate Courts [Civ. P.O., s. 17].

(b) The High Court may transfer any suit before it to a Subordinate Court [Civ. P.O., s. 18(a)].

(c) The High Court may transfer any suit in a Subordinate Court for trial by itself, or by any other Subordinate Court [Civ. P.O., s. 18(b)].

(*iii*) *Criminal matters.*—(a) Any court, upon finding that it has no jurisdiction to hear a case, may transfer it for trial to any other court having jurisdiction [Crim. P.C., s. 72].

(b) Any magistrate holding a Subordinate Court of the first class may:—

> (*i*) transfer any case to be tried by any other Subordinate Court having jurisdiction, and
> (*ii*) direct or empower any magistrate holding a second or third class court to transfer the case for trial by himself [Crim. P.C., s. 73].

(c) A magistrate holding a second or third class court may submit the case to a first class magistrate, and ask him to transfer the case under his powers as set out at (b) above [Crim. P.C., s. 74].

(d) The High Court may order (1) that any particular criminal case be transferred from a criminal court subordinate to its authority to any other criminal court of equal or superior jurisdiction, and (2) that an accused person be committed for trial to itself [Crim. P.C., s. 76].

(8) Inspection, supervision, etc.—The High Court exercises general powers of supervision over all Subordinate Courts, and may at any time call for and inspect or direct the inspection of all records of Subordinate Courts [S.C.O., s. 12].

LAW TO BE ADMINISTERED

As High Court (see under A. 2, pp. 106–107, *ante*).

I. UGANDA (OTHER THAN BUGANDA)

African or native courts may be constituted under and regulated by the Native Courts Ordinance, 1941, cap. 76, or the African Courts Ordinance, 1957, according to (a) the place where a court may be situated, and (b) whether the African Courts Ordinance has or has not been applied in any particular district.

Up to 1957, the system of native courts in Uganda other than Buganda operated under the N.C.O.; it is the policy of the Government to replace the system of native courts by African courts constituted under the A.C.O., and the A.C.O. is being gradually introduced district by district by a proclamation of the Governor made under the A.C.O., s. 1(4). At the time of writing, the A.C.O. had replaced the N.C.O. in one district only (Ankole), though it is expected that it will be extended to several other districts in the near future. It is therefore necessary in the present work to outline the systems of courts under both the old (N.C.O.) and new (A.C.O.) Ordinances.

B. 1 NATIVE COURTS

CONSTITUTION AND POWERS

(1) Establishment.—Constituted under the Native Courts Ordinance, cap. 76. By s. 3 of the N.C.O., a Provincial Commissioner may confirm the establishment of any native court by the issue of a warrant.

No grades of Native Courts are recognised in the warrant, but in fact there are three types:—

    (a) Sub-county Courts (the lowest recognised courts);
    (b) County Courts;
    (c) District Native Courts.

(2) Composition.—The constitution of a Native Court is prescribed by the warrant [N.C.O., s. 4(1)]. A court usually consists of a President and a panel of members, either official (e.g. chiefs) or non-official. The usual quorum is five.

(3) Jurisdiction—original.—(*i*) *Over persons.*—Subject to its warrant, a Native Court may exercise jurisdiction over all causes and matters where, in proceedings of a civil nature, all parties are Africans, or where, in proceedings of a criminal nature, the accused is an African [N.C.O., s. 8(1)]. By the terms of its warrant a Native Court may also be empowered to exercise jurisdiction over classes of persons who are not Africans, but who, having regard to their general mode of life, may, in the opinion of the Provincial Commissioner with the approval of the Governor, nevertheless be made amenable to the jurisdiction of such court [N.C.O., s. 8(2)].

(*ii*) *Territorial limits.*—Subject to its warrant, the jurisdiction of a Native Court extends only to causes and matters arising within the local area of jurisdiction of the court, and to causes and matters arising elsewhere when the defendant is ordinarily resident within such area, save that causes and matters relating to immovable property is heard in the Native Court exercising jurisdiction in the area in which such property is situate [N.C.O., s. 9].

(*iii*) *Cases excluded from jurisdiction.*—These are as follows:—

    (a) any proceedings in which a person is charged with an offence in consequence of which death is alleged to have occurred;
    (b) any proceedings concerning marriage or divorce regulated by the Marriage Ordinance, the Marriage of Africans Ordinance, or the Divorce Ordinance, unless concerning a claim existing only in regard to bride-price or adultery and founded only on native law and custom;
    (c) any proceedings affecting the title to or any interest in land registered under the Registration of Titles Ordinance, or any Ordinance amending or replacing the same;
    (d) any proceedings taken under any Ordinance or any English or Indian law in force in the Protectorate, unless such court has been authorised to administer or enforce such Ordinance or law by the terms of an Ordinance, or under an Order of the Governor;
    (e) any proceedings removed from the jurisdiction of such court by the terms of its warrant;
    (f) any other proceedings which the Governor may remove from the jurisdiction of Native Courts;
    (g) cases of rape are always excluded by the terms of the warrant establishing the court [N.C.O., s. 10].

(4) Jurisdiction—appellate.—The system of appeals from Native Courts is laid down in the warrant establishing such court [N.C.O.,

s. 25(1)]. There is usually a hierarchy of appeals laid down in each court's warrant. This consists of appeal from the sub-county court to the County Court, thence to the District Native Court and finally to the District Magistrate. The High Court exercises no appellate jurisdiction in regard to proceedings originating in Native Courts.

CONTROL OF COURTS

(5) Appeals from.—See (4), *supra.*

(6) Review/revision.—Any magistrate may of his own motion in regard to the Native Courts within the area of his jurisdiction revise any original or appellate proceedings of a Native Court by reversing, amending, varying or quashing the decision given [N.C.O., s. 24(1)]. The High Court also has the same power [N.C.O., s. 26].

(7) Transfer.—(*i*) Where any proceedings are before a Native Court, such court or any magistrate may at any time before judgment, transfer the case to any other Native Court or Subordinate Court of competent jurisdiction; or, if the case is one that appears proper to be heard by the High Court, it may report the matter to the High Court which in its turn may transfer the case to itself or to any other Native or Subordinate Court of competent jurisdiction [N.C.O., s. 21].

(*ii*) By s. 18(1) (a) of the Civ. P.O., the High Court may transfer any civil suit before it to a Native Court.

(8) Inspection, supervision, etc.—(*i*) Every magistrate has access at all times to the Native Courts in the area to which he is posted and may send for and examine the record of any proceedings before a Native Court [N.C.O., s. 23(1)].

(*ii*) Any Chief who is authorised by a Provincial Commissioner may exercise the power conferred on a magistrate by s. 23(1), in relation to such Native Courts as are placed by the Provincial Commissioner under his supervision [N.C.O., s. 23(2)].

LAW TO BE ADMINISTERED

(9) General law.—A Native Court may administer the following:—

   (*i*) the provisions of all rules or orders made by a Provincial Commissioner, District Commissioner, or African Authority under the African Authority Ordinance, cap. 72, and all Ordinances amending or replacing the same and in force in the area in respect of which the Court is constituted [N.C.O., s. 11(b)];

  (*ii*) the provisions of any Ordinance or other law which the court is authorised to administer or enforce by the terms of any Ordinance [N.C.O., s. 11(c)];

 (*iii*) the provisions of any Ordinance, applied Act and regulation and any order, rule and proclamation made thereunder which the court may be authorised to administer by order of the Governor or the Provincial Commissioner with the approval of the Governor [N.C.O., s. 11(d)].

(10) Customary or African law.—The native law and custom prevailing within the area of the jurisdiction of the court, so far as it is applicable and is not repugnant to natural justice or morality, or is not, in principle, in conflict with the provisions of any law in force in the Protectorate [N.C.O., s. 11(a)].

(11) Islamic or other law.—Nil.

B. 2 AFRICAN COURTS

Constitution and Powers

(1) Establishment.—The African Courts Ordinance, no. 1 of 1957, establishes:—

> (*i*) in every district to which the Ordinance has been applied, a District African Court, which exercises jurisdiction throughout the district in which it is established [A.C.O., s. 3(1)];
>
> (*ii*) in every county of such district, a county court, which exercises jurisdiction throughout the county in which it is established [A.C.O., s. 3(2)];
>
> (*iii*) in every sub-county of such district, a sub-county court, which exercises jurisdiction throughout the sub-county in which it is established [A.C.O., s. 3(3)].

(2) Composition.—Prescribed by warrant of the Chief Justice [A.C.O., s. 4(1)], but the Omukama of Bunyoro, the Omukama of Toro and the Omugabe of Ankole, with the consent of the Governor, prescribe the constitution of the courts in each of their kingdoms, respectively [A.C.O., s. 4(2)].

(3) Jurisdiction—original.—(*i*) *Over persons.*—As Native Courts (see B. 1(3), (*i*), p. 110, *ante*); in addition " an African court shall have jurisdiction to hear and determine any proceedings instituted by or against the Crown or any district administration or any African local government where the other party is any person subject to the jurisdiction of such court:

Provided that in the case of proceedings against the Crown the leave of the Attorney General shall first be obtained and in the case of any proceedings against any district administration or any African local government the leave of the district commissioner shall first be obtained " [A.C.O., s. 6].

(*ii*) *Territorial limits.*—As Native Courts (see B. 1(3), (*ii*), p. 110, *ante*) [A.C.O., s. 7].

(*iii*) *Civil Jurisdiction.*—District African Court—may take cognizance of any case where the property in dispute or the compensation claimed does not exceed shs. 10,000 [s. 16(1), A].

County Court—may take cognizance of any case where the property in dispute or the compensation claimed does not exceed shs. 5000 [s. 16(1), B].

Sub-county Court—may take cognizance of any case where the property in dispute or the compensation claimed does not exceed shs. 1000 [s. 16(1), C].

(*iv*) *Criminal Jurisdiction.*—District African Court—maximum punishment: 6 years' imprisonment; shs. 5000 fine; 18 strokes in cases of crimes of violence; forfeiture where there is provision for forfeiture in any written law [s. 16(1), A].

County Court—maximum punishment: 4 years' imprisonment; shs. 4000 fine; 12 strokes in cases of crimes of violence; forfeiture where there is provision for forfeiture in any written law [s. 16(1), B].

Sub-county Court—maximum punishment: 6 months' imprisonment; shs. 500 fine; 6 strokes in cases of crimes of violence [s. 16(1), C].

(v) *Cases excluded from jurisdiction.*—These are as follows:—

   (a) " any proceedings in which a person is charged with an offence in consequence of which death is alleged to have occurred, or in which a person is charged with an attempt to cause anybody's death ";

   (b) " any proceedings concerning marriage or divorce regulated by the Marriage Ordinance, the Marriage of Africans Ordinance or the Divorce Ordinance, unless it is a claim arising only in regard to bride-price or adultery and founded only on native law and custom ";

   (c) any proceedings taken under any Ordinance or any English or Indian law in force in the Protectorate unless such court has been authorised to administer or enforce such Ordinance or law by the terms of any Ordinance, or under the order of the Governor [A.C.O., s. 8].

(4) Jurisdiction—appellate.—County Courts and District African Courts exercise appellate jurisdiction (see (5), *infra*).

CONTROL OF COURTS

(5) Appeals from.—This is laid down in s. 30. The system of appeals, subject to certain limitations as to value in civil cases and penalty in criminal cases, is as follows [A.C.O., s. 31]:—

   (*i*) appeals from a Sub-county court lie to the County Court and from an appellate decision of the County Court to the District African Court by leave of such court [A.C.O., s. 30(1)];

   (*ii*) appeals from a County Court in its original jurisdiction lie to the District African Court [A.C.O., s. 30(2)];

   (*iii*) appeals from a District African Court in its original jurisdiction lie to the High Court [A.C.O., s. 30(3)];

   (*iv*) appeals from a District African Court in its appellate jurisdiction lie to the High Court with the consent of a Courts Adviser [A.C.O., s. 30(4)].

Where leave to appeal is required under the above sections, it can only be granted if the decision to be appealed against involves an important question of law or is a decision appearing to have caused a substantial miscarriage of justice [A.C.O., s. 30(5)].

(6) Review/revision.—The High Court or a Courts Adviser may on their own motion revise any original or appellate proceedings of an African court [A.C.O., s. 27(1) and (2)].

(7) Transfer.—An African court may with the consent of the High Court, on its own motion or by application of any party, transfer a case to any other African court or to a Subordinate Court [A.C.O., s. 24].

113

E

(8) Inspection, supervision, etc.—The High Court and every Courts Adviser have at all times access to all African courts and may send for and examine the record of any proceedings before an African court for the purpose of satisfying themselves as to the correctness, legality or propriety of any judgment, sentence or order, recorded or passed, or as to regularity of any proceedings in any such court [A.C.O., s. 26(1)]. Any permanent judge of a District African Court or any chief so authorised in writing by the Chief Judge with the approval of the District Commissioner, may exercise the same power [A.C.O., s. 26(2)].

Law to be Administered

(9) General law.—(*i*) " The Governor may by order in the Gazette confer jurisdiction on all or any African court or class of African court to administer and enforce all or any provisions of any Ordinance or English or Indian law in force in the Protectorate subject to such limitations and restrictions that he may impose " [A.C.O., s. 10(1)].

(*ii*) " The provisions of all rules or orders made under the African Authority Ordinance and all Ordinances amending or replacing the same and in force in the area in which the court has jurisdiction " [A.C.O., s. 9(b)].

(*iii*) " Any bylaws, orders or directions lawfully made by the district council or any minor council in respect of the area in which the court has jurisdiction " [A.C.O., s. 9(1)].

(10) Customary law.—" The native law and custom prevailing in the area of the jurisdiction of the court, so far as it is applicable and is not repugnant to natural justice or morality and is not in conflict with the provisions of any law in force in the Protectorate or any bylaw in force in the district in which the court has jurisdiction " [A.C.O., s. 9(a)].

Note.—The new Ordinance contains important provisions with regard to the practice and procedure to be followed in African courts. Basically, the practice and procedure of African courts remain to be regulated " in accordance with native law and custom " [A.C.O., s. 11]. This section is qualified, however, by sections 12, 13 and 14 which provide as follows:—

" In matters of a criminal nature African courts shall in regard to their practice and procedure be guided by the provisions of the Criminal Procedure Code and the practice and procedure of subordinate courts " [s. 12].

" In all cases where an African court is trying any person for an offence under native law and custom and a similar offence is to be found in the Penal Code or in any other Ordinance, the court shall so far as circumstances permit be guided in its decision by the relevant provisions of the Penal Code or the other Ordinance, as the case may be " [s. 13].

" An African court in deciding whether or not to admit any evidence at any trial shall be guided in its decision by the provisions of the Evidence Ordinance " [s. 14].

Finally, s. 15 provides that the fact that an African court has not been guided or properly guided by the provisions of any Ordinance referred to in the above sections does not of itself entitle any person to be acquitted or any order of the court to be set aside.

II. BUGANDA

B. 1 THE PRINCIPAL COURT

CONSTITUTION AND POWERS

(1) Establishment.—The establishment of the Court is recognised by s. 3(1) of the Buganda Courts Ordinance, cap. 77.

(2) Composition.—The Kabaka, the Omulamuzi (Minister of Justice), the Katikiro (Prime Minister), the Omuwanika (Minister of Finance), the Omubezi w'Omulamuzi (Assistant to Omulamuzi), the Abelamuzi Abate (junior Judge) and the Ababezi abote ab'omulamuzi (Junior Assistant Judge), who are the permanent members of the court [B.C.O., s. 3(2)]. The Kabaka may appoint chiefs not below the rank of ggombolola chief to be additional judges [B.C.O., s. 3(2), (b)]. The Court shall be duly constituted if it consists of not less than three members presided over by a permanent member [B.C.O., s. 3(3), (a)].

(3) Jurisdiction—original.—The Court has full jurisdiction, civil and criminal, throughout Buganda over all Africans [B.C.O., s. 6(1)].
It does not have jurisdiction in any proceedings [B.C.O., s. 9]:—

- (a) in which a person is charged with an offence in consequence of which death is alleged to have occurred;
- (b) concerning marriage or divorce regulated by the Marriage Ordinance, the Marriage of Africans Ordinance or the Divorce Ordinance;
- (c) taken under any ordinance or any English or Indian law in force in the Protectorate, unless such court has been authorised to administer or enforce such ordinance or law by the terms of an ordinance, or by order of the Kabaka with the consent of the Governor;
- (d) removed from its jurisdiction by the terms of its warrant;
- (e) to which Uganda Agreement (Clan Cases), 1924, relates;
- (f) for the sale or delivery by way of execution of any land registered under the Registration of Titles Ordinance, or any Ordinance amending or replacing the same.

(4) Jurisdiction—appellate.—Hears appeals from courts subordinate to it.

CONTROL OF COURT

(5) Appeals from.—By s. 26(1) appeals lie to the High Court:—

- (a) in criminal cases where a court has passed a sentence of imprisonment exceeding five years, or a fine exceeding shs. 2000;
- (b) in civil cases where the amount or value of the subject matter of the case exceeds shs. 2000.

Where an appeal does not lie to the High Court, an appeal lies to the court of the Judicial Adviser and from thence to the High Court on a matter of law only [B.C.O., s. 26(3)].

(6) Review/revision.—(*i*) The Judicial Adviser may at all times have access to all courts, and to the records and proceedings of such courts and may exercise revisionary powers in respect of them [B.C.O., s. 24].

(*ii*) The High Court must confirm the proceedings of the Principal Court in any case involving questions of title to or any interest in land registered in the Mailo Register under the Registration of Titles Ordinance, where the value of the subject matter exceeds shs. 2000 [B.C.O., s. 11(2)].

(7) Transfer.—A civil or criminal case can be transferred from any Protectorate court to the Buganda courts [B.C.O., s. 7].

(8) Inspection, supervision, etc.—See (6), *supra*.

LAW TO BE ADMINISTERED

(9) General law.—(*i*) The provisions of any ordinance or other law which the court is authorised to administer or enforce by the terms of any ordinance [B.C.O., s. 10(d)].

(*ii*) The provisions of any ordinance, applied Act and regulations and any order, rule and proclamation made thereunder which the court may be authorised to administer or enforce by order of the Kabaka with the consent of the Governor [B.C.O., s. 10(e)].

(10) Customary law.—(*i*) The provision of any native law [B.C.O., s. 10(a)].

(*ii*) The native customary law prevailing in Buganda on or after the commencement of the Ordinance [B.C.O., s. 10(b)].

(*iii*) The provisions of all lawful orders made by a Chief in pursuance of native law and custom [B.C.O., s. 10(1)].

(11) Islamic or other law.—Nil.

B. 2 COURTS SUBORDINATE TO THE PRINCIPAL COURT

CONSTITUTION AND POWERS

(1) Establishment.—By s. 4(1) of the B.C.O., " other courts which shall be subordinate to the Principal Court may be established by the Kabaka, with the consent of the Governor, by the issue of a warrant . . ." There are two types of courts subordinate to the Principal Court:—

    (a) Magistrates' Courts;
    (b) Ggombolola Courts—these are further sub-divided into:—

        (*i*) Special Ggombolola Courts; and
        (*ii*) Petty Ggombolola Courts.

(2) Composition.—This is prescribed by the warrant [B.C.O., s. 5(1)]. The Magistrates' Courts consist of a magistrate appointed by the Kabaka and two private individuals drawn from a panel of local worthies selected by the chief in each administrative Ggombolola. Ggombolola Courts are composed of a chief or his deputy, together with two parish miruka) chiefs in that administrative sub-county.

(3) Jurisdiction—original.—(*i*) *Over persons.*—As Uganda Native Courts [B.C.O., s. 6(1)] (see I.B. 1(3), (*i*), p. 110 *ante*).

(*ii*) *Territorial limits.*—As Uganda Native Courts [B.C.O., s. 8] (see I.B. 1(3), p. 110, *ante*).

(*iii*) *Cases excluded from juristiction.*—As Principal Court (see II. B. 1(3), p. 115, *ante*).

(*iv*) *Extent of jurisdiction.*—This is defined by the warrant. The Petty Ggombolola Courts deal with petty criminal matters only and usually have a power to fine, but not to imprison without an option to pay a fine.

(4) Jurisdiction—appellate.—Nil.

Control of Courts

(5) **Appeals from.**—This is laid down in the warrant [B.C.O., s. 26(4)]. Appeals lie to the Principal Court alone.

(6) **Review/revision.**—As Principal Court (see II. B. 1(6), p. 115, *ante*). The Principal Court may itself also revise subordinate Buganda court proceedings [B.S.O., s. 25].

(7) **Transfer.**—As Principal Court (see II. B. (17), p. 116, *ante*).

(8) **Inspection, supervision, etc.**—Every inspecting officer has at all times access to courts subordinate to the Principal Court in the area to which he is posted, and may send for and examine the record of any proceedings before such court [B.C.O., s. 23(1)].

Law to be Administered

As Principal Court (see II. B. 1(9)–(11), p. 116, *ante*).

ZANZIBAR[1]

The organisation of the courts in Zanzibar is peculiar on account of the " dual jurisdiction " exercised by the British and Zanzibar Courts. On the British side, there is a High Court and lower courts called British subordinate courts; and, on the Zanzibar side, an exactly parallel system prevails, at the head of which stands His Highness the Sultan's Court for Zanzibar and courts subordinate thereto corresponding to the subordinate British courts. In the present survey, the High Court (called the British Court) and the Zanzibar Court will be dealt with together, and the subordinate courts—British and Zanzibar—will also be treated together.

A. 1(a) THE PRIVY COUNCIL
As for KENYA, *q.v.*, p. 89, *ante*.

A. 1(b) THE COURT OF APPEAL FOR EASTERN AFRICA
As for KENYA, *q.v.*, p. 89, *ante*.

A. 2 THE HIGH COURT AND THE ZANZIBAR COURT
CONSTITUTION AND POWERS

(1) Establishment.—British Court established by art. 17(1) of the Zanzibar Order in Council, 1924 (as amended in 1925); Zanzibar Court established by s. 8(1) of the Courts Decree, cap. 3.

(2) Composition.—Both courts have the same personnel, i.e. a Chief Justice and an unspecified number of High Court Judges.

(3) Jurisdiction—original.—Both courts have full criminal and civil jurisdiction.
Jurisdiction over persons.—British Court.—By the Jurisdiction Decree, cap. 2, s. 3, the British Court has jurisdiction over:—
- (a) British subjects;
- (b) British protected persons;
- (c) the subjects and citizens or persons under, or claimed as being under the protection of those powers who, by treaty or otherwise, have agreed with His Britannic Majesty for or consented to the exercise of jurisdiction by His Britannic Majesty;
- (d) the subjects and citizens of all Christian Powers;
- (e) all persons in the regular service of the above.

In addition, the British Court alone has jurisdiction under certain Decrees, e.g., the Insolvency Decree and the Fugitive Offenders' Decree.
Zanzibar Court.—Has jurisdiction in all other cases.

---

[1] For diagram of courts system, see p. 218, *post*.

(4) Jurisdiction—appellate.—The British Court hears appeals from British subordinate courts in civil and criminal matters [British Subordinate Courts Order, 1923, s. 15(1)]; and the Zanzibar Court hears appeals in civil and criminal cases from the Zanzibar subordinate courts, provided that in civil matters the amount involved exceeds shs. 200, or that leave to appeal is granted by the Zanzibar Court [C.D., s. 23(1)].

Law to be Administered

(9) General law.—(*i*) Decrees of the Sultan, provided they have been countersigned by the British Resident [Zanzibar Order in Council, 1924, art. 23].

(*ii*) Orders in Council [Z.O-in-C, art. 24].

(*iii*) Certain specifically applied U.K. legislation [Z.O-in-C, art. 25].

(*iv*) " The substance of the common law, the doctrines of equity and the statutes of general application in force in England on the 7th day of July, 1897 [subject to (*i*) and (*ii*) and (*iii*) *supra*] and provided always that the said common law, doctrines of equity and statutes of general application shall be in force in Zanzibar so far only as the circumstances of the Protectorate and its inhabitants and the limits of His Majesty's jurisdiction permit, and subject to such qualifications as local circumstances render necessary " [Z.O-in-C, art. 24].

(10) Customary law.—" Native law " may be applicable on appeals from Mudirial Courts: see p. 122, *post.*

(11) Islamic law.—(*i*) In civil matters the law of Islam is the fundamental law of the Protectorate [C.D., s. 7].

(*ii*) In matrimonial matters and questions of inheritance and succession, Islamic, Hindu and Buddhist law are applied as the " personal law " of the parties, e.g. under the Succession Decree, s. 7.

(*Note.*—All the above laws can be applied both by the British Court and the Zanzibar Court. There is no practical difference in the law which the two courts administer, save for the law applicable in civil proceedings. While the *corpus juris* in the Sultan's courts consists of the Sharia law as locally applied, in the British courts it consists of the common law and the doctrines of equity.)

For details see Anderson, J. N. D., *Islamic Law in Africa*, pp. 58–80; Vaughan, J. H., *The Dual Jurisdiction in Zanzibar*; and Kingdon, H. E., *The Conflict of Laws in Zanzibar.*

A. 3 SUBORDINATE COURTS

Constitution and Powers

(1) Establishment.—British subordinate courts established by s. 4(1) of the British Subordinate Courts Order, 1923. Zanzibar subordinate courts established by s. 10(1) of the C.D., 1923, cap. 3. Subordinate courts may be:—

    (a) First Class subordinate courts;
    (b) Second Class subordinate courts;
    (c) Third Class subordinate courts;
    (d) Kathis' Courts;

(e) Mudirial Courts;
(f) Juvenile courts.

(2) Composition.—The same officers preside over British and Zanzibar subordinate courts. The courts are presided over as follows:—

first class subordinate court: Resident Magistrate or Provincial Commissioner;

second class subordinate court: such persons as may be specifically appointed by the British Resident;

third class subordinate court: District Officer or other person specifically appointed.

Kathis' Courts: Kathi (see Kathis' Courts, p. 123, *post*);

Mudirial Courts: Mudir (see Mudirial Courts, p. 121, *post*);

juvenile courts: Chairman, who is a Resident Magistrate or Magisterial Officer and two other persons drawn from a panel (see Juvenile Courts, p. 123, *post*).

(3) Jurisdiction—original.—(*i*) *Civil.*—[British S.C.O., s. 9; C.D., s. 14].

First class subordinate court: where value of subject matter does not exceed shs. 5000;

second class subordinate court: where value of subject matter does not exceed shs. 3000;

third class subordinate court; where value of subject matter does not exceed shs. 1000.

(*ii*) *Criminal.*—First class subordinate court: maximum punishment, 4 years' imprisonment, shs. 4000 fine or corporal punishment not exceeding 12 strokes [Criminal Procedure Decree, cap, 8, s. 7]. But sentences exceeding 12 months' imprisonment are subject to the " instant perusal " of the High Court [Crim. P.D., s. 12(a)].

Second class subordinate court: maximum punishment, 12 months' imprisonment, shs. 750 fine or, if so empowered by the British Resident, corporal punishment not exceeding 10 strokes [Crim. P.D., s. 8]. But sentences exceeding 3 months' imprisonment, or a fine of shs. 150, or corporal punishment, if any, are subject to the " instant perusal " of the High Court [Crim. P.D., s. 12(b)].

Third class subordinate court: maximum punishment, 3 months' imprisonment; shs. 200 fine [Crim. P.D., s. 9]. But sentences exceeding one month's imprisonment or shs. 100 fine are subject to the " instant perusal " of the High Court [Crim. P.D., s. 12(1)].

(4) Jurisdiction—appellate.—Nil.

CONTROL OF COURTS

(5) Appeals from.—Appeals from all subordinate courts, civil and criminal, lie to the High Court (either the British Court or the Zanzibar Court).

(6) Review/revision.—(*i*) *Civil.*—The High Court has the power to call for, review and revise the proceedings of a lower court in a civil case in which no appeal lies [Civil Procedure Decree, cap. 4, ss. 81 and 82].

(*ii*) *Criminal.*—(a) The High Court may call for records and examine any criminal proceedings before any subordinate court and revise them [Crim. P.D., ss. 346 and 348].

(b) Any magistrate may call for and examine the record of any criminal proceedings before a subordinate court of a class inferior to his and report any irregularity to the High Court [Crim. P.D., s. 347(1) and (2)].

(7) Transfer.—(*i*) *Civil.*—(a) The High Court has the power to transfer suits which may be instituted in any one of two or more subordinate courts [Civ. P.D., s. 17].

(b) The High Court may at any stage transfer any suit, appeal or other proceeding before it, for trial to a court subordinate to it, or transfer a case being tried by a subordinate court for trial by itself or any other subordinate court [Civ. P.D., s. 18].

(*ii*) *Criminal.*—(a) If upon hearing a complaint it appears that the cause of complaint arose outside the limit of the jurisdiction of the court, the court may transfer the case to a court having jurisdiction [Crim. P.D., s. 72(1)].

(b) Any first class magistrate may transfer any case before him to a second or third class subordinate court within the local limits of his jurisdiction, or may direct any subordinate court of the second or third class to transfer the case for trial by himself [Crim. P.D., s. 73].

(c) The High Court may transfer any case from a criminal court subordinate to its authority to any other criminal court of equal or superior jurisdiction, or may order that an accused person be committed for trial to itself [Crim. P.D., s. 75].

(8) Inspection, supervision, etc.—See under (6), *supra.*

Law to be Administered

As High Court (see p. 119, *ante*).

B. MUDIRIAL COURTS

Constitution and Powers

(1) Establishment.—Although classed under subordinate courts by the British S.C.O. and the Courts Decree, they are established under the District (Mudirial) Courts Proclamation, 1947 (G.N. 105/47). By s. 3(1) the British Resident may by warrant under his hand establish such Mudirial Courts as he thinks fit.

(2) Composition.—Determined by the warrant. The courts are presided over by Mudirial Officers appointed by the British Resident.

(3) Jurisdiction—original.—(*i*) *Over persons.*—Mudirial Courts have full jurisdiction over cases and matters in which all the parties are declared by its warrant to be subject to the jurisdiction of the court, and are resident or within the area of the jurisdiction of such court [D.(M.)C.P., s. 6].

(*ii*) *Criminal jurisdiction.*—As third class subordinate courts, and extending to all criminal charges in which any person is accused of having wholly, or in part, within the jurisdiction of the court committed or been accessory to the committing of an offence [D.(M.)C.P., s. 8].

(*iii*) *Civil jurisdiction.*—As third class subordinate courts, and extending to all civil suits in which the defendant is ordinarily resident within the area of the jurisdiction of the court, or in which the cause of action arose within that area, but civil proceedings relating to immovable property must be taken in the Mudirial Court within the area of whose jurisdiction the property is situate [D.(M.)C.P., s. 9(1)].

(*iv*) *Cases excluded from jurisdiction.*—Mudirial Courts cannot:—

    (a) hold a preliminary enquiry in criminal cases;
    (b) hold an inquest;
    (c) try any case connected with personal status, guardianship, marriage, divorce, succession, inheritance, wills, testamentary dispositions, or waqf;
    (d) try any cognizable offence committed in any place which, under the Towns Decree or any other law in force in the Protectorate, is declared to be a Town [D.(M.)C.P., s. 10(1)].

But a Mudirial Court is declared competent to try:—

    (a) any case in which the parties are both of the same religion and the claim is one for dowry only; or
    (b) any case in which the claim is one for the maintenance of a wife or legitimate or illegitimate child; or
    (c) any case in which the claim is in respect of land which is alleged to be native land by any of the parties [D.(M.)C.P., s. 10(2)].

(4) Jurisdiction—appellate.—Nil.

CONTROL OF COURTS

(5) Appeals from.—These go to the High Court, as from a third class subordinate court [D.(M.)C.P., s. 22].

(6) Review/revision.—(*i*) The Provincial Commissioner or the District Commissioner may call for and examine the record of any civil or criminal proceedings in a Mudirial Court and report any irregularity to the High Court [D.(M.)C.P., s. 16].

(*ii*) The High Court may call for and examine the records of any civil or criminal proceedings before a Mudirial Court, and revise them [D.(M.)C.P., ss. 17 and 18].

(7) Transfer.—Nil.

(8) Inspection, supervision, etc.—See under (6), *supra*.

(9) General law.—The British Resident may empower a Mudirial Court to administer any of the provisions of any law in force in the Protectorate [D.(M.)C.P., s. 12(1)].

(10) Customary law.—Mudirial Courts administer native law mostly in matters relating to native land. " Native law " is defined in the Mudirial Courts Rules 1947, s. 2, as " any custom which is recognised by any natives residing in the Protectorate as being binding upon themselves as having the force of law and which is not repugnant to justice and morality or inconsistent with any other law for the time being in force in the Protectorate." When any case involving " native law " arises, a Mudirial Court must call in the aid of two or more assessors specially qualified [D.(M.)C.P., s. 7(1)].

(11) Islamic or other law.—The " native law " (see (10), *supra*) has in fact assimilated a good deal of Islamic law, mostly Shafei with some slight traces of Shi'i influence.

C. KATHIS' COURTS

CONSTITUTION AND POWERS

(1) Establishment.—Kathis' Courts are established under the British Subordinate Courts Order and the Courts Decree.

(2) Composition.—Presided over by a Kathi.

(3) Jurisdiction—original. They have no criminal jurisdiction and their civil jurisdiction is limited to:—

(a) matters relating to personal status, marriage, divorce, guardianship and (subject to the provisions of any other law for the time being in force) the custody of children in cases in which the parties are Muslims of the Ibathi sect or the Shafei sect;

(b) matters relating to waqfs, religious and charitable trusts, gifts *inter vivos* and inheritance where the claim in respect of any such matter does not exceed shs. 3000, and the parties are Muslims of the Ibathi sect or the Shafei sect;

(c) claims for maintenance (where such claim is for a lump sum not exceeding shs. 1000, or for a periodical payment to be made at a rate not exceeding shs. 100 per month) and the parties are Muslims of the Ibathi sect or the Shafei sect; and

(d) suits and proceedings of a civil nature in which the subject matter can be estimated at a money value and does not exceed shs. 1000 [C.D., s. 14(5); British S.C.O., s. 9(3)].

(4) Jurisdiction—appellate.—Nil.

CONTROL OF COURTS

As subordinate courts (see under A. 3, p. 120, *ante*).

LAW TO BE ADMINISTERED

As subordinate courts, but they mainly administer Islamic law in the matters set out under (3), *supra.*

D. JUVENILE COURTS

CONSTITUTION AND POWERS

(1) Establishment.—Although established as subordinate courts, their constitution and composition is defined in the Children and Young Persons Decree, No. 10 of 1951, s. 3(1) (a).

(2) Composition.—By s. 3(1) (b) of the C.Y.P.D., the personnel of these courts is drawn from panels consisting of 12 or more persons in each of the islands of Zanzibar and Pemba, formed by the British Resident. The Chairman of each Juvenile Court is a Resident Magistrate, or a Magisterial Officer, or, in the absence of both, a person appointed by the Chief Justice. The quorum is the Chairman sitting with two other members of the panel who must include one man and, so far as is practicable, one woman.

(3) Jurisdiction—original.—The courts have jurisdiction to hear and determine any case in which a person under the age of 16 years is charged with an offence other than murder or manslaughter [C.Y.P.D., s. 8].

(4) Jurisdiction—appellate.—Nil.

CONTROL OF COURTS

(5) Appeals from.—To the High Court.

LAW TO BE ADMINISTERED

As subordinate courts (see A. 3, p. 119, *ante*).

SUDAN

The administration of justice in the Sudan is entrusted to an independent body called "the Judiciary" [Judiciary Act, 1959[1] (1959, Act no. 7), s. 3(1)]. The Judiciary consists of two divisions, the Civil Division and the Sharia Division, of which the Chief Justice and the Grand Kadi are the respective Presidents and judicial heads [J.A., s. 4]. The Civil Division comprises:—

A. Civil courts and criminal courts, which administer primarily the general territorial law; and

B. Local courts, which administer primarily native customary law.

The Sharia Division comprises all the Modammedan courts.[2]

I. CIVIL DIVISION[3]

A. 1 COURT OF APPEAL

This Court is part of the High Court of Justice (see A. 2(1), *infra*).

CONSTITUTION AND POWERS

(1) Establishment.—Established by s. 11 of the Civil Justice Ordinance, *Laws of the Sudan*, Vol. 10, Title XXVI, sub-title 1.

(2) Composition.—Chief Justice, judges of the High Court, province judges [C.J.O., s. 15]. Quorum is 2 [C.J.O., s. 16]. Any other fit and proper persons of sufficient legal experience may also be appointed to the Court by the Chief Justice.

(3) Jurisdiction—original.—Nil.

(4) Jurisdiction—appellate.—An appeal lies to the Court of Appeal from every decree made in a suit of value more than £200 if the value of the relief claimed in the appeal is more than £200, but in any Province in which a Judge of the High Court is exercising his functions no appeal lies from the decree of a District Judge [C.J.O., s. 168(1) as amended in 1954].

LAW TO BE ADMINISTERED

See under HIGH COURT, p. 126, *post*.

---

[1] This Act re-enacts most of Chapter IX, ss. 92–102 of the Transitional Constitution of the Sudan, 1956, (which had in part re-enacted the Self-Government Statute, 1953) dealing with the "Judiciary". The Transitional Constitution was suspended by the Supreme Army Council Order, No. 1 of 17th November, 1958.

[2] For another account of the Sudan legal system, see Guttmann, E., "The Sudan Legal System", [1956] S.L.J.R.

[3] For diagram of courts system, see p. 219, *post*.

A. 2 THE HIGH COURT OF JUSTICE

CONSTITUTION AND POWERS

(1) Establishment.—Established by s. 10(a) of the C.J.O. The High Court of Justice consists of (a) the Court of Appeal (see p. 125, *ante*) and (b) courts of original jurisdiction [C.J.O., s. 11].

(2) Composition.—Chief Justice and Judges of the High Court [C.J.O., s. 12].

(3) Jurisdiction—original.—The original jurisdiction is exercised by High Court Judges sitting singly, and the High Court has jurisdiction throughout the Sudan to hear and determine all suits [C.J.O., s. 33].

(4) Jurisdiction—appellate.—Nil. (But see appellate jurisdiction of Court of Appeal, which is part of the High Court of Justice, p. 125, *ante*.

CONTROL OF COURT

(5) Appeals from.—These lie to the Court of Appeal.

(6) Review/revision.—The Court of Appeal may revise proceedings in the High Court [C.J.O., s. 175(b)], and may review such proceedings for the purpose of correcting a clerical error, or other error manifestly the result of an oversight [C.J.O., s. 184]. The High Court may also review its own decisions.

(7) Transfer.—(*i*) Where a suit may be instituted in any one or two or more courts, and is instituted in one of such courts, the court in which the suit was instituted may transfer the suit to the other court [C.J.O., s. 49].

(*ii*) The Chief Justice may with regard to any suit pending in any civil court, (a) withdraw the case from one court and transfer it to another, or (b) transfer any suit being tried by himself to any other court, subordinate to his authority [C.J.O., s. 50(2)].

(8) Inspection, supervision, etc.—The Chief Justice has general superintendence and control over the civil courts [C.J.O., s. 19].

LAW TO BE ADMINISTERED

(9) General law.—Ordinances and (after 1956) Acts. " In cases not provided for by this or any other enactment for the time being in force the Court shall act according to justice, equity and good conscience " [C.J.O., s. 9[1]].

---

[1] This section has been interpreted by judges to mean English law (statute law, equity and the common law) which is in practice freely applied. (See, however, OWEN, J.'s, *dictum* in *Heirs of Ibrahim Khalil* v. *Abdel Moneim* AC–App–6–1926, where he held that the Sudan courts were to be " guided but not bound by English common and statute law ".)

(10) Customary law and Islamic law.—It is far from clear[1] what law is intended to apply in s. 5 of the Civil Justice Ordinance, which reads:—

> "Where in any suit or other proceeding in a Civil Court any question arises regarding succession, inheritance, wills, legacies, gifts, marriage family relations or the constitution of wakfs, the rule of decision shall be:—
>
>> (a) any custom applicable to the parties concerned, which is not contrary to justice, equity or good conscience and has not been by this or any other enactment altered or abolished and has not been declared void by the decision of a competent court;
>>
>> (b) the Mohammedan law, in cases where the parties are Mohammedans, except in so far as that law has been modified by such custom as is above referred to ".

A. 3 PROVINCE COURTS

CONSTITUTION AND POWERS

(1) Establishment.—By s. 10(b) of the C.J.O., there must be a court in each Province which is to be subordinate to the High Court [C.J.O., s. 20].

(2) Composition.—The judges consist of:—

(a) a Province Judge (except in the Province of Khartoum and in any province in which a judge of the High Court is stationed—in this case the High Court judge exercises the functions of a Province Judge).

(b) District Judges, who may be of three grades [C.J.O., s. 21].

(3) Jurisdiction—original.—The various grades of judges have jurisdiction as follows:—

(*i*) Province Judge: no limit as regards value.

(*ii*) District Judge, first grade: no limit as regards value.

(*iii*) District Judge, second grade: value not exceeding £100

(*iv*) District Judge, third grade: value not exceeding £50 when case is undefended; not exceeding £30 when case is defended [C.J.O., s. 35 as amended in 1954].

(4) Jurisdiction—appellate.—By the Province Courts (Conferment of Powers) Act, 1955/1956, art. no. 27, s. 2, the appellate powers of

---

[1] The difficulty arises in the interpretation of the term "custom". Two conflicting interpretations have been given. In *Abdulla Cherchaflia* v. *Marie Batyarellis*, AC–App–12–1934, GORMAN, J., held that the term referred to the *lex domicilii* where the parties are not domiciled in the Sudan and was prepared to hold that the word "custom" would include the canon or religious law of the parties. In *Bamboulis* v. *Bamboulis*, Ac–Rev–58–53, however, LINDSAY, C. J., held that "custom" in this context "refers to local custom originating by usage in the Sudan, and is not applicable to . . . the personal law of foreigners ". In the recent case of *Kattan* v. *Kattan*, [1957] S.L.J.R., the Court of Appeal seems to have pronounced in favour of the latter interpretation though not committing itself to a final decision on the matter.

the High Court are exercisable by a Province Court where the enactments referred to in the Schedule of the Act provide for an appeal to the High Court.

Control of Courts

(5) Appeals from.—These lie to the Court of Appeal (see A. 1(4), p. 125, *ante*).

(6) Review/revision.—As High Court, except that revision of a District Judge's order goes to the Province Judge [C.J.O., s. 175(a)].

(7) Transfer.—As High Court.

(8) Inspection, supervision, etc.—As High Court. Moreover, the Province Judge supervises Province Courts [C.J.O., s. 26].

Law to be Administered

As High Court.

A. 4 TOWN COURTS

Constitution and Powers

(1) Establishment.—By s. 10(c) of the C.J.O., Town Courts[1] are to be established in such provinces as the Chief Justice may direct and they are to be subordinate to the Province Court of that Province [C.J.O., s. 27].

(2) Composition.—The Chief Justice may appoint any fit and proper person to be a member [C.J.O., s. 29]. A Town Court is constituted by three or five members sitting together [C.J.O., s. 30(1)].

(3) Jurisdiction—original.—Has jurisdiction to try any question of fact which is in issue in a suit and which is referred to such Town Court for trial by the court in which such suit is pending, provided:—

    (a) no such question may be referred in a suit in which the Government is a party; and

    (b) in a suit in which the title to immovable property is in issue no such questions may be referred [C.J.O., s. 36].

(4) Jurisdiction—appellate.—Nil.

Control of Courts

(5) Appeals from.—These lie to the Court of Appeal.

(6) Review/revision.—The court which referred the matter to the Town Court has the power of revision [C.J.O., s. 175(c)]. The Court of Appeal also has power to review.

(7) Transfer.—As High Court. Moreover, the Court of a Province Judge may:—

    (*i*) Withdraw any suit pending in a court subordinate to itself and transfer the suit for trial to any court subordinate to itself and competent to try it;

---

[1] So far as is known, only one Town Court has ever been set up, at Rufaa, but it never sat. It appears that the idea of Town Courts has been abandoned, but they still exist in the statute book.

(*ii*) transfer any suit pending before itself for trial to any court subordinate to itself and competent to try it [C.J.O., s. 50(1)].

(8) Inspection, supervision, etc.—Subject to the general control of the Province Judge, the District Commissioner or Assistant District Commissioner of the District in which the Town Court sits exercises control over the court [C.J.O., s. 32].

A. 5 CRIMINAL COURTS

CONSTITUTION AND POWERS

(1) Establishment.—There are six classes of Criminal Courts in the Sudan, all established by s. 8 of the Code of Criminal Procedure, vol. 9, Title XXV, sub-title 1. They are:—

- (a) Major Courts;
- (b) Minor Courts;
- (c) Courts of magistrates of the first class;
- (d) Courts of magistrates of the second class;
- (e) Courts of magistrates of the third class;
- (f) Benches of magistrates.

(2) Composition.—(a) *Major Courts.*—A judge of the High Court and two magistrates; or three magistrates one of whom must be a Province Judge or a first class magistrate [C.C.P., s. 9(1)].

(b) *Minor Courts.*—Three magistrates of whom at least one is to be of the first or second class [C.C.P., s. 9(2)].

(c) *First class magistrate.*—The following are *ex-officio* magistrates of the first class:—every Governor [" Governor " in this context means Provincial Governor], Deputy Governor, Judge of the High Court, Province Judge and District Judge of the first class [C.C.P., s. 10].

(d) *Second class magistrate.*—Every District Commissioner is an *ex-officio* magistrate of the second class [C.C.P., s. 10].

(e) *Third class magistrate.*—Every Mamur is an *ex-officio* magistrate of third class [C.C.P., s. 10].

(f) *Benches of magistrates.*—Three third class magistrates [C.C.P., s. 10(a)].

Note.—It is no longer usual for a member of the Administration to be a member of a court, though they are sometimes called upon to conduct magisterial enquiries.

(3) Jurisdiction—original.—(a) *Major Court.*—Unlimited [C.C.P., s. 16].

(b) *Minor Court.*—Maximum punishment: 7 years' imprisonment; fine not exceeding £500; whipping; detention ⌈C.C.P., s. 17].

(c) *First class magistrate.*—Maximum punishment: 2 years' imprisonment; fine not exceeding £200; whipping; detention [C.C.P., s. 18], except when trying an offence summarily, when it may pass a sentence of not more than 3 months' imprisonment or £20 fine or flogging or whipping.

(d) *Second class magistrate.*—Maximum punishment: 6 months' imprisonment; fine not exceeding £50; whipping and detention [C.C.P., s. 19], except when trying an offence summarily when it may pass a sentence of not more than one months' imprisonment; £5 fine; flogging or whipping.

(e) *Third class magistrate.*—May only try cases summarily; maximum punishment: 7 days' imprisonment; fine not exceeding 50 P.T. (10s.) [C.C.P., s. 20].

(f) *Bench of magistrates.*—Powers of first class magistrate; or second class magistrate; or third class magistrate; or second class magistrate trying an offence summarily, as the Chief Justice directs [C.C.P., s. 10(a)].

(4) Jurisdiction—appellate.—Nil.

CONTROL OF COURTS

(5) Appeals from.—Only a very limited right of criminal appeal exists in the Sudan. Within 7 days of sentence being passed, a convicted person can appeal from the judgment of a court of a magistrate of the first class or of the second class provided the sentence imposed by the court exceeded the penalty which that court could have imposed on a summary trial. An order to give security to keep the peace, a residence order, an order to abate a nuisance, which has been made absolute, and an order forfeiting a bond taken by a court can also be appealed against [C.C.P., s. 253]. Appeals lie to the Judge of the High Court or to the Province Judge where such has been appointed to a circuit. The Judge of the High Court may delegate his powers to a first class magistrate [C.C.P., s. 262(a)].

Confirmation.—Although there is no appeal from the judgment of Major Courts or of Minor Courts, such judgments require to be confirmed by the Chief Justice or the Judge of the High Court respectively [Crim. P.C., ss. 250, 251]. The convicted person may submit a written petition of appeal indicating why the judgment should not be confirmed [Crim. P.C., s. 252], but there is no right to be heard in person or through an advocate [C.C.P., s. 260].

(6) Review/revision.—(*i*) In all criminal cases, the Chief Justice may call for and examine the records of any proceedings for the purpose of satisfying himself as to the correctness, legality or propriety of any finding, sentence or order recorded or passed and as to the regularity of the proceedings of the court [C.C.P., s. 259(1)].

(*ii*) A Judge of the High Court or the Province Judge, where such has been appointed to a circuit, has the same powers within his circuit, except that he cannot revise the proceedings of a Major Court. His decision however may be subjected to a further revision by the Chief Justice.

(*iii*) A Judge of the High Court may delegate his powers under (*ii*), *supra* to a first class magistrate [C.C.P., s. 262(a)].

(7) Transfer.—(*i*) A Province Judge or a High Court Judge, may, whenever it appears to him that such transfer will promote the ends of justice or will be in the interests of public tranquillity, transfer any case from one court within his province or circuit to another at any stage of the proceedings.

(*ii*) The Chief Justice may make the like transfer from one province to another [C.C.P., s. 127].

(8) Inspection, supervision, etc.—See (6), *supra.*

LAW TO BE ADMINISTERED

(9) General law.—The provisions of the Sudan Penal Code and other Ordinances that deal with criminal offences.

(10) Customary law ⎫
⎬ Nil.
(11) Islamic or other law ⎭

A. 6 COURT OF CRIMINAL APPEAL

In exercising his confirmatory or revisionary powers, the Chief Justice may remit any case before him to a Court of Criminal Appeal composed of the Chief Justice and two magistrates of the first class, of whom at least one must be a Judge of the High Court [C.C.P., s. 261(a). Unlike the case of appeal by way of confirmation, the accused is entitled to be heard before the Court of Appeal [C.C.P., s. 261(a), (3)].

B. 1 CHIEFS' COURTS

CONSTITUTION AND POWERS

(1) Establishment.—By s. 5(1) of the Chiefs' Courts Ordinance,[1] vol. 10, Title XXVI, sub-title 3, the Chief Justice by warrant may establish such Chiefs' Courts as he thinks fit.

(2) Composition.—There are the following classes of Chiefs' Courts [C.C.O., s. 4(1)]:—
(a) a Chief sitting alone;
(b) a Chief or president sitting with members;
(c) a special court.

(3) Jurisdiction—original.—(*i*) *Extent.*—The warrant defines the powers of the court and the limits of its jurisdiction [C.C.O., s. 5(2)].

(*ii*) *Over persons.*—Subject to certain exceptions, the court has full jurisdiction in all civil cases in which the accused person is a native[2] [C.C.O., s. 6].

(4) Jurisdiction—appellate.—Nil.

CONTROL OF COURTS

(5) Appeals from.—In both civil and criminal cases, appeals from the decisions of a Chief's Court are as of right and are to the Chief Justice (or to the Judge of the High Court, Province Judge or Resident Magistrate) or to a Chief's Court thereunto authorised by him.

---

[1] The Ordinance only applies to the Provinces of Bahr el Ghazel, Equatoria, Upper Nile and to the area normally inhabited by the Ngork Dinka tribe of Kordofan Province.

[2] By s. 23 " native " means any native of Africa other than a native of Egypt.

(6) Review/revision.—The Chief Justice has powers to revise the decision of any Chief's Court including a Special Court.[1] But a sentence of *not guilty* cannot be revised. It is, however, possible for the revising authority to cancel all proceedings and, within 6 months of judgment, a re-hearing before a court established under the Code of Criminal Procedure or the Civil Justice Ordinance can be ordered [C.C.O., s. 10].

LAW TO BE ADMINISTERED

(9) General law.—The provisions of any ordinance which the court may be authorised to administer in its warrant or regulations [C.C.O., s. 7(1), (b)].

(10) Customary law.—" The native law and custom prevailing in the area over which the court exercises its jurisdiction, provided that such native law and custom is not contrary to justice, morality or order " [C.C.O., s. 7(1) (a)].

(11) Islamic or other law.—Nil.

B. 2 NATIVE COURTS

CONSTITUTION AND POWERS

(1) Establishment.—By s. 6(1) of the Native Courts Ordinance (which applies to all areas of the Sudan except those covered by the Chiefs' Courts Ordinance), the Chief Justice may establish Native Courts in such places as he thinks fit.

(2) Composition.—There are the following classes of Native Courts [N.C.O., s. 5]:—

(a) a Sheikh's Court, that is a court with a Sheikh as president sitting with members;
(b) a court of a Sheikh sitting in *meglis,* that is a court of a Sheikh sitting with elders;
(c) a Village Court;
(d) a court of a Sheikh sitting alone;
(e) a Special Court.

The warrants establishing these courts have introduced a further classification applicable to Sheikh's Courts, which are divided into (1) Main Courts, (2) Regional Courts and (3) Branch Courts. Regional Courts have powers intermediate between Main and Branch Courts.

(3) Jurisdiction—original.—(*i*) *Extent.*—Set out in the warrant establishing the court [N.C.O., s. 7(1)].

(*ii*) *Cases excluded from jurisdiction.*—These are as follows [N.C.O., s. 8(1)]:—

(a) any civil case in which neither party is subject to the jurisdiction of the court, except with the consent of both parties;
(b) any civil case in which one party is subject to the jurisdiction and the other not, except with the consent of the party not subject to the jurisdiction;

---

[1] This power may be delegated to a magistrate of the second class or to a Governor. See for delegation of powers the Judiciary Act, 1959, s. 11; the Code of Criminal Procedure, s. 12(a); and the Miscellaneous Amendments Act, 1956, (Act no. 13), s. 4.

(c) any case concerning the ownership of land, except a claim for partition of land registered under the Land Settlement and Registration Ordinance, and owned in undivided shares by co-heirs;

(d) any criminal case in which the accused is a Government official;

(e) any criminal case in which the accused is a policeman or a non-commissioned officer, or soldier in the Sudan Defence Force;

(f) certain other offences such as homicide, offences against the State, or relating to the military forces or offences relating to slavery.

Moreover, a Village Court cannot:—

(*i*) try offences of assault, hurt, criminal trespass, insult, affray, theft and similar offences; or

(*ii*) hear any civil case in which the value of the subject matter in dispute exceeds £5.

(4) Jurisdiction—appellate.—Appellate powers may be granted to a Native Court by the warrant establishing it [N.C.O., s. 12(1)]. Wherever the warrant provides for appeals, such appeals are as of right [N.C.O., s. 12(2)].

CONTROL OF COURT

(5) Appeals from.—This is set out in the warrant, but the procedure has become generally standardised. Appeals from a Sheikh sitting in *meglis* go to the Branch Court and from the Branch Court to the Regional Court, where such a court exists, otherwise to the Main Court. From a Regional or a Main Court appeals go to the Resident Magistrate (i.e. a District Judge of the first grade and a magistrate of the first class), within whose local jurisdiction the court is situated and thence to the Judge of the High Court or Province Judge.

(6) Review/revision.—The Chief Justice has power to revise the decisions of Native Courts [N.C.O., s. 14]. The Chief Justice may delegate his power to a Judge of the High Court or Province Judge, or to a magistrate of the first or second class.

LAW TO BE ADMINISTERED

(9) General law.—The provisions of any ordinance, where such provisions are not part of native law and custom, and where the court has been expressly authorised in its warrant, order or regulations to administer such provision [N.C.O., s. 9(1), (b)].

(10) Customary law.—" The native law and custom prevailing in the area or in the tribe over which the court exercises its jurisdiction provided that such native law and custom is not contrary to justice, morality or order " [N.C.O., s. 9(1), (a)].

(11) Islamic or other law.—The Sharia is applied by some Native Courts in cases of personal status since a locally trained *Alim*, who is under the supervision of the Sharia courts, sits with the court.[1]

---

[1] For details, see M. ABU RANNAT, C.J.: " The relationship between Islamic and customary law in the Sudan," [1960] J.A.L. 9–16.

Note.—A Bill aimed at consolidating the Chiefs' Courts Ordinance and the Native Courts Ordinance and bringing them under one Ordinance is now in preparation. The Bill will also regulate the practice and procedure in these courts.[1]

II. SHARIA DIVISION[2]

C. MOHAMMEDAN COURTS

The Sudan Mohammedan Law Courts comprise a Court of Appeal, a High Court, courts of first class Kadis and courts of second class Kadis. These will all be dealt with together briefly.

CONSTITUTION AND POWERS

(1) Establishment.—All established by s. 2 of the Sudan Mohammedan Law Courts Ordinance, 1902, vol. II, Title XXVII, Sub-Title 1.

(2) Composition.—(*i*) The Court of Appeal consists of the Grand Kadi, who presides, the Mufti and the Inspectors of the Mohammedan Law Courts. The quorum is three [S.M.L.C.O., s. 2].

(*ii*) The High Court consists of a single High Court Kadi [S.M.L.C.O., s. 4].

(*iii*) First class courts consist of a single first class Kadi [S.M.L.C.O., s. 5(1)].

(*iv*) Second class courts consist of a single second class Kadi [S.M.L.C.O., s. 5(2)].

(3) Jurisdiction—original.—Courts of first and second class Kadis and the High Court exercise original jurisdiction [S.M.L.C.O., ss. 4 and 5], but the Court of Appeal only exercises appellate and revisionary jurisdiction. All the courts are competent to decide [S.M.L.C.O., s. 6]:—

(a) any question regarding marriage, divorce, guardianship of minors or family relationships, provided that the marriage to which the question related was concluded in accordance with Modammedan law, or the parties are all Mohammedans;

(b) any question regarding waqf, gift, succession, wills, interdiction or guardianship of an interdicted or lost person, provided that the endower, dower or the deceased or the interdicted or lost person is a Mohammedan;

(c) any question other than those in (a) or (b), *supra*, provided that all the parties, whether being Mohammedans or not, make a formal demand signed by them asking the court to entertain the question and stating that they agree to be bound by the ruling of Mohammedan law.

(4) Jurisdiction—appellate.—First class Kadis, the High Court and the Court of Appeal exercise appellate jurisdiction.

CONTROL OF COURTS

(5) Appeals from.—Appeals go from Kadis of the second class to Kadis of the first class [the Sudan Mohammedan Law Courts Organisation and Procedure Regulations, 1916, as amended by the Mohammedan

---

[1] See Rannat, *op. cit.*, p. 16, for details of the main proposals in the Bill.
[2] For diagram of courts system, see p. 218, *post.*

Law Courts Organisation and Procedure (Amendment) Regulations, 1957 (1957, L.R.O. No. 40), reg. 25]; and to the High Court from decisions of a first class Kadi or second class Kadi not appealable to a first class Kadi [reg. 29(d)]; and appeals from the High Court go to the Court of Appeal [reg. 30]. The Grand Kadi also has powers to hear appeals from any Court of a Kadi sitting alone.

(6) Review/revision.—(*i*) The High Court can revise the decisions of Kadis of the first and second class.

(*ii*) The Court of Appeal has powers of revision over the decisions of first class Kadis, High Court Kadis and of the Grand Kadi whether given in the exercise of his original or appellate jurisdiction [regs. 31 and 34].

(7) Transfer.—The Grand Kadi may transfer any suit pending before any court to another court [S.M.L.C.O.P.R., reg. 51].

(8) Inspection, supervision, etc.—A Committee of Supervision composed of the Chief Justice, the Grand Kadi, the Mufti and the Inspector of the Mohammedan law courts supervise the work of all the Mohammedan law courts, except the High Court [S.M.L.C.O.P.R., reg. 43].

LAW TO BE ADMINISTERED

(9) General law ⎫
⎬ Nil.
(10) Customary law ⎭

(11) Islamic or other law.—The Courts administer Islamic law as expounded by the Hanafi school of jurists [reg. 53].

D. COURT OF JURISDICTION

The Judiciary Act, 1959 (1959 Act no. 7), s. 7 (re-enacting article 96 of the Transitional Constitution of the Sudan) provides:—

" In the event of any conflict of jurisdiction arising between the Civil and the Sharia divisions, the same shall be referred for decision to a Court of Jurisdiction which shall consist of the Chief Justice as president, the Grand Kadi, two judges of the Civil High Court and one judge of the Sharia High Court."
As far as is known, this Court has never yet sat.

SOMALI REPUBLIC[1]

On June 26, 1960, the former British Protectorate of Somaliland received its independence, and at the same time ceased to form part of the British Commonwealth.

The Constitution of Somaliland is to be found in an Annex to the Somaliland Order in Council, 1960 S.I. 1960 No. 1060. This Constitution introduced certain changes of substance, of which the most important is the abolition of appeals from the High Court to the Court of Appeal for Eastern Africa and thence to the Judicial Committee of the Privy Council [O-in-C 1960, s. 3]. By s. 54, the existing laws of the Somaliland Protectorate were retained for independent Somaliland.

On July 1, 1960, Somaliland united with Somalia (previously a Trust Territory under Italian administration) to form a single state, the Somali Republic. On union the two constituent portions of the new state retained their existing legal, judicial and administrative systems, which remain in force until altered by the National Assembly of the Somali Republic. Article 3(1) of the Act of Union[2] provides that:—

" The laws in force in Somaliland and Somalia at the time of the establishment of the Union shall remain in full force and effect in the respective jurisdictions subject to the provisions of the Constitutions, this law or any future law."

And art. 3(2) provides that:—

" Subject to the provisions of article 94 of the Constitution concerning the jurisdiction of the Supreme Court, and any future law, the Courts as presently constituted in Somaliland and Somalia shall continue to exercise the respective jurisdiction conferred upon them by law."

However, by art. 9(1), it is provided that:—

" Any provision of any law of Somaliland or Somalia, including the Somaliland Order in Council, 1960 (being the Constitution of Somaliland), which is inconsistent with the Constitution of the Somali Republic or this law is hereby repealed."

Apart from verbal and other changes consequent on independence and union, and the adaptation of the existing laws in accordance with the provisions of the Act of Union and the Constitution of the Somali Republic,[3] the Protectorate legislation relating to the law and courts in Somaliland (now the Northern Region of the Republic) is still applicable.

---

[1] For diagram of courts system, see p. 220, *post*.

[2] Adopted on January 18, 1961, by the National Assembly, but has retroactive effect as from July 1, 1960.

[3] This Constitution provisionally came into force on July 1, 1960, but still has to be submitted to a popular referendum for approval.

136

I. NORTHERN REGION (SOMALILAND)

The courts comprise:—

A. The High Court and District Courts, which primarily administer the general law;

B. Subordinate Courts, which primarily administer customary law;

C. Cadis' Courts, which only administer Islamic law.

A. 1 APPEAL COURTS

Appeals to the Court of Appeal for Eastern Africa and to the Privy Council have been abolished. However, a draft Ordinance, which has not yet come into effect, makes provision for appeals to lie from the High Court in Hargeisa (whether in its original or appellate capacity) to the Supreme Court in Mogadishu. In such cases the Supreme Court is to be composed of the President, two Counsellors and two honorary magistrates who are experts in the law of the Northern Region.

A. 2 THE HIGH COURT

CONSTITUTION AND POWERS

(1) Establishment.—Established by s. 39 of the Som. O-in-C, 1960, continuing the High Court established under the Som. O-in-C 1950, art. 2.

(2) Composition.—" There shall be for Somaliland a High Court which shall consist of such number of Judges as may from time to time be appointed by the Council of Ministers " [Somaliland Constitution, art. 39(1)].

(3) Jurisdiction—original.—" The High Court shall be a Court of record and shall have unlimited original jurisdiction in civil and criminal matters and such appellate and revisional jurisdiction as may be prescribed by any law " [Som. O-in-C, 1960, art. 39(2)].

(4) Jurisdiction—appellate.—Hears appeals from District Courts in civil matters [Som. O-in-C, 1929–46, art. 27(1)] and criminal matters [Crim. Procedure Ordinance, s. 299].

LAW TO BE ADMINISTERED

(9) General law.—Article 42 of the Somaliland Constitution provides:—

" (1) The criminal and civil jurisdiction of the Courts of Somaliland shall, so far as circumstances permit, be exercised in conformity with the enactments set out in the Second Schedule to this Constitution and subject thereto and so far as the same do not extend or apply shall be exercised in conformity with the substance of the common law, the doctrines of equity and the statutes of general application in force in England on the 16th day of March, 1900, and with the powers vested in and according to the procedure and practice observed by and before the Courts of Justice and Justices of the Peace in England according to their respective jurisdiction and authorities at that date, save in so far as the said enactments and the said common law, doctrines of equity and statutes of general application, and the said powers, procedure and practice have been, or hereafter may be, modified, amended or replaced by any written law made for Somaliland:

Provided always that the said common law, doctrines of equity and statutes of general application shall be in force in Somaliland so far only as the circumstances of Somaliland and its inhabitants permit and subject to such qualifications as local circumstances render necessary.

(2) For the purpose of facilitating the application of the enactments set out in the Second Schedule to this Constitution:—

    (a) A court may construe any such enactment with such alterations not affecting the substance as may be necessary or proper in order to adapt the same to the matter before the Court;

    (b) the Council of Ministers may by order direct by what authority any jurisdiction, powers or duties incident to the operation of any such enactment and for the exercise or performance of which no convenient provision has been otherwise made shall be exercised or performed;

    (c) any order of the Council of Ministers made in pursuance of this sub-section shall be published in the Gazette and shall have effect as from a date to be specified in the order."

The law which the High Court might administer immediately prior to independence consisted of:—

    (a) Ordinances of the Somaliland Protectorate;

    (b) applied Indian laws, including the Indian Penal Code, Indian Evidence Act, Indian Civil Procedure Code; but no amendments passed in India after September 1, 1923, were applied in the Protectorate;

    (c) certain specifically applied U.K. legislation;

    (d) the common law, doctrines of equity and the statutes of general application in force in England on March 16, 1900, except where they have been modified, amended or replaced by (a), (b), and (c), *supra*.

(10) Customary law.—Article 43 of the Somaliland Constitution provides:—

" In all cases, civil and criminal, to which only Somalis are parties, every Court shall—

    (a) be guided by Somali customary law (including Somali customary law which is based upon Islamic law) so far as it is applicable and is not repugnant to justice, equity and good conscience or is inconsistent with any written law in force in Somaliland or any regulation or rule made thereunder; and

    (b) decide all such cases according to substantial justice, without excessive regard to technicalities of procedure and without undue delay."

(11) Islamic or other law.—See art. 43 of the Constitution under (10), *supra*.

A. 3 DISTRICT COURTS

CONSTITUTION AND POWERS

(1) Establishment.—"There shall be for Somaliland such Courts subordinate to the High Court and possessing such jurisdiction and powers as may be prescribed by any law " [Somaliland Constitution, art. 41].

Under the Judicial Districts and Appointment of Judges Ordinance, 1939, cap. 3, District Courts were established. District Criminal Courts were established by s. 6 of the Crim. P.O. There are two classes of District Courts, viz.: (a) District Courts of the first class and (b) District Courts of the second class.

(2) Composition.—(a) The District Officer, or Assistant District Officer, in charge of the district is the Judge in civil cases [J.D.A.J.O., s. 4], and the Magistrate in criminal cases of a first class District Court [Crim. P.O., s. 7(1)].

(b) The Assistant District Officer in charge of the district is the Judge in civil cases [J.D.A.J.O., s. 7(2)], and the magistrate of a second class District Court in criminal cases [Crim. P.O., s. 7(2)].

Any suitable person can also be appointed (by the Governor) as a Joint Judge of the District Court.

(3) Jurisdiction—original.—(a) *Civil.*—First class District Court: unlimited;

Second class District Court: where the subject matter in dispute does not exceed shs. 1500 [J.D.A.J.O., s. 8].

(b) *Criminal.*—First class District Court: may not impose punishment exceeding 4 years' imprisonment; shs. 4500 fine; whipping of males under 16 [Crim. P.O., s. 14(1)].

Second class District Court may not impose punishment exceeding 6 months imprisonment; shs. 1125 fine; whipping of males under 16 [Crim. P.C., s. 14(2)].

(4) Jurisdiction—appellate.—Exercises appellate jurisdiction in both criminal and civil matters when hearing appeals from subordinate courts.

CONTROL OF COURTS

(5) Appeals from.—These lie to the High Court (see under A. 2(4), p. 137, *ante*).

(6) Review/revision.—The High Court may call for the records of any criminal [Crim. P.O., s. 318] or civil [Som. O-in-C, art. 27(1)] proceedings in District Courts and revise them.

(7) Transfer.—The High Court may transfer any criminal proceedings from a court subordinate to its authority to any other such criminal court of equal or superior jurisdiction, or order that an accused person be committed to itself for trial [Crim. P.O., s. 153(1)].

(8) Inspection, supervision, etc.—The High Court may call for and inspect the records of any proceedings in a District Court (see under

(6), *supra*). Any magistrate may also call for the records of any proceedings before any inferior criminal court situated within his jurisdiction and report any irregularity to the High Court [Crim. P.O., s. 317(1)].

LAW TO BE ADMINISTERED

As High Court.

B. SUBORDINATE COURTS

CONSTITUTION AND POWERS

(1) Establishment.—Under the Subordinate Courts Ordinance, s. 3(1), the [Governor] was empowered to establish subordinate courts by warrant. This Ordinance repealed the Kadis' Courts Ordinance, 1937, which established Kadis' Courts, and classified Kadis' Courts under Subordinate Courts. (Kadis' Courts are dealt with separately at p. 142, *post*.)

(2) Composition.—The constitution of subordinate courts is determined by the warrant. Appointments are made administratively.

(3) Jurisdiction—original.—(*i*) *Over persons.*—(a) Subject to any limitations contained in its warrant, a subordinate court may exercise jurisdiction over all causes and matters where, in civil suits, all parties are natives, or where, in criminal cases, the accused is a native [S.C.O., s. 7(a)].

(b) By terms of its warrant a subordinate court may be empowered also to exercise jurisdiction over classes of persons who are not natives, but who having regard to their general mode of life, may, in the opinion of the [Governor], nevertheless be made amenable to the jurisdiction of such court [S.C.O., s. 7(b)].

(*ii*) *Local limits.*—Jurisdiction extends only:—

    (a) to causes and matters arising within the local limits of the jurisdiction of the court; and

    (b) to causes and matters arising elsewhere when the defendant is ordinarily resident within such limits, or when he is a member of a tribe that is specifically subject to the jurisdiction of the court; provided that causes and matters relating to immovable property must be heard in the subordinate court within the local limits of whose jurisdiction such property is situate [S.C.O., s. 9].

(*iii*) *Cases excluded from jurisdiction.*—By s. 10 of the S.C.O., no subordinate court has jurisdiction in:—

    (a) any criminal proceedings in which a person is charged with an offence in consequence of which death is alleged to have occurred;

    (b) any proceedings concerning marriage or divorce except when the marriage was contracted solely under and in accordance with native law and custom, or when the claim arises only in regard to bride-price or adultery or is founded only on native law and custom;

(c) any proceedings affecting the title to or any interest in land other than those arising out of any question of gift, succession or wills under native law and custom;

(d) any proceedings taken under any Ordinance or any English or Indian law in force in the [Protectorate] unless such court has been authorised to enforce such Ordinance or law by the terms of an Ordinance or by Order of the [Governor];

(e) any proceedings excluded from the jurisdiction of the subordinate court by the terms of its warrant or by order of the [Governor].

(*iv*) *Extent of jurisdiction.*—This is laid down in the warrant, [S.C.O., s. 3(1)]. The jurisdiction does not normally exceed shs. 5000 in civil matters. The courts usually have power to try minor criminal offences with power to impose a sentence of imprisonment not exceedings six months or a fine not exceeding shs. 750.

(4) Jurisdiction—appellate.—Nil.

CONTROL OF COURTS

(5) Appeals from.—This is prescribed in the warrant, and it is probable that in future appeals in civil matters will lie to the High Court sitting with an assessor. In civil matters, appeals lay in the past to the Subordinate Court of Civil Appeal, composed of the Commissioner for Somali Affairs as President, and two subordinate court judges; however, the court was abolished recently.

The pattern of appeals from subordinate courts is usually as follows:—

appeals lie to a first class magistrate of a District Court, and thence in *criminal* matters to the High Court.

(6) Review/revision.—Any magistrate has access to any subordinate court within the local limits of his jurisdiction, and may send for and examine the proceedings of the court and may revise the proceedings therein [S.C.O., s. 30(1)].

(7) Transfer.—A subordinate court, or any magistrate, may at any time before judgment transfer any civil or criminal case to some other subordinate court, or a District Court having jurisdiction, or make a report to the High Court, who may transfer the case to itself or to any other subordinate court or District Court [S.C.O., s. 27].

(8) Inspection, supervision, etc.—See under (6), *supra.*

LAW TO BE ADMINISTERED

(9) General law.—(*i*) The provisions of any Ordinance or other law which the court is authorised to administer or enforce by the terms of any Ordinance [S.C.O., s. 11(b)].

(*ii*) The provisions of any Ordinance or other law which the court may have been authorised to administer or enforce by order of the [Governor] [S.C.O., s. 11(c)].

(10) Customary law.—" The native law and custom prevailing within the limits or among the tribal community, as the case may be, that is subject to the jurisdiction of the court so far as it is applicable and is not repugnant to natural justice or morality or is not, in principle, in conflict with the provisions of any law in force in [the Protectorate] " [S.C.O., s. 11(a)].

(11) Islamic or other law.—Administered in Kadis' courts, *q.v.*, *infra*.

C. KADIS' COURTS

CONSTITUTION AND POWERS

(1) Establishment.—Established by Kadis' Courts Ordinance, 1937, but deemed to be subordinate courts under the S.C.O., s. 35(1).

(2) Composition.—Kadi.

(3) Jurisdiction—original.—Has jurisdiction in the following:—

> (*i*) any question regarding marriage, including divorce and maintenance, guardianship of minors and family relationship, under the Sheriat Law;
> (*ii*) any question regarding waqf, gift, succession or wills under the Sheriat Law [S.C.O., s. 10(2), (a)].

It does not have jurisdiction in the following:—

> (*i*) criminal proceedings;
> (*ii*) any matter upon which jurisdiction is not expressly conferred upon it [S.C.O., s. 10(2), (b)].

(4) Jurisdiction—appellate.—Nil.

CONTROL OF COURTS

(5) Appeals from.—Appeals lie to the Court of the Chief Kadi.

(6) Review/revision.—The Chief Kadi has in relation to Kadis' courts the same powers of revision as are conferred upon a magistrate by the S.C.O.

LAW TO BE ADMINISTERED

(9) General law ⎱
⎰ Nil.
(10) Customary law ⎰

(11) Islamic or other law.—The courts administer the Shariat Law in the matters specified under S.C.O., s. 10(2), (a) (see under C. (3), *supra*).

II. SOUTHERN REGIONS (SOMALIA)

The organisation of courts and the laws administered in the Southern Regions of the Republic differ fundamentally from the Northern Region. The system of Courts is briefly as follows [Ordinance No. 5 of 2 February 1956, as amended by Law No. 9 of 19 February 1958]:—

(1) *Kadis' Courts.*—Their jurisdiction is limited to disputes between Muslims in *civil* matters only, but with no limit as to value.

(2) *Tribunal of Kadis.*—This is composed of three Kadis and hears appeals from Kadis' Courts. A further appeal lies to the Court of Justice (see 8, *infra*).

(3) *District Judge.*—There are a few such Judges in some Districts, but in most areas the function of District Judge is still exercised by District Commissioners. They have jurisdiction in *criminal* cases punishable by imprisonment up to 3 years. Appeals lie to a Regional Judge and thence to the Court of Justice.

(4) *Regional Judge.*—He has his seat in the capital of each Region. He is competent to hear all cases, civil and criminal, not falling within the competence of Kadis or District Judges (with the exception of those offences exclusively triable by the Assize Court).

(5) *Judge of Appeal.*—His function is to hear appeals from the Regional Judge.

(6) *Assize Court.*—This is composed of the Judge of Appeal as Chairman and of six assessors. It has jurisdiction in serious criminal cases, e.g. offences against the state, homicide, and slavery. Appeals lie to the Assize Court of Appeal and then to the Court of Justice.

(7) *Assize Court of Appeal.*—This hears appeals from the Assize Court.

(8) *Court of Justice.*—Its main functions are appellate and revisionary. It is composed of a President, the Magistrate of Accounts, two counsellors and two Kadis and is divided into three sections: ordinary, Shariat and special accounts.

(9) *Supreme Court.*—Article 94 of the Somali Republic Constitution provides:—

" The Supreme Court shall be the highest judicial organ of the Republic. It shall have jurisdiction over the whole territory of the State in civil, penal, administrative and financial matters and in any other matter specified by the Constitution and the laws."

The Court also sits as a Constitutional Court to decide on questions of constitutional legality [art. 99].

The law administered in all courts other than Kadis' courts is generally based on Italian law. Kadis' courts administer Islamic law tempered by Somali customary law.

Note.—A Consultative Commission for Integration has recently been set up. This Commission has been given the task of promotin; the integration of the legislation and institutions of the Northern and Southern Regions of the Republic. The integration of the judicial and legal systems will undoubtedly be one of the foremost preoccupations of the Commission.

PART III

CENTRAL AFRICA

By

W. T. McCLAIN, LL.B., LL.M.,

of the Bar of Indiana; Research Officer, Restatement of African Law Project, School of Oriental and African Studies.

F

SUMMARY

                                                                          PAGE

FEDERATION OF RHODESIA AND NYASALAND   .   .   .   147

NORTHERN RHODESIA   150

SOUTHERN RHODESIA   160

NYASALAND   169

FEDERATION OF RHODESIA AND NYASALAND[1]

The Federation, consisting of the self-governing Colony of Southern Rhodesia and the two Protectorates, Northern Rhodesia and Nyasaland, was established by the Federation of Rhodesia and Nyasaland (Constitution) Order in Council, 1953.

A. 1 THE PRIVY COUNCIL

Federal legislation may provide for right to appeal to the Privy Council, but has not, as yet, done so. [R. and N. (Const.) O-in-C, arts. 61–63].[2]

A. 2 FEDERAL SUPREME COURT

CONSTITUTION AND POWERS

(1) Establishment.—Established by the Federal Supreme Court Act, No. 11 of 1955, s. 3, pursuant to the Federation of Rhodesia and Nyasaland (Constitution) O-in-C, art. 46(1).

(2) Composition.—The Court is composed of a Chief Justice and a number of other judges who are appointed by the Governor-General, together with the Chief Justices of the three territories. The number of judges, in addition to the Chief Justice, appointed by the Governor-General, must be not less than two and not more than six except on address of the Federal Assembly to the Governor-General praying for appointment of additional judges [R. and N. (Const.) O-in-C, 1953, arts. 46(1), (a), (b), (c), 47(1), (2)].

(3) Jurisdiction—original.—(*i*) Exclusive original jurisdiction as follows:—

  (a) disputes between the Federation and Territory, or between Territories, if the dispute involves legal rights;
  (b) to determine:—
    (*i*) whether by reason of circumstances prescribed by a law of the Federal Legislature or the Constitution, a vacancy exists in the Federal Assembly; or
    (*ii*) a petition complaining of an undue return or an undue election of a member of the Federal Assembly by reason of want of qualification or by reason of disqualification,

---

[1] For diagram of courts system, see p. 221, *post*.

[2] In the absence of territorial legislation establishing an appeal as a matter of right or a Parliamentary Act specifying that the Judicial Committee of the Privy Council shall not hear appeals from a particular territory, appeals may be heard by special leave. See *Mungoni* v. *Attorney-General of Northern Rhodesia*, [1960] A.C. 336, the first appeal from the Federal Supreme Court of Rhodesia and Nyasaland. The appeal was by special leave.

corrupt or illegal practice or irregularity or by reason of any other cause whatsoever;

(c) to determine a matter in which a writ or order of mandamus or prohibition or injunction or interdict is sought against an officer or authority of the Federation;

(d) to determine a question of interpretation of the Constitution referred to the Court. [R. and N. (Const.) O-in-C, art. 53, amended 1957, art. 54(1)–(4)].

(*ii*) Other original jurisdiction: Federal or Territorial legislation may confer non-appellate jurisdiction upon the Court. The Territorial legislation requires approval of the Federal Assembly and the Court cannot have original jurisdiction in criminal matters [R. and N. (Const.) O-in-C, art. 57(a), (b)].

(4) Jurisdiction—appellate. [1]—(*i*) Exclusive appellate jurisdiction to hear and determine appeals from any Territorial High Court as to the interpretation of the Federal Constitution or Territorial Constitution [R. and N. (Const.) O-in-C, art. 55].

(*ii*) Other appellate jurisdiction: Federal legislation may confer jurisdiction upon the Court to hear and determine appeals from the the High Court of any Territory on any matter except that the Court cannot exercise jurisdiction in any matter " for the time being within the legislative competence of Territorial legislation with respect to which legislation has provided that the decision of the High Court is to be final " [R. and N. (Const.) O-in-C, art. 56].

Pursuant to this authorisation the Federal Supreme Court Act, No. 11 of 1955, provided for criminal and civil appeals from the Territorial High Courts as follows:—

(a) *Criminal appeals.*—Any person convicted on trial by a High Court may appeal to the Supreme Court against his conviction on a question of law, of fact, or mixed fact and law or any other ground which is certified by the trial judge or a Supreme Court judge as sufficient ground for appeal. A conviction in Northern Rhodesia or Nyasaland by an inferior court in which a death sentence is given, when confirmed by the High Court, may be appealed as if tried in such High Court [F.S.C.A., s. 12(1), (a)].[2]

A person convicted by an inferior court may appeal from judgment of a Territorial High Court in the exercise of appellate jurisdiction, or in Northern Rhodesia or Nyasaland in the exercise of the High Court's

---

[1] The Administration of Justice (Appeals) Act, 1931, of Southern Rhodesia provided that appeals from the High Court of Southern Rhodesia in both criminal and civil matters should lie only to the Appellate Division of the Supreme Court of the Union of South Africa. The Southern Rhodesian Court of Appeal Act, 1938, provided for appeals in criminal matters to the newly established Court of Appeal for Rhodesia and Nyasaland.

The Court of Appeal for Rhodesia and Nyasaland functioned as a Court of Appeal in criminal matters for all three territories and in civil matters for Northern Rhodesia and Nyasaland only [Northern Rhodesia Court of Appeal Ordinance, 1938 and the Rhodesia and Nyasaland Court of Appeal Ordinance, 1946, cap. 102 of Nyasaland]. With the establishment of the Federal Supreme Court, the operation of these Acts and Ordinances was terminated.

[2] In Nyasaland any person aggrieved by a decision of the High Court in its appellate jurisdiction in criminal matters may appeal to the Federal Supreme Court on a matter of law, but such decision is final as to matters of fact and severity of sentence [Nyasaland Criminal Procedure Code, cap. 24, s. 28, as amended in 1958].

revisional jurisdiction, or in Southern Rhodesia from the High Court's judgment on review [S.C.A., s. 12(2)].

(b) *Civil appeals.*—The Supreme Court has jurisdiction in civil appeals from any judgment of a High Court except from certain preliminary rulings, interlocutory orders or judgments, with the exception of specified orders. The judgments of the High Court in the exercise of appellate or revisional jurisdiction are appealable by leave of the High Court or the Supreme Court [F.S.C.A., s. 23].

CONTROL OF COURT

(5) Appeals from.—Appeals from the Supreme Court lie, if at all, to the Privy Council [Const. O-in-C, arts. 61–63].

LAW TO BE ADMINISTERED

(9) General law. [1]—In hearing and determining an appeal the law to be applied is the law applicable to the case in the Territory from which appeal is brought [F.S.C.A., s. 8].

---

[1] The general law of Northern Rhodesia and Nyasaland is based on English law and the general law of Southern Rhodesia on Roman–Dutch law; see: (9) *General law* for each territory for extent of application of the general law and the precise date of its introduction.

NORTHERN RHODESIA[1]

The courts for the administration of justice in the Protectorate comprise:—

A. The High Court and subordinate courts administering primarily the general law; and

B. The Native Courts administering primarily customary law, with separate provision for the Barotseland Protectorate.

A. 1(a) THE PRIVY COUNCIL

See p. 147, *ante*.

A. 1(b) THE FEDERAL SUPREME COURT

See p. 147, *ante*.

A. 2 THE HIGH COURT

CONSTITUTION AND POWERS

(1) Establishment.—Established by art. 27 of the Northern Rhodesia Order in Council, 1924 to 1957, and the provisions of the High Court Ordinance, No. 41 of 1960, cap. 3, s. 3.

(2) Composition.—The Court consists of so many judges as the Governor may appoint, in accordance with instructions he may receive from Her Majesty [N.R. O-in-C, 1924–1957, art. 28].

(3) Jurisdiction—original.—The High Court has full jurisdiction civil and criminal, over all persons and all matters within Northern Rhodesia, " subject to the provisions hereinafter contained with regard to native law and custom " [N.R. O-in-C, 1924–1957, art. 27(1)]. Jurisdiction conferred upon subordinate courts by any ordinance does not restrict the jurisdiction of the High Court, but in all matters the Court has an original jurisdiction concurrent with the subordinate courts [Native Courts Ordinance, 1936, cap. 159, as amended, s. 14].

(4) Jurisdiction—appellate.—Provision by Ordinance for the hearing and determining of appeals from the subordinate courts was authorised by Northern Rhodesia Order-in-Council, 1924–1957, art. 33.

(*i*) *Appellate civil jurisdiction.*—Appeals lie to the Court from subordinate courts in accordance with the provisions of the Subordinate Courts Ordinance, as follows:—

> (a) an appeal lies to the Court from a first or second class subordinate court from all final decisions, interlocutory orders and decisions made in the course of any suit [Subordinate Courts Ordinance, 1933, as amended, cap. 4, s. 27(1), (a), (b)].

---

[1] For diagram of courts system, see p. 222, *post*.

(b) an appeal lies to the Court from all judgments, decisions, and orders of a first class subordinate court sitting in its appellate jurisdiction [S.C.O., s. 27(2)].

(*ii*) *Appellate criminal jurisdiction.*—Appeals lie to the Court from subordinate courts in accordance with provisions in the Criminal Procedure Code, as follows:—

(a) any person convicted by a first or second class subordinate court may appeal to the High Court against conviction on any ground of appeal which involves a question of law, a question of fact, or mixed fact and law, or against a sentence not fixed by law [Crim. P.C., cap. 7, s. 294(1) (a), (b), (c)].

(b) any person who has appealed to a Provincial Commissioner's Court against a conviction by a third or fourth class subordinate court, may appeal from the Provincial Commissioner's Court to the High Court [Crim. P.C., s. 294(3)].

(*iii*) *Appellate jurisdiction—Native Courts.*—(a) Appeals from any judgment, order or decision of a District Commissioner's Court, or a Provincial Commissioner's Court under the Native Courts Ordinance lie to the High Court. No such appeal lies if the sentence does not exceed a fine of £10 or imprisonment for three months, or in a civil cause in which the amount in question does not exceed £50 [N.C.O., s. 33].

(b) Appeals lie to the High Court from a Barotse higher native court of appeal, or if there is none, then from a native court of appeal, or if none, then from a Barotse native court of first instance [Barotse Native Courts Ordinance, 1936, as amended in 1954, cap. 160, s. 33(1), (2), (3)].

(c) The High Court in the exercise of jurisdiction under the N.C.O. may make any order that could be made by the court of first instance, or order the cause reheard before the court of first instance, or any other native court, or a subordinate court of competent jurisdiction [N.C.O., s. 35(1), (a), (b)].

(d) Same provisions for Barotse appeals [B.N.C.O., s. 35].

CONTROL OF COURT

(5) Appeals from.—Appeals may lie to Federal Supreme Court.

LAW TO BE ADMINISTERED

(9) General law.—The N.R. O-in-C, 1924, as amended, provides in art. 27(2):—

" Subject to the provisions hereinafter contained with regard to native law and custom such civil and criminal jurisdiction shall, as far as circumstances admit, be exercised upon the principles of and in conformity with the substance of the law for the time being in force in and for England, and with the powers vested in, and according to the course of procedure and practice observed by and before courts of justice and Justices of the Peace in England, according to their respective jurisdictions and authorities, except so far as such law, powers, procedure and practice may be inapplicable or may have been modified by any Order in Council, Regulations, Proclamations, Federal Act or Ordinance or may hereafter be modified by any Order in Council, Federal Act or Ordinance.

Provided that no Act passed by the Parliament of the United Kingdom after the commencement of the Northern Rhodesia Order in Council, 1911, shall be deemed to apply to the said Territory, unless it shall have been applied thereto since the commencement of the said Order, or shall hereafter be applied thereto, by any law for the time being in force in the said Territory."

The jurisdiction of the Court in probate, divorce and matrimonial causes is exercised in substantial conformity with the law and practice for the time being in force in England [H.C.O., cap. 3, s. 11].

(10) Customary law.—Article 36 of the N.R. O-in-C, 1924, as amended, provides:—

" In civil cases between natives every court shall—

    (a) be guided by native law so far as it is applicable and is not repugnant to natural justice or morality or inconsistent with any Order in Council, Ordinance or Proclamation or any Regulation or Rule made under any Order in Council, Ordinance or Proclamation, and shall—

    (b) decide all such cases according to substantial justice without undue regard to technicalities of procedure and without delay. In all other respects the Court shall follow as far as possible the procedure observed in similar cases in England."

(11) Islamic or other law.—There is no provision for the application of Islamic law, although some parts of such law may be in force by reason of having become native law and custom. [1]

A. 3 SUBORDINATE COURTS

Constitution and Powers

(1) Establishment.—The subordinate courts were established by the Subordinate Courts Ordinance, 1933, as amended, cap. 4, s. 4, pursuant to the authority given by the N.R. O-in-C, art. 32.

(2) Composition.—The subordinate courts are composed as follows:—

    (a) first class court—the Court of the Provincial Commissioner;
    (b) first class court—the Court of the Senior Resident Magistrate;
    (c) first class court—the Court of the Resident Magistrate;
    (d) second class court—the Court of the District Commissioner;
    (e) third class court—the Court of the District Officer (not in charge of a District);
    (f) fourth class court—the Court of a cadet in the Provincial Administration [S.C.O., s. 4].

Note.—The Resident Magistrates and the Senior Resident Magistrates are appointed by the Governor [S.C.O., s. 3], whilst, in the absence of any special appointment, every administrative officer other than

---

[1] See Anderson, J. N. D., *Islamic Law in Africa*, p. 170. There does not appear to be any provision for Muslim Asians. Contrast Nyasaland provisions in the Asiatic (Marriage, Divorce and Succession) Ordinance, 1929.

a cadet is deemed to have been duly appointed to hold the appropriate rank of subordinate court [S.C.O., s. 5].

(3) Jurisdiction—original.—(*i*) *Territorial.*—The territorial jurisdiction of subordinate courts whose members are administrative officers is restricted to the Province or District where the officer is situated. The territorial jurisdiction of the Courts of Senior Magistrates and Resident Magistrates is determined by the Chief Justice [S.C.O., s. 6].

(*ii*) *Civil.*—(a) First class courts have jurisdiction: (*i*) in all personal suits, arising from contract or tort, when the amount in dispute is not more than £200, except that in suits before the Senior Resident Magistrates' Courts the amount is £400; (*ii*) guardianship and custody of infants; (*iii*) attachment; (*iv*) ejectment when the value is under £144, except that in cases before the Senior Resident Magistrate the value is £300; (*v*) bastardy support, etc.

Courts do *not* have jurisdiction over: (*i*) title to office; (*ii*) validity of wills; (*iii*)legitimacy; (*iv*) dissolution of marriage (other than polygamous marriages contracted under native custom [S.C.O., as amended by Ordinance No. 17 of 1959, s. 19]).

(b) Senior Resident Magistrates' Courts and Resident Magistrates' Courts have jurisdiction to enforce any judgment or order of the High Court for payment of money where such judgment or order has been transferred to the Magistrate's Court by the High Court [S.C.O., as amended by Ordinance No. 17 of 1959, s. 19].

(c) Second class courts have similar jurisdiction except that the jurisdictional amount is not more than £100 [S.C.O., s. 20].

(d) Third class courts have jurisdiction: (*i*) in all personal suits, tort or contract, where the value in dispute is not more than £25; (*ii*) to appoint guardians of infants and make custody orders; (*iii*) to enforce attachments [S.C.O., s. 21].

(e) Fourth class courts have no civil jurisdiction [S.C.O., s. 21(a)].

(*iii*) *Criminal.*—(a) Subordinate courts of the first, second or third class may try any offence under the Penal Code except treason, murder and offences specified by notice of the Chief Justice [Crim. P.C., as amended No. 16 of 1959, s. 10] and may pass sentence with the following limits: (*i*) the court of the Senior Resident Magistrate may not impose imprisonment exceeding 5 years; and (*ii*) other first, second or third class courts, imprisonment not exceeding 3 years [Crim. P.C., s. 7(1)].

(b) Subordinate courts of the fourth class have a jurisdiction restricted to scheduled offences and may pass the following sentences: imprisonment not exceeding 3 months, fine not more than £25 and corporal punishment on juveniles only [Crim. P.C., s. 7(2)].

(4) Jurisdiction—appellate.—(*i*) *Civil.*—An appeal lies to a court of a Provincial Commissioner from all judgments, orders or decisions of a third class subordinate court [S.C.O., s. 32].

(*ii*) *Criminal.*—An appeal lies to a court of a Provincial Commissioner from a third or fourth class subordinate court upon conviction [Crim. P.C., s. 294(b)].

Appeals may lie to certain administrative officers' courts from the native courts (see NATIVE COURTS, B. 1(5), p. 156, *post*).

CONTROL OF COURTS

(5) Appeals from.—Appeals from decisions of subordinate courts of the first and second class are to the High Court, and from courts of the third and fourth class to the Provincial Commissioner's Court, from which court appeal may be taken to the High Court. (See A. 3(4), p. 153, and A. 2(4), p. 150, *ante*.

(6) Review/revision.—(*i*) The High Court may call for and examine the record of any criminal proceeding before a subordinate court to determine the correctness and legality of a finding, sentence or order [Crim. P.C., ss. 307, 309].

(*ii*) A Provincial Commissioner's Court may call for and examine the record of any criminal proceeding before a subordinate court of the third or fourth class, and may exercise revisionary powers if the finding, sentence or order is illegal or improper [Crim. P.C., s. 308(1), (2)].

(*iii*) A District Commissioner's Court may call for and examine the record of any criminal proceeding before a subordinate court of the fourth class, and may exercise revisionary powers if the finding, sentence or order is illegal or improper [Crim. P.C., s. 308(a)].

(*iii*) *Confirmation.*—(a) Sentences imposed by a Senior Magistrate's Court exceeding 3 years' imprisonment and in the case of any other first class subordinate court exceeding 2 years' imprisonment must be confirmed by the High Court. Fines exceeding £100 may be levied and in default the convicted person may be imprisoned, but the record of the case must be transmitted to the High Court for confirmation[1] [Crim. P.C., s. 8(1), (2)].

(b) Sentences imposed by a second class subordinate court exceeding 1 year's imprisonment must be confirmed by the High Court. Fines exceeding £50 may be levied and in default the convicted person may be imprisoned, but the record of the case must be transmitted to the High Court for confirmation[1] [Crim. P.C., s. 8(3), (4)].

(c) Sentences imposed by a third class subordinate court exceeding 6 months' imprisonment must be confirmed and no fine exceeding £25 may be levied in respect of the excess, until the record of the case has been transmitted to and the sentence or order is confirmed by the Provincial Commissioner's Court within whose jurisdiction the third class court is situate. If the sentence exceeds that which the Provincial Commissioner's Court may impose without confirmation, or exceeds £100, then confirmation by the High Court is necessary [Crim. P.C., s. 8(5)].

(d) Sentences imposed by fourth class subordinate courts exceeding one month's imprisonment must be confirmed and no fine exceeding £5 may be levied in respect of the excess until the record of the case has been transmitted to and the sentence or order is confirmed by the District Commissioner's Court within whose jurisdiction the fourth class court is situate [Crim. P.C., s. 8(7)].

---

[1] The High Court upon transmittal of the record in cases of fines exceeding specified amounts, may " exercise all the powers conferred upon it by subsection (3) of section 12 ". Section 12(3) of the Crim. P.C., provides: " The confirming court may exercise the same powers in confirmation as are conferred upon it in revision by Part X of this Code."

(e) A sentence of death passed by any subordinate court is subject to confirmation by the High Court [Crim. P.C., s. 8(6)].

(7) Transfer.—(*i*) Any civil cause may be transferred from the court of one magistrate of the first class to another magistrate's court of the first class [S.C.O., s. 26(a)].

(*ii*) In criminal proceedings the magistrate holding a subordinate court of the first class may transfer any case to another subordinate court with jurisdiction to try such case, or may direct or empower any subordinate court of the second or third class to transfer a case to the Provincial Commissioner's Court, or to another specified court competent to try the accused [Crim. P.C., as amended by Ordinance No. 16 of 1959, s. 73(a), (b)].

(*iii*) The High Court may order any offence to be tried or inquired into by any competent court, or may order transfer of a case or class of cases from a subordinate court to any other subordinate court, or order the accused to stand trial before the High Court when it appears:—

    (a) that a fair trial cannot be had in the subordinate court; or
    (b) that some unusual question of law is likely to arise; or
    (c) that a view of the place of the offence is required; or
    (d) that the convenience of the parties or the ends of justice will be served [Crim. P.C., s. 75(1)].

(*iv*) Any cause or matter may be transferred by the High Court from one subordinate court to another, or to the High Court, or from such Court, to any subordinate court [H.C.O., s. 22(1), (2)].

(8) Inspection, supervision, etc.—(*i*) The Chief Justice may, by order, authorise an increased jurisdiction in civil cases and matters to be exercised by an administrative officer or a resident magistrate [S.C.O., s. 23].

(*ii*) The magistrates are subject to orders and directions of the High Court [S.C.O., s. 57].

(*iii*) The High Court may make rules to regulate the operation of the subordinate courts [S.C.O., s. 61].

Law to be Administered

(9) General law.—See S.C.O., s. 12, under which subordinate courts administer substantially the same law as the High Court (p. 151, *ante*).

(10) Customary law.—See S.C.O., s. 16, under which subordinate courts administer substantially the same law as the High Court (p. 152, *ante*).

B. 1 NATIVE COURTS (First Instance)

Constitution and Powers

(1) Establishment.—The Native Courts are established under the Native Courts Ordinance, 1936, as amended, cap. 158, s. 3(1) for all the Territory with the exception of the Barotseland Protectorate, which is provided for by the Barotse Native Courts Ordinance, 1936, as amended, cap. 160, s. 3. Hereafter reference will be made to the Barotse Native Courts when they differ in any aspect from the other Northern Rhodesian Native Courts. The Governor may by warrant authorise a

Provincial Commissioner to recognise by warrant such Native Courts as he may think fit [N.C.O., cap. 158, s. 3(1)]. The Barotse Native Courts are recognised by the Governor by warrant [B.N.C.O., cap. 160, s. 3].

(2) Composition.—The Native Court is constituted in accordance with " the native law or custom of the area ", with the provision in the N.C.O. that the Provincial Commissioner may, subject to directions of the Governor, prescribe the constitution of the Native Court [N.C.O., s. 4].

(3) Jurisdiction—original.—The Native Courts have jurisdiction to the extent set out in their warrants, over causes and matters in which all parties are natives [N.C.O., s. 3(1)]. No court has jurisdiction, except by express provision, to try cases:

(a) in which a person is charged with an offence in consequence of which death is alleged to have occurred, or which is punishable with death or life imprisonment;

(b) relating to witchcraft, except with the approval of a District Officer authorised to give such approval;

(c) in which a non-native is a witness [N.C.O., s. 11].

(*i*) *Civil.*—Extends to the trial of civil suits within the limits of the warrant, including suits for recovery of civil debts due to Her Majesty and jurisdiction is conferred upon all or any Native Courts by the Governor by order to administer specified laws [N.C.O., ss. 8, 13].

(*ii*) *Criminal.*—Every Native Court has the criminal jurisdiction set out in its warrant, and such additional jurisdiction as is conferred by the Governor by order [N.C.O., ss. 10, 13].

(4) Jurisdiction—appellate.—Nil.

CONTROL OF COURTS

(5) Appeals from.—Appeals from the Native Courts lie to the Native Court of Appeal, or, if there is none, to the District Officer's Court, or if there is none, to the District Commissioner's Court, unless the Provincial Commissioner directs that the case or class shall be appealed to the Provincial Commissioner's Court [N.C.O., ss. 32(2), 33(1)]. Appeals from the Barotse Native Courts of first instance lie to the Native Court of Appeal and from such court of appeal to a higher Native Court of Appeal or, if there is no such court of appeal, to the High Court [N.C.O., s. 33]; (for appeal to High Court provisions, see A. 2(4), p. 151, *ante*).

(6) Review/revision.—(*i*) Every Provincial Commissioner, District Commissioner and District Officer in his capacity as a holder of a subordinate court may revise any sentence or decision of a Native Court. If the sentence is increased, there may be an appeal from the order of a District Officer to the Provincial Commissioner's Court and from the Provincial Commissioner or District Commissioner to the High Court [N.C.O., s. 31].

(*ii*) Revision of Barotse Native Court proceedings is limited to criminal cases [B.N.C.O., s. 31].[1]

---

[1] The only substantial difference between the Barotse Native Court Ordinance, s. 31, and the Native Court Ordinance is the use of the adjective "criminal" before " causes and matters " and before " records ". It would appear that the Barotseland administrative officer under this section is limited to revision of criminal causes and matters.

(*iii*) Revision under the N.C.O. by the District Commissioner's Court or the Provincial Commissioner's Court, on appeal or otherwise, may be appealed to the High Court [N.C.O., s. 31(a)].

(7) Transfer.—(*i*) Every Provincial Commissioner, District Commissioner and District Officer may transfer any cause from a Native Court to a subordinate court of the first or second class, or to any subordinate court on application of the defendant [N.C.O., ss. 29, 31].

(*ii*) A Native Court of Appeal, subordinate court, or the High Court, may order the cause to be reheard before the court of first instance or any competent subordinate court [N.C.O., s. 35].

(*iii*) Any subordinate court may transfer any civil or criminal proceedings to any Native Court within the territorial jurisdiction of the transferring court. Such native court must, however, be a court which has the jurisdiction and power to entertain the particular proceedings. This transfer power is applicable to native courts recognised both under the N.C.O. and under the B.N.C.O. [S.C.O., s. 13(2)].

(*iv*) Any cause or matter may be transferred by a Judge from the High Court to any Native Court having power to entertain such cause or matter. Such transfer may be to a Native Court recognised under the N.C.O. or the B.N.C.O. [H.C.O., s. 25 (1), (2)].

(8) Inspection, supervision, etc.—(*i*) The Governor may direct the Native Court to submit reports of all cases tried to the Provincial Commissioner, or to the District Commissioner [N.C.O., s. 22].

(*ii*) District Officers may sit as advisers to Native Courts [N.C.O., s. 24].

(*iii*) Every Provincial Commissioner, District Commissioner and District Officer has access to the records of the Native Courts [N.C.O., s. 31].

(*iv*) The Governor in Council is authorised to make rules for the courts [N.C.O., s. 39, see cap. 158, s. 39, Subsidiary Legislation for rules].

Law to be Administered

(9) General law.—(*i*) The Native Courts may enforce provisions of Ordinances and Federal Acts designated by the Governor's Order [N.C.O., s. 13]. Some 28 Ordinances have been scheduled, e.g. African Education Ordinance, Markets Ordinance, Municipal Corporations Ordinance [Native Courts (Jurisdiction) Ordinance, s. 13, subsidiary legislation].

(*ii*) The courts also administer the provisions of Ordinances when the particular Ordinance so specifies, and administer the provisions of the Native Authority Ordinance [N.C.O., s. 12].

(10) Customary law.—The Native Court administers " the native law and custom prevailing in the area of the jurisdiction of the court, so far as it is not repugnant to justice or morality or inconsistent with the provisions of any order of the Queen in Council, or with any other law in force in the Territory " [N.C.O., s. 12].

(11) Islamic or other law.—There is no provision for the application of Islamic law, although some parts of such law may be in force by reason of having become native law and custom. [1]

B. 2 NATIVE COURTS OF APPEAL

CONSTITUTION AND POWERS

(1) Establishment.—(*i*) By the N.C.O., 1936, as amended, cap. 158, s. 32, a Provincial Commissioner may, with the Governor's approval, by warrant recognise a single chief (as defined by the Native Authority Ordinance) or a body of chiefs or natives to be a court of appeal from the Native Courts.

(*ii*) The Barotse Native Court of Appeal is recognised by the Governor by warrant [B.N.C.O., s. 32].

(2) Composition.—Defined in the warrant [N.C.O., s. 32].

(3) Jurisdiction—original.—According to its warrant.

(4) Jurisdiction—appellate.—Hears appeals from Native courts of first instance.

CONTROL OF COURTS

(5) Appeals from.—(*i*) (a) Appeals from the Native Courts of Appeal lie to the District Commissioner's Court, unless the Provincial Commissioner directs that the case be appealed to his court. No appeal lies when the sentence does not exceed a fine of £5, or imprisonment for more than 1 month, or from a decision in a civil cause in which the amount in dispute does not exceed £25 [N.C.O., s. 33(2)].

(b) Appeals from the District Officer's Court (see B. 2(5), *supra*) lie to the Provincial Commissioner's Court with the same limitations as (a), *supra*[2] [N.C.O., s. 33(3)].

(c) Appeals lie from the District Commissioner or Provincial Commissioner to the High Court from any order or decision made under the N.C.O. by such District Commissioner or Provincial Commissioner [N.C.O., s. 33(4)].

(*ii*) Appeal from a Barotse Native Court of Appeal is to any higher Barotse Native Court of Appeal—if any—and then to the High Court [B.N.C.O., s. 33(2), (3)].

(6) Review/revision

(7) Transfer ⎫ As Native Courts of first instance.

(8) Inspection, supervision, etc. ⎭

---

[1] See Anderson, J. N. D., *Islamic Law in Africa*, p. 170. There does not appear to be any provision for Muslim Asians. Contrast Nyasaland provisions in the Asiatic (Marriage, Divorce and Succession) Ordinance, 1929.

[2] It should be noted that while s. 33(3) provides for appeal from the District Officer's Court to the Provincial Commissioner's Court, there is no express authority for appeal from the District Commissioner's Court to the Provincial Commissioner's Court.

LAW TO BE ADMINISTERED

As Native Courts of first instance.

Note.—Under the N.C.O. there have been established urban native courts. There is no specific authority for the creation of such courts, and apparently they are established or constituted under the provision in s. 4 which permits the Provincial Commissioner to prescribe the constitution of any Native Court subject to the approval of the Governor. The urban Native Courts have jurisdiction to enforce all the provisions of Ordinances which are given to Native Courts, and in addition may enforce the provisions relating to the migration of natives under the N.A.O. [N.C.O., s. 13, subsidiary legislation, s. 13]. For a description of the constitution, organisation and operation, including appeals, of the urban Native Courts, see Moffat, R. L., " African Courts and native customary law in the urban areas of Northern Rhodesia ", (1957) 9 J.A.A., 71, and Epstein, A., *The Administration of Justice and the Urban African*, 1953, London, H.M.S.O.

(Since the manuscript of this section went to press, a new Ordinance, the Native Courts Ordinance, 1960, No. 14 of 1961, has been passed by the Northern Rhodesian Legislative Council, but it has not at the time of writing been brought into operation.)

SOUTHERN RHODESIA[1]

The courts for the administration of justice in the Colony of Southern Rhodesia comprise:—

A. The High Court and magistrates' courts administering primarily Roman–Dutch law; and

B. The Native Court of Appeal, the courts of the native commissioners and the native courts administering primarily customary law.

A. 1(a) THE PRIVY COUNCIL

See p. 147, *ante*.

A. 1(b) THE FEDERAL SUPREME COURT

See A. 2, pp. 147–149, *ante*.

A. 2 THE HIGH COURT

CONSTITUTION AND POWERS

(1) Establishment.—First established by the Southern Rhodesia Order in Council, 1898, art. 49(1) and now constituted by the High Court Act, cap. 8, s. 2.

(2) Composition.—The High Court consists of so many judges as the Governor may appoint, one of whom is the Chief Justice [Southern Rhodesia Constitution Letters Patent, 1923, s. 38; H.C.A., s. 3].

(3) Jurisdiction—original.—The High Court is a Court of Record, with full jurisdiction, civil and criminal, over all persons and matters within the Colony, subject to the very restricted but significant exclusive original jurisdiction of the Federal Supreme Court [H.C.A., s. 2].

The High Court has discretionary jurisdiction to determine existing, future or contingent rights or obligations, but a party cannot claim relief upon determination [H.C.A., s. 19].

(4) Jurisdiction—appellate.—(*i*) *Civil.*—Appeals lie to the High Court from magistrates' courts against judgments for the plaintiff on his claim; or the defendant on his defence; or judgments of absolution; or judgment as to costs; or rescission or alteration of judgment; or against a rule or order having the effect of a final judgment; or against the overruling of an exception when the parties consent [Magistrates Court Act, cap. 11, ss. 14, 35, 36]. An appeal lies from the Native Appeal Court to the High Court [Native Affairs Act, cap. 72, s. 17(8)]. There is no appeal in civil matters from a native commissioner's court to the High Court.

---

[1] For diagram of courts system, see p. 221, *post*.

(ii) Criminal.—Any person convicted of any offence in a magistrate's or native commissioner's court may appeal to the High Court against the conviction and sentence [H.C.A., s. 58(1); N.A.A., s. 16(b)].

CONTROL OF COURT

(5) Appeals from.—*(i) Civil.*—Appeals from a High Court judgment in any civil cause or matter lie to the Federal Supreme Court except for certain specified orders and decisions [Federal Supreme Court Act, 1955, ss. 22, 23].

(ii) Criminal.—Appeals from the High Court lie to the Federal Supreme Court: (a) against conviction; (b) against sentence unless fixed by Federal or territorial law; (c) against judgment of the High Court in exercise of its appellate jurisdiction, and (d) against judgment of the High Court on review [F.S.C.A., 1955, s. 12].

LAW TO BE ADMINISTERED

(9) General law.—*(i)* The Southern Rhodesia Constitution Letters Patent, 1923, providing for the Constitution of Responsible Government in the Colony of Southern Rhodesia, contained a saving provision, s. 63(2), which maintained in effect non-repugnant Orders, etc. The Southern Rhodesia Order in Council, 1898, art. 49, provided:—

" The law to be administered by the High Court and by the Magistrates' Courts hereinafter mentioned shall, so far as not inapplicable, be the same as the law in force in the Colony on the 10th day of June, 1891, except so far as that law has been modified by any Order in Council, Proclamation, Regulation or Ordinance in force at the date of the commencement of this Order. . . .

Provided that no Statute of the Colony of the Cape of Good Hope promulgated after the 10th day of June 1891 shall be in effect within the limits of this Order, unless specially applied thereto by Proclamation, Ordinance, or Regulation."

(ii) The H.C.A., s. 13, provides:—

" Subject to the provisions with regard to native law and custom contained in the Native Law and Courts Act, the law to be administered by the High Court and by the Magistrates' Courts shall be the same as the law in force in the Colony of the Cape of Good Hope on the tenth day of June, 1891, as modified by subsequent legislation having in this Colony the force of law."

Note.—The law of the Colony of the Cape of Good Hope in force in 1891 was Roman–Dutch law and the effect of the S. Rhodesia High Court Act is to make Roman–Dutch law applicable as the general law of Southern Rhodesia to the extent it was in force in 1891.

(10) Customary law.—*(i)* The S.R. O-in-C, 1898, art. 50, provides:—

" In civil cases between natives the High Court and the Magistrates' Courts shall be guided by native law so far as that law is not repugnant to natural justice or morality, or to any Order made by Her Majesty in Council, or to any Proclamation or Ordinance. In such case the court may obtain the assistance of one or two native assessors, to advise the court upon native law and custom, but the decision of the court shall be given by the Judge or Magistrate alone. In all other respects the court shall follow as far as possible the procedure observed in similar cases in the courts of the Colony."

(*ii*) Native law and custom are provided for in s. 13 of the H.C.A., and in the Native Law and Courts Act, cap. 73, ss. 2, 3, which Act defines " native law and custom " as follows:—

"Means, in relation to a particular tribe, the general law and custom of such tribe, except in so far as such law or custom is repugnant to natural justice or morality or to the provisions of any statute law from time to time in force in the Colony:

Provided that nothing in the statute law of the Colony relating to the age of majority, the status of women, the effect of marriage on the property of the spouses, the guardianship of children or the administration of deceased estates shall affect the application of native law and custom except in so far as such statute law has been specifically applied to natives by statute " [s. 2].

The Native Law and Courts Act, s. 3(1), provides:—

" Notwithstanding the provisions of section 13 of the High Court Act (Chapter 8), in the determination of any civil case between natives by any court of law, the decision shall be in accordance with native law and custom, but if native law and custom is inapplicable to the cause or matter before the court—(a) any court of law other than a native court shall determine the case in accordance with the law of the Colony."

The N.L.C.A., s. 4(1) expressly provides that in civil cases polygamous marriages may be treated as valid, in so far as such marriages are " recognised by native law or custom ".

(11) Islamic or other law.—Nil.

A. 3 MAGISTRATES' COURTS

CONSTITUTION AND POWERS

(1) Establishment.—Establishment of magistrates' courts was authorised by the S.R. O-in-C, 1898, arts. 69 and 70, and the present establishment is by the Magistrates' Courts Act, s. 5(1).

(2) Composition.—The Minister of Justice may determine the number of courts required and assign to each the local limits of the district within which it is to have jurisdiction [M.C.A., s. 6]. The Minister of Justice may appoint any person to be a magistrate, additional magistrate or assistant magistrate and after consultation with the Chief Justice of the Colony and the Attorney-General, may appoint any person who holds the office of magistrate or additional magistrate, to be a special magistrate for a specified case or area [M.C.A., s. 7(1), (2), (3)].[1] Any person appointed exercises all the jurisdiction of the court [M.C.A., s. 7(4)].

---

[1] Magistrates are appointed from the District Courts subdivision of the civil service and must have the required practical experience and academic qualifications.

(3) Jurisdiction—original.—(*i*) *Civil.*—Every court has in all civil cases the following jurisdiction:—

- (a) with regard to persons:—(*i*) residing, carrying on business or employed within district; (*ii*) partnership with premises or any member within district; (*iii*) any person when proceedings are instituted by him; (*iv*) any person when cause or action arose wholly within district;
- (b) with regard to causes of action:—(*i*) negotiable instrument to the amount of £500; (*ii*) action for the delivery of property or the cancellation of an agreement as to the property when the value is not more than £200; (*iii*) ejectment where the right does not exceed £200 value to occupier; (*iv*) in all other actions where the claim does not exceed £200 [M.C.A., s. 10].

A court does not have jurisdiction in civil cases in which the rights of natives only are concerned unless:—(a) both parties consent thereto; or (b) one of the parties is a native to whom a certificate has been issued under s. 12 of the N.L.C.A.[1]

Note.—The jurisdiction above is subject to provisions as to separation of claims, computations of jurisdictional amounts, etc., and with the exception of the following actions, agreement of the parties gives the court jurisdiction. Magistrates' courts have no jurisdiction in the following:—

- (a) dissolution of marriage or separation;
- (b) validity or interpretation of wills;
- (c) mental capacity status;
- (d) specific performance without an alternative of damages with exceptions relating to the delivery of property and to the rendering of an account;
- (e) decree of perpetual silence;
- (f) namptissement (provisional sentence);
- (g) without exceptions, when future rights are involved [M.C.A., s. 12].

(*ii*) *Criminal.*—The court has jurisdiction over all offences except treason and murder [M.C.A., s. 49(1), (b)].

(4) Jurisdiction—appellate.—Nil.

Control of Courts

(5) Appeals from.—Appeals from decisions of the magistrates' courts go to the High Court. (See A. 2(4), p. 160, *ante*.)

(6) Review/revision.—(*i*) The High Court has the power and jurisdiction to review all proceedings of all inferior courts of justice, and, if necessary, to set aside or correct the proceedings. The basis for review is: (a) incompetency of court as to presiding officer; (b) incompetency of court as to jurisdiction; (c) malice or corruption; (d) gross irregularity; (e) admission of illegal or incompetent evidence [H.C.A., s. 15, as amended 1949, and s. 16]. The review is by application of a party to the

---

[1] Section 12 of the N.L.C.A. provides that on the application of any individual native, the Chief Native Commissioner may, subject to the approval of the Ministry of Native Affairs, certify the applicant for the purposes of the Act only not to be a native.

civil or criminal proceedings supported by affidavits [High Court Practice and Procedure Act, cap. 9, Order 25, rule 6].

(*ii*) All criminal cases heard in inferior courts are reviewable by a judge of the High Court in chambers. However, automatic review is only given to such cases in which the sentence exceeds three months' imprisonment or a fine of £25, or lashes or strokes are imposed. In such cases, the clerk of the court must forward to the registrar of the High Court the record of the proceedings [M.C.A., s. 54(1), (a)]. If upon consideration, the proceedings appear to be not in accord " with real and substantial justice " the High Court judge has full power to alter, reverse, correct or remit them to the inferior court with instructions [M.C.A., as substituted by s. 2 of Act 3 of 1949].

(7) Transfer.—The High Court may, on the motion of the defendant and showing that the plaintiff would be unable to pay the costs, transfer or remit the cause for trial in an inferior court of competent jurisdiction. In addition it may remove action *in forma pauperis* to such court [M.C.A., s. 16].

(8) Inspection, supervision, etc.—(*i*) The magistrates' courts have the power in civil cases to rescind, vary or correct errors in their judgment. The exercise of such powers is subject to right of appeal [M.C.A., s. 35].

(*ii*) The Attorney General may remit a case to the magistrate's court which may have the effect of increasing the jurisdiction of the magistrate if the Attorney General so directs [Criminal Procedure and Evidence Act, cap. 28, s. 95].

LAW TO BE ADMINISTERED

(9) General law.—As High Court (see A. 2(9), p. 161, *ante*).

(10) Customary law.—In civil cases between natives where a magistrate's court has jurisdiction, the court may " hear and receive evidence as to native law and custom in so far as the same may be relevant to the action or proceedings " [M.C.A., s. 10(2), (3)].

B. 1 NATIVE COURTS (of First Instance)

CONSTITUTION AND POWERS

(1) Establishment.—The Governor may by warrant constitute such native courts as he thinks fit [N.L.C.A., s. 5(1)].

(2) Composition.—The Governor appoints a native chief or headman who is assisted in the hearing of every case by at least two counsellors approved by the native commissioner of the district. Counsellors act only in an advisory capacity [N.L.C.A., s. 5(2), (3)]. " ' Chief ' means a native appointed by the Governor to exercise control over a tribe as chief, acting chief or deputy of a chief " [Native Affairs Act, cap. 72, s. 2].

(3) Jurisdiction—original. [1]—Jurisdiction is conferred by the

---

[1] Although these courts have a sanctioned but restricted power of summoning and subpoenaing natives, no powers or processes are provided for the enforcement of a judgment of such court [N.L.C.A., ss. 6(1)(b), 8]. Consequently, the efficacy of a judgment is dependent on voluntary compliance or enforcement by social sanctions, which are fairly effective within the narrow confines of a tribal community.

provisions of the Native Law and Courts Act within the limits defined by the Governor's warrant [N.L.C.A., s. 5(1)]. Jurisdiction of the native court extends to the hearing, trial and determination of all civil actions and suits, provided that:—

(a) all the parties must be natives;

(b) the defendant must ordinarily be a resident and reside within the jurisdiction of the court at the time of summons;

(c) the action or suit must be capable of being decided according to native law and custom.

A native court has no jurisdiction in an action or suit:—

(a) in which dissolution of marriage is sought; or

(b) which arises from any act or omission (other than adultery) which is a punishable offence; and

(c) a native court has no criminal jurisdiction [N.L.C.A., s. 6].

(4) Jurisdiction—appellate.—Nil.

CONTROL OF COURTS

(5) Appeals from.—Any party to a civil case who is dissatisfied with the judgment of a native court may apply to the court of the native commissioner of the district for re-hearing and re-trial of the case. The native court's judgment has no effect in such a case [N.L.C.A., s. 10].

The native commissioner may, on application or on his own initiative, order the case to be re-tried before the same native court or before any native court of competent jurisdiction [N.L.C.A., s. 9(b)].

(6) Review/revision.—Every native commissioner has at all times access to native courts in his district and to the records of such courts, and on application or on his initiative he may revise any of the proceedings of the native court and make any order which the native court could have made [N.L.C.A., s. 9(a)].

(7) Transfer.—(a) The native commissioner may, on application or on his own initiative intervene in any case at any stage of the proceedings and transfer the case to his own court, or to any other court of competent jurisdiction.

(b) In a case in which native law and custom is inapplicable the native court must state all proceedings to the native commissioner of the district for decision or transfer to a court of competent jurisdiction [N.L.C.A., s. 9].

(c) The Governor may make regulations for the administration of native courts [N.L.C.A., s. 11].

LAW TO BE ADMINISTERED

(9) General law.—Nil.

(10) Customary law..." ' Native law and custom ' means, in relation to a particular tribe, the general law and custom of such tribe, except in so far as such law or custom is repugnant to natural justice or morality or to the provisions of any statute law from time to time in force in the Colony:

Provided that nothing in the statute law of the Colony relating to the age of majority, the status of women, the effect of marriage on the property of the spouses, the guardianship of children or the administration of deceased estates shall affect the application of native law and custom, except in so far as such statute law has been specifically applied to natives by statute " [N.L.C.A., s. 2].

Where the parties to a civil case between natives reside in areas where different native laws and customs are in operation, the native law and custom, if any, to be applied by the court is the law prevailing in the place of residence of the defendant [N.L.C.A., s. 3(2)].

Polygamous marriages contracted between natives according to native law and custom may be treated as valid, and native law and custom as to the pronibition of marriage between persons on account of relationship of blood or affinity in regard to natives prevails over the law of the Colony, except marriages contracted in accordance with the terms of the Marriage Act [N.L.C.A., s. 4(1), (2)].

(11) Islamic or other law.—Nil.

B. 2 NATIVE COMMISSIONERS' COURTS

Constitution and Powers

(1) Establishment.—Section 39(1) of the Constitution Letters Patent, 1923, as amended, provides for the appointment by the Governor in Council of a chief native commissioner and native commissioners and assistant native commissioners. The Native Affairs Act of 1927, as amended by s. 3 of No. 16 of 1958, establishes courts of native commissioners [N.A.A., s. 14(1)].

(2) Composition.—Each district has a native commissioner and the Governor may appoint assistant native commissioners as required [N.A.A., s. 13]. When a native commissioner is unable to act, an assistant native commissioner in the district may exercise the judicial powers granted to the court of the native commissioner [N.A.A., s. 14(6)].

(3) Jurisdiction—original.—(*i*) *Civil.*—A native commissioner's court has jurisdiction to hear and determine civil cases in which the rights of natives only are concerned, save that this court is subject to the same limitations of jurisdiction in respect of cause of action as is a magistrate's court [N.A.A., s. 14(2)].

A native commissioner's court may call any chief to its assistance as an assessor to advise it on any matter concerning native law and custom [N.A.A., s. 14(4)].

(*ii*) *Criminal.*—In criminal proceedings in which the accused is a native, a native commissioner's court has the same jurisdiction as a magistrate's court. In addition, it has jurisdiction in respect of all offences created by the N.A.A., 1927, save a limited group over which only the Provincial Native Commissioner has jurisdiction [N.A.A., s. 14(5)].[1]

---

[1] Criminal proceedings in respect of contempt or failure to comply with any lawful order or a native commissioner are heard by the court of the Provincial Native Commissioner, which for this purpose is deemed to be a court of a native commissioner.

(4) Jurisdiction—appellate.—The native commissioner exercises a kind of appellate jurisdiction in entertaining appeals from native courts of first instance. The N.L.C.A., s. 10(1), (2), provides that an aggrieved party may apply to the native commissioner and he may hear and determine the case, the judgment of the native court being of no effect.

CONTROL OF COURTS

(5) Appeals from.—The Native Appeal Court is empowered to hear appeals from the courts of native commissioners in civil cases [N.A.A., s. 17(1)]. An appeal lies from the decisions of this court to the High Court [N.A.A., s. 17(8)].

(6) Review/revision.—The High Court has jurisdiction to review all proceedings of all inferior courts of justice, including native commissioners' courts [H.C.A., ss. 15, 16].

The provisions which govern the sending of records of criminal proceedings in the magistrates' courts for review and their review by a judge of the High Court in chambers, apply to criminal cases heard by native commissioners' courts [N.A.A., s. 16(b), as substituted by s. 3, Act No. 16 of 1958].

(7) Transfer.—Nil.

(8) Inspection, supervision, etc.—The Governor may make rules regulating civil and criminal proceedings in native commissioners' courts and appeals from such courts [N.A.A., s. 22].

LAW TO BE ADMINISTERED

(9) General law ⎱ As High Court (see A. 2(9), (10), p. 161,
(10) Customary law ⎰ *ante*).

B. 3 NATIVE COURT OF APPEAL

CONSTITUTION AND POWERS

(1) Establishment.—A Court of Appeal for native civil cases was established by the Native Affairs Act in 1927. This court was reconstituted by the 1958 amendment to the Act [N.A.A., s. 17(1)].

(2) Composition.—The Court of Appeal consists of three members, one of whom is president of the Court. The President is either a retired judge or an advocate of not less than twelve years standing appointed by the Governor. The other two members of the Court are selected by the President from a list of present or former native commissioners [N.A.A., s. 17(1), (2), (3), (4)].

(3) Jurisdiction—original.—Nil.

(4) Jurisdiction—appellate.—(*i*) *Civil.*—The Court of Appeal is empowered to hear appeals from the court of a native commissioner in civil cases [N.A.A., s. 17(1)].

(*ii*) *Criminal.*—The Court of Appeal has no criminal jurisdiction.

CONTROL OF COURT

(5) Appeals from.—An appeal lies from the decisions of this court to the High Court [N.A.A., s. 16].

(6) Review/revision.—The High Court has jurisdiction to review all proceedings of all inferior courts of justice [H.C.A., ss. 15, 16].

(7) Transfer.—Nil.

(8) Inspection, supervision, etc.—The President of the Court of Appeal may, with the approval of the Chief Justice of the Colony make rules to regulate the procedure of the Court of Appeal [N.A.A., s. 18(1), (2), (3)].

LAW TO BE ADMINISTERED

(9) General law
(10) Customary law } As High Court (see A. 2(9), (10), p. 161, *ante*).

NYASALAND[1]

The courts for the administration of justice in the Protectorate of Nyasaland comprise:—

A. the High Court and subordinate courts administering primarily the general law; and

B. the African courts administering primarily customary law.

A. 1(a) THE PRIVY COUNCIL
See p. 147, *ante*.

A. 1(b) THE FEDERAL SUPREME COURT
See pp. 147–149, *ante*.

A. 2 HIGH COURT

CONSTITUTION AND POWERS

(1) Establishment.—Established by the Nyasaland (Constitution) Order in Council, 1961, s. 74.

(2) Composition.—The High Court consists of as many judges as the Governor, under the N. (Const.) O-in-C, s. 75, may appoint, one of whom is the Chief Justice [N. (Const.) O-in-C, s. 74(1)].

(3) Jurisdiction—original.—The High Court is a court of record and is given unlimited original jurisdiction, civil and criminal, within Nyasaland by the N. (Const.) O-in-C, s. 82. Specific jurisdiction without prejudice to general jurisdiction is given to the High Court by s. 15 of the Courts Ordinance, 1958, and may be summarized as follows:—

    (a) to appoint and control guardians, property and persons of infants;

    (b) to order land to be charged or mortgaged where the Court has jurisdiction to order sale;

    (c) to grant relief by interpleader;

    (d) to provide for interim preservation of property by sale, injunction appointment of receiver or registration of caveat or *lis pendens*;

    (e) to enforce judgment of the High Court or a subordinate court in any manner it may prescribe;

    (f) to direct interest to be paid on debts, including judgment debts, and to direct payment of judgment debt by instalment;

    (g) to arrest the defendant and attach property of the defendant before judgment, subject to the provisions of any Ordinance;

    (h) to order service out of the jurisdiction, and;

    (i) shall have all jurisdiction and powers, civil and criminal, which belong to any subordinate court.

---

[1] For diagram of courts system, see p. 223, *post*.

(4) Jurisdiction—appellate.—(*i*) *Appellate civil jurisdiction.*— The appellate civil jurisdiction of the High Court consists of appeals from subordinate courts as provided by law. An appeal lies to the High Court from a subordinate court from all final judgments, from all interlocutory judgments and orders made in the course of a civil action. No appeal shall lie, except by leave of the subordinate court or High Court, from an order made *ex parte*, or by consent, or as to costs only [C.O., ss. 21, 22(1), (a), (b)].

(*ii*) *Appellate criminal jurisdiction.*—The appellate criminal jurisdiction of the High Court consists of hearing appeals from subordinate courts according to the law for the time being in force [C.O., s. 20]. The Criminal Procedure Code, as amended, 1958, ss. 314, 316, provides that any person aggrieved by any finding, sentence or order made by any subordinate court may appeal to the High Court on a matter of law or fact. No appeal is allowed on a plea of guilty except as to the legality of sentence.

CONTROL OF COURT

(5) Appeals from.—Appeals from the High Court lie to the Federal Supreme Court with some exceptions [Federal Supreme Court Act, 1955, ss. 12(2), 23]:—

(a) Persons may appeal to the Federal Supreme Court from a decision of the High Court in its appellate jurisdiction on a matter of law, but no appeal may be taken on matters of fact or severity of sentence [Criminal Procedure Code, s. 328].

(b) Persons convicted on trial held by the High Court may appeal to the Federal Supreme Court (*i*) on a ground which involves a question of law; (*ii*) with leave of the Court or certificate of the trial judge on a ground which involves a question of fact alone or mixed law and fact, and (*iii*) with leave of the Court against sentence passed on conviction, unless such sentence is fixed by law [Crim. P.C., s. 345].

LAW TO BE ADMINISTERED

(9) General law.—" Subject to the provisions of this Order and of any law for the time being in force in Nyasaland, the civil and criminal jurisdiction of the High Court and of courts subordinate to the High Court, shall, so far as circumstances admit, be exercised in conformity with:—

(a) the statutes of general application in force in England on the 11th day of August, 1902, and

(b) the substance of English common law and doctrines of equity,

and with the powers vested in and according to the course of procedure and practice observed by and before courts of justice and justices of the peace in England " [N. (Const.) O-in-C, s. 83(1)].

(10) Customary law.—" In cases in which all the parties are Africans of Nyasaland, that is to say, members of a tribe or race of Africa which ordinarily resides in Nyasaland, or persons who ordinarily reside in Nyasaland as members of such a tribe or race, the civil and criminal jurisdiction of the High Court and of courts subordinate to the High

Court shall, until a law enacted under this order otherwise provides, be exercised in accordance with the provisions of Article 20 of the British Central Africa Order in Council, 1902, notwithstanding the revocation of that Order " [N. (Const.) O-in-C, s. 83(2)]. Article 20 of the 1902 O-in-C provides as follows:—

" In all cases, civil and criminal, to which natives are parties every Court (a) shall be guided by native law so far as it is applicable and is not repugnant to justice and morality or inconsistent with any Order in Council or Ordinance, or any Regulation or Rule made under any Order in Council or Ordinance; and (b) shall decide all such cases according to substantial justice without undue regard to technicalities of procedure and without undue delay."

(11) Islamic or other law.—There is no general provision for the application of such law, although some parts of such law may be in force by reason of having become native law and custom.[1] The Asiatics (Marriage, Divorce and Succession) Ordinance, 1929, authorises the recognition by the courts of certain laws of the parties.

A. 3 SUBORDINATE COURTS

CONSTITUTION AND POWERS

(1) Establishment.—The establishment of subordinate courts was authorised by the B.C.A.O-in-C, 1902, s. 18 (now repealed) and pursuant to this authorisation, the Courts Ordinance, 1958, s. 53, provides for the Resident Magistrate's Court. Section 54(1) of the C.O. provides that the following are to be magistrates and hold subordinate courts:—

(a) Provincial Commissioners—first class subordinate courts;
(b) District Commissioners—second class subordinate courts;
(c) Administrative officers, who have been confirmed, other than District Commissioners—third class subordinate courts;
(d) Administrative officers on probation—fourth class subordinate courts.

The Governor may by order invest an administrative officer with the power to hold a second class court (with the recommendation or approval of the Chief Justice) and an administrative probationary officer with the power to hold a third class court and by warrant confer upon any person the power to hold a Resident Magistrate's court, or a subordinate court of any class [C.O., s. 54(2), (a)–(c)].

(2) Composition.—See (1), *supra*.

(3) Jurisdiction—original.—(*i*) *Territorial jurisdiction.*—The territorial jurisdiction of the subordinate courts is as follows:—

Resident Magistrate's court—jurisdiction within the limits of the Protectorate;
First class court—jurisdiction in the province where it is situate;
Second, third and fourth class courts—jurisdiction in the districts where they are situate.

---

[1] See Anderson, J. N. D., *Islamic Law in Africa*, pp. 162–170.

(ii) Civil jurisdiction.—Jurisdiction over all civil actions and suits where the amount in dispute does not exceed:—

Resident Magistrate's court—not over £200;
Second class court—not over £100;
Third and fourth class courts—not over £25.

Subordinate courts do not have jurisdiction in the following: title to or ownership of land; specific performance or rescission of contract; for injunction; cancellation or rectification of instruments; to enforce trusts; to issue or revoke grants of administration in decedents' estates; legitimacy; guardianship or custody and disputes relating to title to any right, duty or office [C.O., s. 59(1)–(4)]. No subordinate court has jurisdiction in matters involving the validity or dissolution of any marriage except as specifically provided by law [C.O., s. 59(4), *(i)*].

(iii) Criminal jurisdiction.—Jurisdiction conferred by Crim. P.C., as amended 1958, s. 8(1)–(3) :—

(a) courts of the first and second class may try any offence under the Penal Code other than treason, instigating invasion, concealment of treason, murder and manslaughter or attempts to commit or aid and abet or procure the commission of these offences;
(b) courts of the third class may try any offence in the 5th Schedule, which specifies a number of misdemeanours and lesser offences;
(c) courts of the fourth class may try any offence in the 6th Schedule, which is more limited in the number of offences than the 5th.

The Resident magistrate's court has the criminal jurisdiction conferred by the Crim. P.C., and by any other law upon it or upon subordinate courts of the first class [C.O., s. 83(1)].

(4) Jurisdiction—appellate.—Appeals may be taken from African courts of first instance or appeal to the District or Provincial Commissioner [African Courts Ordinance, s. 33(1)–(3)].

CONTROL OF COURTS

(5) Appeals from.—*(i) Civil.*—To the High Court [C.O., s. 22(1)].

(ii) Criminal.—Any person convicted on a trial held by any subordinate court may appeal to the High Court, except upon a plea of guilty [Crim. P.C., ss. 314, 316].

(6) Review/revision.—*(i)* The High Court has general supervisory and revisionary jurisdiction over all subordinate courts and may, either of its own motion, or at the instance of any interested party or person, at any stage of civil or criminal proceedings in any subordinate court, call for the record and may remove the proceeding into the High Court or give directions to the subordinate court [C.O., s. 28(1), (2)]. Revision in any civil matter is not entertained at the instance of a party who could have appealed [C.O., s. 29].

(ii) The High Court may examine the record of any criminal proceedings before a subordinate court [Crim. P.C., s. 330], and may:—

(a) reverse an order of acquittal and order a new trial;
(b) exercise, in case of conviction, any of the appellate powers

conferred by ss. 322, 324 and 325 of the Crim. P.C., including the enhancement of sentence;

(c) alter or reverse any other finding, sentence or order;

(d) make any other order; or

(e) direct further inquiry [Crom. P.C., s. 323(1), (a)–(e)].

Certain limitations are placed on the power of the High Court. The High Court may not inflict a greater punishment under this provision than might have been imposed by the inferior court. An acquittal may not be converted into a conviction, except under the specific conditions set out in s. 322. There is the further guarantee of an opportunity to be heard for the accused, in person or by his legal representative [Crim. P.C., s. 332(2)–(4)]. No proceeding by way of revision in any criminal matter is entertained at the instance of a party who could have appealed [Crim. P.C., s. 332(5)].

(7) Transfer.—(*i*) *Civil.*—The High Court may transfer civil proceedings from place to place, or to or from any subordinate court [C.O., s. 15(7)].

(*ii*) *Criminal.*—Criminal proceedings may be transferred by the High Court from one magistrate to another on report of a magistrate [Crim. P.C., s. 74], or whenever it appears to the High Court (a) that a fair trial may not be had in the subordinate court; or (b) where an unusual question of law is present; or (c) a view is necessary; or (d) convenience of the parties or ends of justice will be served, the High Court may transfer from one court to another or from a subordinate court to itself [Crim. P.C., s. 75(1), (2)].

(8) Inspection, supervision, etc.—(*i*) Any magistrate may call for and examine the record of criminal proceedings of a court of an inferior class and, if the magistrate considers that the proceedings are improper, illegal or irregular, he must forward the record to the High Court [Crim. P.C., s. 331];

(*ii*) No sentence may be carried into effect until the High Court has confirmed it in the following cases:—

(a) first class court—penalty exceeding 2 years' imprisonment, or sentence in default of payment, or both or 12 strokes;

(b) second class court—penalty exceeding 6 months' imprisonment, or sentence in default of payment, or both or 12 strokes;

(c) third class court—penalty of 6 months' imprisonment; and

(d) in any court in which there is an order for payments more than £50 [Crim. P.C., s. 9(1)].

No sentence of corporal punishment in addition to a sentence of imprisonment may be carried into effect until confirmed by the High Court [Crim. P.C., s. 7].

LAW TO BE ADMINISTERED

(9) General law

(10) Customary law   As High Court (see A. 2(9)–(11), pp. 170–171, *ante.*

(11) Islamic or other law

B. 1 AFRICAN COURTS (of First Instance)

CONSTITUTION AND POWERS

(1) Establishment.—The Governor may by warrant authorise a Provincial Commissioner to establish by warrant such African courts as he thinks fit [African Courts Ordinance, 1933, cap. 75, s. 3(1)].

(2) Composition.—The African court is constituted in accordance with the native law or custom of the area of jurisdiction, provided that the Provincial Commissioner may, with the Governor's approval, prescribe the constitution of the court [A.C.O., s. 4].

(3) Jurisdiction—original.—No African court has jurisdiction, except by express provision, to try:—

    (a) cases in which a person is charged with an offence which is alleged to have resulted in death or which is punishable by death or imprisonment for life; or

    (b) cases in connexion with marriage other than a marriage contracted under Mohammedan or native law or custom, except where both parties are of the same religion and the claim is for dowry only [A.C.O., s. 11].

The Governor may confer upon all or any African courts jurisdiction to enforce any or all of the provisions of a specified law or laws [A.C.O., s. 13].

(*i*) *Civil jurisdiction.*—Every African court has the civil jurisdiction set out in its warrant, subject to the A.C.O. provisions, over causes and matters in which all the parties are Africans, and the defendant was at the time that the cause of action arose resident or within its jurisdiction. Such jurisdiction extends to suits for the recovery of civil debts due to Her Majesty under the provisions of any law where jurisdiction has been expressly conferred. Civil proceedings relating to immovable property are taken in a court within the area where the property is situate [A.C.O., s. 8].

(*ii*) *Criminal jurisdiction.*—Every African court has the criminal jurisdiction set out in its warrant, subject to the A.C.O. provisions [A.C.O., s. 10].

(4) Jurisdiction—appellate.—Nil.

CONTROL OF COURTS

(5) Appeals from.—Appeals from African courts lie to an African Court of Appeal, or if there is none, or if the Provincial Commissioner directs, appeals may lie to the District Commissioner's Court. Further appeal lies either from the African Court of Appeal to the District Commissioner, or from the District Commissioner to the Provincial Commissioner and then to the High Court [A.C.O., ss. 32(1), (2), 33(1)].

(6) Review/revision.—Every Provincial Commissioner and District Commissioner has access to African courts in his area, and may, on application or of his own motion, revise any civil or criminal proceedings of an African court [A.C.O., s. 31].

District Commissioners may not exercise revisory powers in cases where they have sat in an advisory capacity under s. 24 of the A.C.O. [A.C.O., s. 31(2)].

(7) Transfer.—(*i*) A Provincial Commissioner, on the application of a defendant, may direct that a case before an African court be tried by any competent subordinate court [A.C.O., s. 29].

(*ii*) Every Provincial Commissioner and District Commissioner, on application or his own motion, may order any case to be retried before any other competent African court, or may transfer any cause at any stage of the proceedings to any first or second class subordinate court [A.C.O., s. 31(c)].

(8) Inspection, supervision, etc.—Every Provincial Commissioner and District Commissioner has, within his province or district, access to African courts and the records of such courts [A.C.O., s. 31].

LAW TO BE ADMINISTERED

(9) General law.—African courts administer:—

- (a) provisions of certain Ordinances which the Governor, by order, made under s. 13 of the African Courts Ordinance, specifies (e.g. Public Health Ordinance, Game Ordinance, African Tax (Registration) Rules) [A.C.O., s. 13].
- (b) the provisions of all rules or orders made by the Provincial Commissioner, District Commissioner or Native Authority under the N.A.O., in force in the area of the jurisdiction of the court;
- (c) provisions of any Ordinance which the court is, by such Ordinance, authorised to administer [A.C.O., s. 12(b), (c), (d)].

(10) Customary law.—An African court administers: " the native law and custom prevailing in the area of the jurisdiction of the court, so far as it is not repugnant to justice or morality or inconsistent with the provisions of any Order of the Queen in Council or with any other law in force in the Protectorate " [A.C.O., s. 12(a)].

(11) Islamic or other law.—As High Court (see A. 2(11), p. 171, *ante*).

B. 2 AFRICAN COURTS OF APPEAL

CONSTITUTION AND POWERS

(1) Establishment.—A Provincial Commissioner may, with the Governor's approval, by warrant appoint a single chief or a body of chiefs or any other African or Africans, or combination, sitting with or without assessors, to be a Court of Appeal from all or any of the African courts in the province [A.C.O., s. 32(1)].

(2) Composition.—Defined by warrant.

(3) Jurisdiction—original.—As defined by warrant.

(4) Jurisdiction—appellate.—As defined by warrant, which may be " from all or any of the African courts in the province in respect of all or any of the cases arising therein " [A.C.O., s. 32(1)].

CONTROL OF COURTS

(5) Appeals from.—Any person aggrieved by an order or decision of an African Court of Appeal may appeal to the District Commissioner

[A.C.O., s. 32(2)]. Appeals from the District Commissioner's order or decision may be taken to the High Court. A District Commissioner may not exercise appellate jurisdiction in cases where he has sat as adviser [A.C.O., s. 33(3), (4)].

(6) Review/revision

(7) Transfer

(8) Inspection, supervision, etc.

As African courts of first instance (see B. 1, pp. 174–175, *ante*).

LAW TO BE ADMINISTERED

As African courts of first instance (see B. 1, p. 175, *ante*).

PART IV

HIGH COMMISSION TERRITORIES

By

W. T. McCLAIN, LL.B., LL.M.,

of the Bar of Indiana; Research Officer, Restatement of African Law Project, School of Oriental and African Studies.

SUMMARY

		PAGE
HIGH COMMISSION TERRITORIES	. . . . .	179
BASUTOLAND	. . . .	181
BECHUANALAND	. . . .	191
SWAZILAND	. . . .	199

HIGH COMMISSION
TERRITORIES[1]

The High Commission Territories comprise Basutoland, Bechuanaland Protectorate, and Swaziland.

A. 1(a) THE PRIVY COUNCIL

The Basutoland, Bechuanaland Protectorate and Swaziland (Appeals to the Privy Council) Order in Council, 1954, provided in s. 4 that an appeal shall lie as of right from a final judgment of the Basutoland, Bechuanaland Protectorate and Swaziland Court of Appeal where the matter or claim in dispute amounts to the value of £500 or more, and from final judgment of divorce or nullity of marriage. Appeal lies to the Privy Council at the discretion of the Court of Appeal from any other judgment of the Court of Appeal.

A. 1(b) THE BASUTOLAND, BECHUANALAND PROTECTORATE AND SWAZILAND COURT OF APPEAL

CONSTITUTION AND POWERS

(1) Establishment.—Established by the Basutoland, Bechuanaland Protectorate and Swaziland Court of Appeal Order in Council, 1954, as a superior court of record of the Territories [B., B.P., and S.C.A. O-in-C, s. 4].

(2) Composition.—The judges of the court are:—

    (*i*) the person who holds the substantive offices of Chief Justice of the High Courts of Basutoland, of Bechuanaland Protectorate and of Swaziland, who is the President of the Court;

    (*ii*) the other judges, if any, of the High Courts of the Territories; and

    (*iii*) such other persons as the High Commissioner may appoint from time to time.

If under (*i*), *supra*, the three offices of Chief Justice are not held by the same person then every person who holds such office is a judge of the Court and the High Commissioner designates one of these persons to be President [B., B.P., and S.C.A. O-in-C, s. 6(1), (2)].

(3) Jurisdiction—original.—Nil.

(4) Jurisdiction—appellate.—The Court has jurisdiction to hear and determine such appeals from judgments of courts of the Territories, and to exercise such powers and authorities as may be prescribed by any laws for the Territories respectively [B., B.P., and S.C.A. O-in-C, s. 13(1)].

---

1 For diagram of courts system see p. 224, *post*.

LAW TO BE ADMINISTERED

(9) General law.—" In the hearing of any appeal the law to be applied shall be the law applicable to the case in the Court from which the appeal is brought " [B., B.P. and S.C.A. O-in-C, s. 13(3)].

(10) Customary law.—See (9), *supra.*

BASUTOLAND[1]

The courts for the administration of justice in Basutoland comprise:—
    A. the High Court and subordinate courts administering primarily the general law; and
    B. Judicial Commissioners' Courts and a system of Basuto Courts administering primrily Sesuto law.

A. 1(a) THE PRIVY COUNCIL

See p. 179, *ante.*

A. 1(b) THE BASUTOLAND, BECHUANALAND PROTECTORATE AND SWAZILAND COURT OF APPEAL

See pp. 179–180, *ante.*

A. 2 THE HIGH COURT

CONSTITUTION AND POWERS

(1) Establishment.—The High Court was first established pursuant to the authority of the Disannexation of Basutoland from the Colony of the Cape of Good Hope Order in Council, 1884, and was re-established pursuant to s. 65(1) of the Basutoland (Constitution) Order in Council, 1959.[2]

(2) Composition.—The High Court is composed of a Chief Justice, who is the President of the Court, and such number of puisne judges as may from time to time be appointed [B.(C.) O-in-C, s. 65(1)]. Appointments of the Chief Justice and puisne judges are made by the High Commissioner pursuant to instructions given to him by Her Majesty through a Secretary of State [B.(C.) O-in-C, s. 66(1)].

(3) Jurisdiction—original.—(*i*) The High Court has within Basutoland unlimited original jurisdiction in civil and criminal matters [B.(C.) O-in-C, s. 66(2)]. No civil cause or action within the jurisdiction of a subordinate court of the First Class may be instituted or removed to the High Court except with the leave of a judge upon application [High Court Proclamation, s. 4, as replaced by s. 4 of the High Court (Constitutional Amendment) Proclamation, 1960].

(*ii*) Where any person holds the office of Chief Justice or puisne judge of the High Court of Basutoland and also holds such office for the High Court of Bechuanaland or Swaziland, such judicial officer may exercise jurisdiction according to the law for the time being in force in Bechuanaland or Swaziland in certain scheduled matters [B.(C.) O-inC, s. 69, Fifth Schedule].

---

1 For diagram of courts system see p. 225, *post.*
2 The Basutoland (Constitution) Order in Council, 1959, came into operation on March 5, 1960, by High Commissioner's Notice No. 20 of 1960.

(4) Jurisdiction—appellate.—The High Court is a Court of Appeal from all subordinate courts in the territory [H.C.P., s. 6].

(*i*) *Civil.*—A party to any civil suit or proceeding in a subordinate court may appeal to the High Court against:—

    (a) judgment for the plaintiff on his claim;
    (b) judgment for the defendant on his defence;
    (c) absolution;
    (d) judgment as to costs;
    (e) any rule or order having the effect of final sentence; and
    (f) a decision on an exception under certain circumstances [Basutoland Subordinate Courts Proc., cap. 4, ss. 30 and 53].

No appeal lies if before the hearing the parties agree in writing that the decision of the court shall be final [S.C.P., s. 52].

(*ii*) *Criminal.*—Any person convicted by a judgment of any subordinate court, including a person discharged after conviction, may appeal to the High Court against the conviction and sentence or order [S.C.P., s. 72].

A case may be required to be stated in any criminal proceedings giving a decision in favour of the accused on a matter of law and the Attorney-General or prosecutor may appeal from the decision to the High Court [S.C.P., s. 72(7), (8)].

(*iii*) *Appeals from Basuto Courts.*—No appeal lies from a Basuto Court directly to the High Court but cases may be appealed to the Court of the Judicial Commissioner from which an appeal to the High Court lies with leave of the Judicial Commissioner or the High Court [Native Courts Proclamation, 1938, s. 28].

CONTROL OF COURT

(5) Appeals from.—Appeals in both criminal and civil cases against the judgment of the High Court lie to the Court of Appeal [Court of Appeal (Basutoland) Proclamation, 1954, ss. 3, 11].

LAW TO BE ADMINISTERED

(9) General law.—The Disannexation of Basutoland from the Colony of the Cape of Good Hope Order in Council, February 2, 1884, Part II, provided *inter alia* that all laws in force in Basutoland at the time when this Order took effect should continue in operation until repealed or altered by proclamation of the High Commissioner. On May 29, 1884, the High Commissioner made a Proclamation, which, as later amended, is as follows:—

" In all suits, actions, or proceedings, civil or criminal, the law to be administered shall, as nearly as the circumstances of the country will permit, be the same as the law for the time being in force in the Colony of the Cape of Good Hope:

Provided, however, that in any suit, action or proceeding in any Court to which all the parties are natives, and in all suits, actions or proceedings whatsoever, before any Native Chief exercising jurisdiction as aforesaid, native law may be administered: And provided, further, that the laws set out in the Schedule hereto and Acts passed after the 29th of September, 1884, by the Parliament of the Colony of the Cape of Good Hope shall not apply to the said territory."

Note.—The effect of the Order in Council, 1884, and the High Commissioner's Proclamation is that the Roman–Dutch law in force in 1884 in the Colony of the Cape of Good Hope and such statutes, not discontinued by proclamation, are in force in Basutoland [General Law Proclamation, 1884, as amended, s. 2].

(10) Customary law.—(*i*) See the proviso cited in (9), *supra*.

(*ii*).—(a) See B. 1(10), p. 187, *post*. A Native Court of Appeal, a subordinate court or the High Court in the exercise of appellate jurisdiction under the Native Courts Proclamation may make any order or pass any such sentence as the court of first instance could have made or passed [N.C.P., s. 30].

(b) The provision under the Basuto Courts Proclamation, not yet in force, is that any court dealing on appeal or review with proceedings which were tried in a Basuto Court shall administer the law which was or should have been administered by the Basuto Court. "Any court" means the Central Court, the Courts of Judicial Commissioners, the High Court and the Basutoland, Bechuanaland Protectorate and Swaziland Court of Appeal [B.C.P., 1958, s. 114(1), (2)].

A. 3 SUBORDINATE COURTS

CONSTITUTION AND POWERS

(1) Establishment.—The subordinate courts were established by the Subordinate Courts Proclamation, 1938, as amended in 1954, s. 2. The courts consist of:—

    (a) subordinate courts of the first class;
    (b) subordinate courts of the second class;
    (c) subordinate courts of the third class.

(2) Composition.—The following persons may hold courts:—

    (a) Every Senior District Officer and every District Commissioner—court of the first class;
    (b) Every District Officer—court of the second class; and
    (c) Every Cadet—court of the third class.

The Resident Commissioner may, with the concurrence of the Chief Justice, by notice, appoint:—

    (a) any person as a magistrate or assistant magistrate to hold a court of a class to be specified;
    (b) any District Officer to hold a court of the first class or any Cadet to hold a court of the second class.

Unless otherwise stated, the appointment is deemed to confer jurisdiction to hold the court within any territorial district [S.C.P., s. 3].

(3) Jurisdiction—original.—(*i*) *Civil.*—(a) The jurisdiction in civil matters is as follows:—

    (*i*) first class courts have jurisdiction where the amount does not exceed £500;

    (*ii*) second class courts have jurisdiction where the amount does not exceed £250;

    (*iii*) third class courts have no civil jurisdiction.

When both parties are natives and the cause of action is, in the opinion of the Clerk of the Court, suitable for a native court, the Clerk of the Court may refuse to issue a summons and may order the plaintiff to commence the action in the appropriate native court [S.C.P., s. 15(1), proviso (2)].

(b) Subordinate courts have no jurisdiction in the following:—

    (*i*) dissolution of marriage or judicial separation where the parties are Europeans;

    (*ii*) validity or interpretation of wills;

    (*iii*) status of persons in respect of mental capacity;

    (*iv*) specific performance without alternative of payment of damages except transfer or delivery or property and rendering account;

    (*v*) decree of perpetual silence; or

    (*vi*) provisional sentence [S.C.P., s. 28].

(*ii*) *Criminal.*—(*i*) Subordinate courts of the first, second and third class have jurisdiction over all offences except treason, murder, sedition, offences relating to coinage or currency, and rape. The Attorney-General may remit a rape case for trial by a subordinate court of the first class [S.C.P., s. 59].

(*ii*) Subordinate courts have the following limitations on their power to punish:—

    (a) a first class court may sentence to imprisonment for not more than 2 years, levy a fine of not more than £100 and prescribe not more than 15 strokes with a cane;

    (b) a second class court may sentence to imprisonment for not more than 1 year, levy a fine of not more than £50 and prescribe not more than 8 strokes with a cane;

    (c) a third class court may sentence to imprisonment for not more than 6 months, levy a fine of not more than £25, but may not impose punishment of whipping [S.C.P., s. 61(1)].

(*iii*) The Attorney-General may remit a case, other than one beyond the jurisdiction of the subordinate court, after holding a preparatory examination. The remittal may expressly give increased jurisdiction. There is no remittal to a third class court [S.C.P., ss. 63, 64].

(4) Jurisdiction—appellate.—Nil.

Control of Courts

(5) Appeals from.—A party to any civil suit, unless the parties have agreed that the decision of the court shall be final, may appeal to the High Court against any judgment, rule or order having the effect of a final sentence, or, when the parties concerned consent to such an appeal to a decision overruling or upholding an exception [S.C.P., ss. 52 and 53].

Every person convicted by judgment of a subordinate court may appeal against such conviction to the High Court [S.C.P., s. 72(1)].

(6) Review/revision.—(*i*) The High Court has full power, jurisdiction and authority to review the proceedings of all subordinate courts and if necessary set aside or correct them [H.C.P., 1954, s. 5(1)].

(*ii*) All sentences in criminal cases imposed by a third class subordinate court are subject to review as of course by an officer appointed to hold a first class court without prejudice to the right of appeal against the sentence [S.C.P., s. 65].

(*iii*) All sentences in criminal cases, in the case of courts of the first class for a period of imprisonment exceeding 6 months or a fine exceeding £50, and, in the case of courts of the second and third class for a period exceeding 3 months or a fine exceeding £25, are subject to review as of course by the High Court without prejudice to right of appeal [S.C.P., s. 66].

(7) Transfer.—(*i*) In proceedings before a subordinate court when both parties are natives and the cause of action in the opinion of the Clerk of the Court is one suitable to be heard in a Basuto court, the Clerk may refuse to issue a summons and may order the plaintiff to commence his action in such a court [S.C.P., s. 15(1)].

(*ii*) A subordinate court may transfer a proceeding to another court of the same class or of a higher class by consent of the parties or upon the application of any party upon a showing that the trial will result in undue expense or inconvenience in the particular court [S.C.P., s. 19].

(*iii*) An action in a second class court where the amount of the claim exceeds £100 may, upon the application of the defendant, be removed to a first class court. Any action in a first or second class court where the claim exceeds £200 may, upon the application of the defendant, be removed to the High Court (with leave of the Judge in Chambers when the amount does not exceed £500) [H.C.P., 1954, s. 4; S.C.P., s. 31(1), (2)].

(*iv*) The Chief Justice or Judge of the High Court, or in their absence the Registrar, may for good cause order a criminal case transferred for trial from the district in which the crime was committed to any other district [S.C.P., s. 60(1) proviso].

(*v*) Under the Criminal Procedure and Evidence Proclamation, the Attorney-General has authority to remit a criminal case except one of murder or treason to a subordinate court after a preparatory examination and may specify in such remittal that the subordinate court shall have increased jurisdiction [C.P. and E.P., s. 88].

Law to be Administered

(9) General law
(10) Customary law } As High Court (see A. 2(9), (10), pp. 182–183, *ante*).

B. 1 NATIVE COURTS

The system of African or native courts was established by the Basutoland Native Courts Proclamation, 1938. Substantial changes in this court system were introduced by the Basutoland Courts Proclamation, 1958 which has not as yet come into force. This survey includes both the operative Basutoland Native Courts Proclamation, 1938 and the

Basutoland Courts Proclamation, 1958, which was intended to replace the earlier law.

CONSTITUTION AND POWERS

(1) Establishment.—The Native Courts Proclamation of 1938 provides that the Resident Commissioner, subject to the approval of the High Commissioner, may recognise or establish such native courts as he thinks fit [N.C.P., s. 2(1)].

In addition to the ordinary native court, the Resident Commissioner may, with the approval of the High Commissioner, appoint any native court to be a court of appeal or a higher native court of appeal [N.C.P., s. 27].

(2) Composition.—The native court is constituted in accordance with native law and custom. The Resident Commissioner, with the approval of the High Commissioner, may prescribe the constitution, order of precedence, and duties and powers of assessors [N.C.P., s. 2(3)].

(3) Jurisdiction—original.—Subject to express provision conferring jurisdiction no native court has jurisdiction to try cases:—

(a) in which a person is charged with an offence in consequence of which death is alleged to have occurred, or which is punishable with death or life imprisonment;

(b) in connexion with marriage, other than marriage contracted under native law and custom, except in so far as the case concerns the return or payment of " dowry " [N.C.P., s. 8(1)].

(*i*) *Civil.*—Every native court has civil jurisdiction to the extent set out in its warrant, over causes and matters in which all the parties are natives and the defendant ordinarily resides within the jurisdiction of the court, or over causes of action which arise within the territorial jurisdiction of such court [N.C.P., s. 6].

(*ii*) *Criminal.*—Every native court has criminal jurisdiction, to the extent set out in its warrant, in charges in which the complainant and the accused are natives and the offence is alleged to have been committed within the territorial jurisdiction of such court [N.C.P., s. 7].

(4) Jurisdiction—appellate.—(*i*) The ordinary native court has no appellate jurisdiction.

(*ii*) Native courts of appeal and higher native courts of appeal have the appellate jurisdiction designated by the Resident Commissioner [N.C.P., s. 27].

CONTROL OF COURTS

(5) Appeals from.—Appeals from the native courts of first instance lie to a native court of appeal and from the native court of appeal to a higher native court of appeal, or if none, to a first class subordinate court. Appeals lie from a higher native court of appeal to the Court of the Judicial Commissioner[1] [N.C.P., s. 28(1), (2), (3)].

---

[1] The Judicial Commissioner's Court is a first class subordinate court and the provisions of the Basutoland Subordinate Courts Proclamation, which apply to first class subordinate courts, apply *mutatis mutandis*, except that no civil suit or action may commence in the courts of Judicial Commissioners [Basutoland Judicial Commissioners' Proclamation, 1950, s. 3(1)].

(6) Review/revision.—Every District Officer or Assistant District Officer, as holder of a subordinate court, has access to all native courts in his district and to the records of such courts, and may on his own motion or on application of the accused in a criminal case, or of either of the parties in a civil cause, take the following action:—

    (a) revise any proceedings of the native court and may make any order which the native court could have made or passed. Certain limitations are placed upon the officer, e.g., requiring an opportunity for the parties to be heard.

    (b) order the case re-tried before the same or any other native court of competent jurisdiction [N.C.P., s. 26].

(7) Transfer.—(*i*) Every District Officer or Assistant District Officer, as holder of a subordinate court, may on his own motion or on the application of the accused in a criminal case, or of either of the parties in a civil cause, transfer any civil or criminal matter at any stage of the proceedings to any subordinate court of competent jurisdiction [N.C.P., s. 26(c)].

(*ii*) If a native court unreasonably delays the hearing or adjudication of a cause, application by any party, after notice, may be made to the native court of appeal, or if the delaying court is a native court of appeal, application may be made to a District Officer as holder of a subordinate court for hearing. The court hearing the application may direct the inferior court to take appropriate action, or may itself hear the cause or matter [N.C.P., s. 31].

(*iii*) Proceedings may be transferred from a subordinate court to a native court when both parties are natives and the clerk of the court believes the action to be suitable to be heard in a native court [S.C.P., amended 1952, s. 15(1)].

(8) Inspection, supervision, etc.—(*i*) The High Commissioner may by rule provide for fees, practice and procedure and for the carrying into effect of the provisions of the Basutoland Native Court Proclamation [N.C.P., s. 34].

(*ii*) For powers of administrative officers, see under (6), *supra*.

LAW TO BE ADMINISTERED

(9) General law.—The native court administers:—

    (*i*) the provisions of any law which the court is authorised to administer by order of the High Commissioner;

    (*ii*) the provisions of all rules or orders made by a Paramount Chief, Chief, sub-chief or headman under the Native Administration Proclamation, 1938;

    (*iii*) the provisions of any Proclamation which the court is authorised to administer by the terms of such Proclamation [N.C.P., s. 9].

(10) Customary law.—The native court administers: " the native law and custom prevailing in the Territory, so far as it is not repugnant to justice or morality or inconsistent with the provisions of any law in force in the Territory " [N.C.P., s. 9(a)].

B. 2 BASUTO COURTS

CONSTITUTION AND POWERS

(1) Establishment.—(*i*) Basuto Courts will be established under ss. 3 and 4 of the Basuto Courts Proclamation, 1958, which provided that these courts were to be divided into two grades: (1) first grade—the Central Basuto Court, which is to have a headquarters division and regional divisions; and (2) second grade—local Basuto Courts; and in the First Schedule established one Central Court (Headquarters Division) and 11 Central Courts (Regional divisions) and 53 local courts.

(*ii*) The Paramount Chief on the advice of the Executive Council may by notice in the Gazette establish or abolish (a) regional divisions of the Central Basuto Court; and (b) Local Basuto Courts [B.C.P., as amended in 1959, s. 4(2)].

(2) Composition.—The power to hold a Basuto Court is to be vested in an officer known as the President. The appointment, transfer, or dismissal of Presidents, members and officers of Basuto Courts is to be effected by the Paramount Chief on the recommendation of an appointments committee [B.C.P., 1958, ss. 14 and 16).

(3) Jurisdiction—original.—No Basuto Court has jurisdiction over any person other than Africans or jurisdiction to try any civil or criminal case where any of the parties or witnesses are not Africans [B.C.P., 1958, s. 26]. Territorial jurisdiction is that included in the Schedule [B.C.P., 1958, s. 27].

(*i*) The civil jurisdiction of Basuto Courts in respect of value of subject matter is as follows:—

    (a) Central Courts—unlimited;
    (b) Local Courts—maximum £500;

No local court has power to try cases involving:—

    (a) dissolution of marriage;
    (b) grant of ejectment order [B.C.P., 1958, s. 44(1), (2)].

No Basuto Court has jurisdiction to try cases in connection with marriage other than marriage contracted under or in accordance with African law or custom, except where the case concerns payment or return of dowry [B.C.P., s. 46].

(*ii*) Criminal jurisdiction of the Basuto Courts is that which is given by provision of law, or order of the High Commissioner or under Sesuto law and custom [B.C.P., s. 68].

No Basuto Court has jurisdiction, in the absence of an express provision of law, to try cases in which a person is charged with an offence, as the consequence of which death is alleged to have occurred, or which is punishable under law by death [B.C.P., s. 69].

(4) Jurisdiction—appellate.—(a) Local Courts have no appellate jurisdiction; (b) Central Courts may hear appeals from the local courts [B.C.P., s. 112(1)].

CONTROL OF COURTS

(5) Appeals from.—Appeals from Basuto local courts lie to the division of the Central Court and appeals from the Central Courts lie to the Courts of Judicial Commissioners [B.C.P., s, 112(1)].

(6) Review/revision.—(a) Every administrative officer entitled to or appointed to hold a first or second class subordinate court has at all times access to all Basuto Courts in his district.

(b) He may on his own motion or on the application of the accused revise any of the criminal proceedings whether of first instance or appeal [B.C.P., s. 80(1), (2)].

(7) Transfer.—(a) Proceedings may be transferred from a subordinate court to a Basuto Court [S.C.P., s. 15(1)].

(b) Every administrative officer may of his own motion or upon application of the accused (*i*) transfer any criminal case from one Basuto Court to another, or (*ii*) transfer any criminal case to a subordinate court of competent jurisdiction [B.C.P., 1958, s. 80(5)].

(c) The Basuto Court must transfer a civil case to a Basuto Court of competent jurisdiction or to a subordinate court when it appears that the matter is beyond the jurisdiction of the Basuto Court [B.C.P., s. 50].

(d) Any civil case may be transferred by the court to another competent Basuto Court with the consent of all parties [B.C.P., s. 51].

(e) A party may apply for transfer of the case to a Basuto court of greater jurisdiction or to a subordinate court on the grounds of the gravity of the case or for any other good reason [B.C.P., ss. 52, 53].

(f) When a court is not empowered by law to administer the law, any party may by application request the court to transfer the case to a subordinate court [B.C.P., s. 54].

(8) Inspection, supervision, etc.—(*i*) The Paramount Chief may issue instructions to provide for the duties and training of court officials, inspection of Basuto Court records, and the efficient functioning of the Basuto Courts [B.C.P., 1958, s. 8].

(*ii*) For the powers of administrative officers, see under (6), *supra*.

(*iii*) The Resident Commissioner has the right to intervene and take any action which he may deem necessary if he has reasonable grounds to believe this intervention necessary to the proper administration of justice in the Basuto Courts [B.C.P., 1958, s. 121].

LAW TO BE ADMINISTERED

(9) General law.—The Basuto Court administers the provisions of any law which the Court is, by or under such law, authorised to administer and the provisions of any law which the Court may be authorised to administer by the High Commissioner [B.C.P., 1958, ss. 24(c), (d), 25].

(10) Customary law.—The Basuto Court administers:—

" (a) The Sesuto law and custom prevailing in the Territory so far as it is not repugnant to justice or morality or inconsistent with the provisions of any law in force in the Territory: and the Provisions of this Proclamation;

(b) the provisions of all rules or orders made by the Paramount Chief or by a principal chief, ward chief, chief or headman under any law in force . . ." [B.C.P., 1958, s. 24].

B. 3 JUDICIAL COMMISSIONERS' COURTS

Constitution and Powers

(1) Establishment.—The Courts of Judicial Commissioners were established by Proclamation No. 25 of 1950 [Judicial Commissioners' Courts Proclamation, 1950, s. 1].

(2) Composition.—The Judicial Commissioners are appointed by the High Commissioner [J.C.C.P., s. 2].

(3) Jurisdiction—original.—Such courts possess the jurisdiction, power and authority vested in subordinate courts of the first class except that no civil suit or proceeding may be commenced therein [J.C.C.P., ss. 1(2), 3(1)].

(4) Jurisdiction—appellate.—(*i*) Appeals lie from a decision of a higher native court of appeal to the Courts of Judicial Commissioners [J.C.C.P., s. 4 (amending N.C.P., s. 28)].

(*ii*) The provisions of the as yet inoperative Basuto Courts Proclamation of 1958 are as follows:—

> (a) appeals from Basuto Central Courts lie to the Courts of the Judicial Commissioners [B.C.P., 1958, s. 112(1), (b)].
> (b) revision by administrative officers altering an acquittal or sentence may be appealed to the Courts of Judicial Commissioners [B.C.P., 1958, s. 80].

Control of Courts

(5) Appeals from.—There is no appeal to the High Court from decisions of the Courts of Judicial Commissioners except in the following cases:—

> (*i*) upon a question of law or native law and custom reserved by a Judicial Commissioner at the instance of either party, or on his own motion; or
> (*ii*) upon certificate of a judicial commissioner that it is a fit case for appeal on any other ground. The High Court may consider the motion of the party aggrieved by refusal of the judicial commissioner to allow an appeal [J.C.C.P., s. 4 (amending N.C.P., s. 28)]. The recent Basuto Courts Proclamation of 1958 makes no change in this appellate provision [B.C.P., 1958, s. 112(2)].

(6) Review/revision

(7) Transfer

(8) Inspection, supervision, etc.

As first class subordinate courts (see A. 3(6), (7), p. 185, *ante*).

Law to be Administered

(9) General law

(10) Customary law

As High Court (see A. 2(9), (10), pp. 182–183, *ante*).

BECHUANALAND PROTECTORATE[1]

The courts for the administration of justice in the Bechuanaland Protectorate comprise:—

A. the High Court and subordinate courts administering primarily the general law; and

B. a system of African courts administering primarily customary law.

A. 1(a) THE PRIVY COUNCIL

See p. 179, *ante*.

A. 1(b) THE BASUTOLAND, BECHUANALAND PROTECTORATE AND SWAZILAND COURT OF APPEAL

See pp. 179–180, *ante*.

A. 2 THE HIGH COURT

CONSTITUTION AND POWERS

(1) Establishment.—The High Court was established pursuant to the authority of the General Administration Order in Council, 1891, and in 1954 the law relating to the High Court was consolidated by the Bechuanaland Protectorate High Court Proclamation [B.H.C.P., 1954, s. 2(1)].

(2) Composition.—The High Commissioner for Bechuanaland may appoint a Chief Justice and a puisne judge of the High Court [H.C.P., 1954, s. 3(1)].

(3) Jurisdiction—original.—(*i*) The High Court has all the jurisdiction, powers and authority vested in the Supreme Court of South Africa [H.C.P., 1954, s. 2(2)]. The jurisdiction is over all causes and proceedings both civil and criminal, except that no civil cause to which Africans only are a party, and no civil cause to which either party is a European when the amount in dispute does not exceed £500 may be instituted in or removed to the High Court without leave of the judge. This exception does not apply to those matters over which the subordinate courts are expressly denied jurisdiction [H.C.P., ss. 2(2), 4; Bechuanaland Protectorate Subordinate Courts Proclamation, s. 28].

(*ii*) The Chief Justice or puisne judge may exercise jurisdiction in the Territory in respect of specified matters arising in either of the other Territories [H.C.P., s. 12].

---

[1] For diagram of courts system see p. 224, *post*.

(4) Jurisdiction—appellate.—The High Court is a Court of Appeal from all subordinate courts in the Territory [H.C.P., s. 6].

(*i*) *Civil.*—A party to any civil suit or proceeding in a subordinate court may appeal to the High Court against:—

(a) judgment for the plaintiff on his claim;
(b) judgment for the defendant on his defence;
(c) absolution;
(d) judgment as to costs;
(e) any rule or order having the effect of final sentence [S.C.P., ss. 31, 62, 63].

No appeal lies if before the hearing the parties agree in writing that the decision of the court shall be final.

(*ii*) *Criminal.*—Any person convicted by judgment of any subordinate court including a person discharged after conviction may appeal to the High Court against the conviction and sentence or order [S.C.P., s. 82].

A case may be required to be stated in any criminal proceedings giving a decision in favour of the accused on a matter of law and the Attorney-General or prosecutor may appeal from the decision to the High Court [S.C.P., s. 83(1), (2)].

(*iii*) *Appeals from African Courts.*—No appeal lies directly from an African court to the High Court, but cases may be appealed through the appellate hierarchy to a first class subordinate court from which an appeal lies to the High Court where the amount of judgment exceeds £100 or imprisonment exceeding 6 months, or corporal punishment in excess of 8 strokes, or in other cases by special leave of the High Court Judge [Bechuanaland Native Courts Proclamation, 1944, s. 32(4)].

CONTROL OF COURT

(5) Appeals from.—Appeals, in both criminal and civil cases, against the judgment of the High Court lie to the Court of Appeal [Court of Appeal (Bechuanaland Protectorate) Proclamation, 1954, ss. 3, 11].

LAW TO BE ADMINISTERED

(9) General law.—(a) Following the High Commissioner's Proclamation of June 10, 1891, doubt arose as to the effect of s. 19 of that Proclamation upon the application of the Roman–Dutch common law in the Protectorate. The General Law Proclamation, 1909, for the purpose of removing any doubt as to the effect of that Proclamation, provided in part:—

" . . . the laws in force in the Colony of the Cape of Good Hope on the 10th day of June, 1891, shall *mutatis mutandis* and so far as not inapplicable be the laws in force and to be observed in the said Protectorate. . . ."

The use of the word " laws " left some uncertainty as to whether or not there was proper authority for the application of both the common law and the statutes of the Colony of the Cape of Good Hope in the Protectorate.

The General Law (Cape Statutes) Revision Proclamation, 1959, clarifies this question of the authority for the application of Roman–Dutch common law by providing:—

" Nothing in this Proclamation shall . . . be construed as affecting the continued application of the Roman–Dutch common law in the territory, or of any other laws other than enactments of the legislative authority of the Colony of the Cape of Good Hope which were in force on the 10th day of June, 1891, and were in force in the territory at the commencement of this Proclamation. " [G.L.(C.S.)R.P., s. 2][1].

(10) Customary law.—The General Administration O-in-C, 1891, in s. 4 provides for the High Commissioner's power to legislate by Proclamation and provides further:—

" The High Commissioner in issuing such Proclamations shall respect any native laws or customs by which the civil relations of any native chiefs, tribes or populations under Her Majesty's protection are now regulated, except so far as the same may be incompatible with the due exercise of Her Majesty's power and jurisdiction."

A. 3 SUBORDINATE COURTS

CONSTITUTION AND POWERS

(1) Establishment.—The subordinate courts were established by the Subordinate Courts Proclamation, 1938, s. 3. The courts consist of:—

    (a) subordinate courts of the first class;
    (b) subordinate courts of the second class;
    (c) subordinate courts of the third class.

(2) Composition.—The following persons may hold courts:—

    (a) every Senior District Officer and every District Commissioner—court of the first class;
    (b) every District Officer—court of the second class; and
    (c) every Cadet—court of the third class.

The Resident Commissioner may, with the concurrence of the Chief Justice, by notice, appoint:—

    (a) any person as a magistrate or assistant magistrate to hold a court of a class to be specified;
    (b) any District Officer to hold a court of the first class or any Cadet to hold a court of the second class.

(3) Jurisdiction—original.—(*i*) *Civil.*—The jurisdiction in civil matters is as follows:—

    (a) first class courts have jurisdiction where the amount in dispute does not exceed £500;
    (b) second class courts have jurisdiction where the amount in dispute does not exceed £250;
    (c) third class courts have jurisdiction where the amount in dispute does not exceed £50.

---

1 By the General Law (Cape Statutes) Revision Proclamation, 1959, s. 2, all Cape Statutes not contained in a Schedule of some thirty-six Acts, or applied to the Territory by some other Proclamation, were discontinued in force.

When both parties are Africans and the cause of action in the opinion of the Clerk of the Court is suitable to be heard by an African court, the Clerk may refuse summons and may order the plaintiff to commence the action in the appropriate African court [S.C.P., s. 16].

(*ii*) *Criminal.*—(a) Subordinate courts of the first, second and third class have jurisdiction over all offences except treason, murder, sedition, offences relating to coinage or currency, and rape; except that cases of rape where natives only are concerned may be tried in first class courts. The Attorney-General may remit a rape case for trial by a subordinate court of the first class [S.C.P., s. 69].

(b) Subordinate courts have the following limitations on their power to punish:—

> (*i*) first class court may sentence to imprisonment for not more than 2 years, levy a fine of not more than £100 and prescribe not more than 15 strokes with a cane;
> (*ii*) second class court may sentence to imprisonment for not more than 1 year, levy a fine of not more than £50 and prescribe not more than 8 strokes with a cane;
> (*iii*) third class court may sentence to imprisonment for not more than 6 months, levy a fine of not more than £25, but may not impose a punishment of whipping [S.C.P., s. 71(1)].

Subordinate courts have no jurisdiction in the following:—

> (a) dissolution of marriage or separation where the parties are Europeans;
> (b) validity or interpretation of wills;
> (c) status of persons in respect of mental capacity;
> (d) specific performance without alternative of payment of damages except transfer or delivery of property and rendering account;
> (e) decree of perpetual silence; or
> (f) provisional sentence [S.C.P., s. 29].

(4) Jurisdiction—appellate.—Subordinate courts have jurisdiction to hear appeals from an African court if there is no African Court of Appeal. Appeals lie from an African Court of Appeal to a Higher African Court of Appeal, and, if there is none, to a first class subordinate court. Appeals lie from a Higher African Court of Appeal to a first class subordinate court [African Courts Proclamation, ss. 31(2), 32(1), (2), (3)].

The appellate jurisdiction of the subordinate courts in respect of African court proceedings is as follows:—

> (a) first class courts—all matters;
> (b) second class courts—all matters where amount in dispute or claimed does not exceed £250 [S.C.P., s. 16(2), as inserted 1957].

CONTROL OF COURTS

(5) Appeals from.—A party to any civil suit, unless the parties have agreed that the decision of the court shall be final, may appeal to the High Court against any judgment, rule or order having the effect of a final sentence or decision overruling or upholding an exception, when the parties concerned consent to such an appeal [S.C.P., ss. 62 and 63].

Every person convicted by judgment of a subordinate court may appeal against such conviction to the High Court [S.C.P., s. 82(1)].

(6) Review/revision.—(*i*) The High Court has full power, jurisdiction and authority to review the proceedings of all subordinate courts and if necessary set aside or correct them [H.C.P., s. 5(1)].

(*ii*) All sentences in criminal cases imposed by a third class subordinate court are subject to review as of course by an officer appointed to hold a first class court without prejudice to the right of appeal against the sentence [S.C.P., s. 75].

(*iii*) All sentences in criminal cases, in the case of first class courts for a period of imprisonment exceeding 6 months or a fine exceeding £50 and, in the case of courts of the second and third class, for a period exceeding 3 months or a fine exceeding £25, are subject to review by the High Court without prejudice to the right of appeal [S.C.P., as amended 1951, s. 76].

(7) Transfer.—(*i*) In proceedings before a subordinate court when both parties are natives and the cause of action in the opinion of the Clerk of the Court is one suitable to be heard in an African court, the Clerk may refuse to issue a summons and may order the plaintiff to commence his action in such a court [S.C.P., s. 16].

(*ii*) A subordinate court may transfer a proceeding to another court of the same class or of a higher class by the consent of the parties or upon application of any party upon a showing that trial will result in undue expense or inconvenience in the particular court [S.C.P., s. 20].

(*iii*) An action in a second class court where the amount of the claim exceeds £100 may, upon application of the defendant, be removed to a first class court. Any action in a first or second class court where the claim exceeds £200 may, upon the application of the defendant, be removed to the High Court (with leave of the Judge in Chambers when the amount does not exceed £500) [S.C.P., s. 32(1), (2); H.C.P., s. 7].

(*iv*) Under the Criminal Procedure and Evidence Proclamation the the Attorney-General has authority to remit a criminal case to a subordinate court after a preparatory examination and may specify in such remittal that the subordinate court shall have increased jurisdiction [C.P. and E.P., s. 90].

LAW TO BE ADMINISTERED

(9) General law ⎱ As High Court (see A. 2(9), (10), pp. 192–
(10) Customary law ⎰ 193, *ante*).

B. 1 AFRICAN COURTS (first instance)

CONSTITUTION AND POWERS

(1) Establishment.—With the approval of the High Commissioner the Resident Commissioner by warrant may establish such African courts as he shall think fit [African Courts Proclamation, 1961, s. 2(3)].

(2) Composition.—The constitution of the African court shall be in accordance with native law or custom of the area, provided the Resident Commissioner may, subject to the directions of the High Commissioner, prescribe the constitution of any African court [A.C.P., s. 3].

(3) Jurisdiction—original.—(*i*) Civil jurisdiction, defined by the warrant, is over causes and matters in which all parties are natives [A.C.P., ss. 2(3), 7].

(*ii*) Criminal jurisdiction, defined by warrant, extends to cases in which the complainant and accused are natives [A.C.P., s. 8].

(*iii*) No African court has jurisdiction in the absence of express provision conferring jurisdiction to try the following:—

> (a) cases in which the person is charged with an offence in which death is alleged to have resulted or which is punishable by death or life imprisonment;
> (b) any cause in case of persons married under the laws of the Territory, which seeks nullity, divorce or separation;
> (c) any cause involving testamentary disposition;
> (d) proceeding relating to witchcraft; and
> (e) any case in which a non-native is a witness [A.C.P., s. 9].

(4) Jurisdiction—appellate.—Nil.

CONTROL OF COURTS

(5) Appeals from.—Any person aggrieved by an order or decision of an African court may appeal to an African Court of Appeal, or if there is none, to a subordinate court of competent jurisdiction [A.C.P., s. 32(1)].

(6) Review/revision.—Every administrative officer as holder of a subordinate court has access to all African courts within his jurisdiction, and on application or on his own motion may revise any proceedings of African courts of first instance or of appeals [A.C.P., s. 29(1), (a)].

(7) Transfer.—(*i*) A party to a dispute within the jurisdiction of the African court of first instance who has reason to believe that the matter cannot be equitably adjudicated or that the trial of the matter is unreasonably delayed, may report the matter to the African Court of Appeal or Higher African Court of Appeal to have the matter transferred to such court for hearing. If the party believes the same conditions will prevail in such higher native court, he may make application to the appropriate subordinate court for a hearing and determination [A.C.P., s. 27(1), (2), (3)].

(*ii*) Every administrative officer as holder of a subordinate court, may transfer any cause, civil or criminal, at any stage of the proceedings to any subordinate court of competent jurisdiction [A.C.P., s. 29(1), (c)].

(8) Inspection, supervision, etc.—(*i*) Every administrative officer as holder of a subordinate court may inspect the records of all African courts and exercise the powers noted at (6) and (7), *supra* [A.C.P., s. 29].

(*ii*) The Resident Commissioner may authorise any chief to have access to the records of the African courts and if the chief considers the finding, order or decision incorrect, he must forward it to the court from which appeal lies from the African court [A.C.P., s. 30].

LAW TO BE ADMINISTERED

(9) General law.—African courts administer:—

    (*i*) the provisions of rules and orders of the Resident Commissioner, an administrative officer or native authority, in force in the area of the jurisdiction of the court;

    (*ii*) the provisions of any proclamation which the court is, by such proclamation, authorised to administer;

    (*iii*) the provisions of any law which the court is authorised to administer by order of the High Commissioner [A.C.P., ss. 11(b), (c), (d), 12].

(10) Customary law.—African courts administer " the native law and custom prevailing in the area of the jurisdiction of the court so far as it is not inconsistent with the provisions of any law in force in the Territory " [A.C.P., s. 11(a)].

" ' Native law or custom ' and ' Native custom ' mean in relation to a particular tribe or in relation to any native community outside any tribal area, the general law or custom of such tribe or community, except so far as the same may be incompatible with the due exercise of His Majesty's power and jurisdiction or repugnant to morality, humanity or natural justice or injurious to the welfare of the natives " [A.C.P., s. 1(2)].

B. 2 AFRICAN COURTS OF APPEAL

CONSTITUTION AND POWERS

(1) Establishment.—The Resident Commissioner may, with the approval of the High Commissioner by warrant recognise or establish any African court, chief or body of chiefs, or other natives to be an African Court of Appeal or a Higher African Court of Appeal [A.C.P., s. 31(1)].

(2) Composition.—See (1) Establishment, *supra.*

(3) Jurisdiction—original.—As defined by warrant (same as African court of first instance) [A.C.P., ss. 31(1), 29].

(4) Jurisdiction—appellate.—Hears appeals from inferior African courts [A.C.P., s. 32].

CONTROL OF COURTS

(5) Appeals from.—Appeals from an African Court of Appeal are to a Higher African Court of Appeal, if any, then to a subordinate court of the first class. Appeals from the subordinate court are to the High Court. The High Commissioner may by order limit appeals from the Higher African Court of Appeal and from the subordinate courts to cases in excess of specified amounts, periods of imprisonment or corporal punishment [A.C.P., s. 32].

(6) Review/revision

(7) Transfer

(8) Inspection, supervision, etc.

As African courts of first instance.

LAW TO BE ADMINISTERED

(9) General law

(10) Customary law

As African courts of first instance.

SWAZILAND[1]

The courts for the administration of justice in Swaziland comprise:—
    A. the High Court and subordinate courts administering primarily the general law; and
    B. Judicial Commissioners' courts and a system of Swazi courts administering primarily customary law.

A. 1(a) THE PRIVY COUNCIL
See p. 179, *ante*

A. 1(b) THE BASUTOLAND, BECHUANALAND PROTECTORATE AND SWAZILAND COURT OF APPEAL
See pp. 178–180, *ante*.

A. 2 THE HIGH COURT
CONSTITUTION AND POWERS

(1) Establishment.—The High Court was first established pursuant to the authority of the Swaziland Order in Council, 1903, and in 1954 the law relating to the High Court was consolidated by the Swaziland High Court Proclamation [H.C.P., s. 2(1)].

(2) Composition.—The High Commissioner for the three territories may appoint a Chief Judge and a puisne judge of the High Court [H.C.P., s. 3(1)].

(3) Jurisdiction—original.—(*i*) The High Court has all the jurisdiction, power and authority vested in the Supreme Court of South Africa [H.C.P., 2(2)]. The jurisdiction is over all causes and proceedings both civil and criminal, except that no civil cause to which either party is a European when the amount in dispute does not exceed £500, may be instituted in or removed to the High Court without leave of a judge. This exception does not apply to those matters over which the subordinate courts are expressly denied jurisdiction [H.C.P., ss. 2(2), 4 and Subordinate Courts Proclamation, s. 28].

(*ii*) The Chief Justice or a puisne judge may exercise jurisdiction in the Territory in respect of specified matters arising in either of the other Territories [H.C.P., s. 12].

(4) Jurisdiction—appellate.—The High Court is a court of appeal from all subordinate courts in the Territory [H.C.P., s. 6].

(*i*) *Civil.*—A party to any civil suit or proceeding in a subordinate court may appeal to the High Court against judgment for the plaintiff on his claim, for the defendant on his defence, absolution, judgment as to costs, any rule or order having the effect of final and definite sentence

---

[1] For diagram of courts system see p. 226, *post*.

and a decision on an exception under certain circumstances [Subordinate Courts Proclamation, cap. 4, ss. 30 and 62]. No appeal lies if before the hearing the parties agree in writing that the decision of the court shall be final [S.C.P., s. 61].

(*ii*) *Criminal.*—Any person convicted by judgment of any subordinate court including a person discharged after conviction, may appeal against conviction and sentence or order to the High Court [S.C.P., s. 81].

A case may be stated in any criminal proceeding giving a decision in favour of the accused on a matter of law and the Attorney-General or prosecutor may appeal from that decision to the High Court [S.C.P., 81(a), (1), (2)].

(*iii*) *Appeals from Native Courts.*—Civil appeals lie from a Higher Native Court of Appeal to the High Court and, if the record of the case is inadequate, a Judge of the High Court may order a civil appeal to be heard by the Judicial Commissioner from whom an appeal lies to the High Court. Criminal appeals from the Judicial Commissioner lie to the High Court [Native Courts Proclamation, 1950, s. 31].

CONTROL OF COURT

(5) Appeals from.—Appeals, in both criminal and civil cases, against the judgment of the High Court lie to the Court of Appeal [Court of Appeal (Swaziland) Proclamation, 1954, ss. 3, 11].

LAW TO BE ADMINISTERED

(9) General law.—The General Law and Administration Proclamation, February 22, 1907, s. 2(1), (2), as amended, provides:—

" (1). The Roman–Dutch Common Law save in so far as the same has been heretofore or may from time to time hereafter be modified by statute shall be the law of Swaziland;

(2). Save and except in so far as the same have been repealed by the Proclamations set out in the 4th Schedule to this Proclamation, the Statutes in force in the Transvaal on the 15th day of October, 1904, and the Statutes of the Transvaal set out in the 1st Schedule to this Proclamation and the statutory regulations thereunder shall *mutatis mutandis* and as far as they may be applicable be in force in Swaziland. . . . "

(10) Customary law.—The Swaziland Order in Council, 1903, as amended, in s. 5 provides for the High Commissioner's power to legislate by Proclamation and provides further:—

" The High Commissioner in issuing such Proclamations shall respect any native laws by which the civil relations of any native chiefs, tribes or populations under Her Majesty's protection are now regulated, except so far as the same may be incompatible with the due exercise of Her Majesty's power and jurisdiction, or clearly injurious to the welfare of the said natives."

The General Law and Administration Proclamation, 1907, s. 17(1) provided:—

" Notwithstanding anything in this Proclamation contained the Paramount Chief and other native chiefs shall continue to exercise jurisdiction according to native law and custom in all civil disputes in which natives only are concerned."

A. 3 SUBORDINATE COURTS

CONSTITUTION AND POWERS

(1) Establishment.—The subordinate courts were established by the Subordinate Courts Proclamation, 1938, cap. 2, s. 2. The courts consist of:—

- (a) subordinate courts of the first class;
- (b) subordinate courts of the second class;
- (c) subordinate courts of the third class.

(2) Composition.—The following persons may hold courts:—

- (a) every Senior District Officer and every District Commissioner—court of the first class;
- (b) every District Officer—court of the second class; and
- (c) every Cadet—court of the third class.

The Resident Commissioner may, with the concurrence of the Chief Justice, by notice, appoint:—

- (a) any person as a magistrate or assistant magistrate to hold a court of a class to be specified;
- (b) any District Officer to hold a court of the first class or any Cadet to hold a court of the second class.

Unless otherwise stated, the appointment is deemed to confer jurisdiction to hold the court within any territorial district [S.C.P., s. 3].

(3) Jurisdiction—original.—(*i*) *Civil.*—The jurisdiction in civil matters is as follows:—

- (a) first class courts have jurisdiction where neither party is a European and all other actions where the amount claimed does not exceed £500;
- (b) second class courts have jurisdiction where neither party is a European and all other actions where the amount claimed does not exceed £250;
- (c) third class courts have no civil jurisdiction [S.C.P., s. 15(1), proviso (2)].

When both parties are natives and the cause of action is, in the opinion of the Clerk of the Court, suitable for a Swazi Court, the Clerk may refuse to issue a summons and may order the plaintiff to commence the action in the appropriate Swazi Court [S.C.P., s. 15, proviso].

(*ii*) *Criminal.*—(a) Subordinate courts of the first, second and third class have jurisdiction over all offences except treason, murder, sedition, offences relating to coinage or currency, and rape. The Attorney-General may remit a rape case for trial by a subordinate court of the first class [S.C.P., s. 68].

(b) Subordinate courts have the following limitations on their power to punish:—

- (*i*) a first class court may sentence to imprisonment for not more than 2 years, levy a fine of not more than £100 and prescribe not more than 8 strokes with a cane;
- (*ii*) a second class court may sentence to imprisonment for not more than 1 year, levy a fine of not more than £50 and prescribe not more than 8 strokes with a cane;

(*iii*) a third class court may sentence to imprisonment for not more than 6 months or levy a fine of not more than £25, but may not impose a punishment of whipping [S.C.P., 1938, as amended 1953, s. 70].

(c) The Attorney-General may remit a case, other than one beyond the jurisdiction of the subordinate court after holding a preparatory examination. The remittal may expressly give increased jurisdiction. There is no remittal to a third class court [S.C.P., ss. 72, 73].

Subordinate courts have no jurisdiction in the following:—

(a) dissolution of marriage or separation where the parties are Europeans;
(b) validity or interpretation of wills;
(c) status of persons in respect of mental capacity;
(d) specific performance without alternative of payment of damages except transfer or delivery of property and rendering account;
(e) decree of perpetual silence; or
(f) provisional sentence [S.C.P., s. 28].

(4) Jurisdiction—appellate.—Nil.

CONTROL OF COURTS

(5) Appeals from.—A party to any civil suit, unless the parties have agreed that the decision of the court shall be final, may appeal to the High Court against any judgment, rule or order having the effect of a final sentence or decision overruling or upholding an exception, when the parties concerned consent to such an appeal [S.C.P., ss. 61, 62, 81(1)].

Every person convicted by judgment of a subordinate court may appeal against such conviction to the High Court [S.C.P., s. 72(1)].

(6) Review/revision.—(*i*) The High Court has full power, jurisdiction and authority to review the proceedings of all subordinate courts and if necessary set aside or correct them [H.C.P., s. 5(1)].

(*ii*) All sentences in criminal cases imposed by a third class subordinate court are subject to review as of course by an officer appointed to hold a first class court without prejudice to the right of appeal against the sentence [S.C.P., s. 74].

(*iii*) All sentences in criminal cases, in the case of courts of the first class for a period of imprisonment exceeding 6 months or a fine exceeding £50, and in case of courts of the second and third class for a period exceeding 3 months or a fine exceeding £25, are subject to review by the High Court without prejudice to the right of appeal [S.C.P., s. 75].

(7) Transfer.—(*i*) In proceedings before a subordinate court when both parties are natives and the cause of action in the opinion of the Clerk of the Court is one suitable to be heard in a Swazi Court, the Clerk may refuse to issue a summons and may order the plaintiff to commence his action in such a court [S.C.P., s. 28].

(*ii*) A subordinate court may transfer a proceeding to another court of the same class or of a higher class by the consent of the parties or upon the application of any party upon a showing that trial will result in undue expense or inconvenience in the particular court [S.C.P., 1938, s. 19].

(*iii*) An action in a second class court where the amount of the claim exceeds £100 may, upon the application of the defendant, be removed to a first class court. Any action in a first or second class court where the claim exceeds £200 may, upon the application of the defendant, be removed to the High Court (with leave of the Judge in Chambers) when the amount does not exceed £500 [S.C.P., 1938, s. 31(1), (2)].

(*iv*) The Chief Justice or a judge of the High Court, or in their absence the Registrar, may for good cause, order a criminal case to be transferred for trial from the district in which the crime was committed to any other district [S.C.P., s. 60].

(*v*) Under the Criminal Procedure and Evidence Proclamation, the Attorney-General has authority to remit a criminal case to a subordinate court after a preparatory examination and may specify in such remittal that the subordinate court shall have increased jurisdiction [C.P. and E.P., s. 88].

LAW TO BE ADMINISTERED

(9) General law

(10) Customary law

As High Court (see A. 2(9), (10), p. 200, *ante*).

B. 1 SWAZI COURTS (First Instance)

CONSTITUTION AND POWERS

(1) Establishment.—The Swaziland Native Courts Proclamation, 1950, s. 2, provides for the recognition or establishment of Swazi courts by warrant of the Paramount Chief with the prior approval of the Resident Commissioner.

(2) Composition.—The Swazi courts are constituted in accordance with the native law and custom of the Territory. The Paramount Chief, with prior approval of the Resident Commissioner, may prescribe the constitution of any Swazi court, order of procedence, or powers and duties of assessors [N.C.P., s. 3].

(3) Jurisdiction—original.—(*i*) *Civil.*—Civil jurisdiction, defined by the warrant, is over causes and matters in which all the parties are natives [N.C.P., ss. 2(2), 6].

(*ii*) *Criminal.*—Criminal jurisdiction, defined by warrant, extends to cases in which complainant and accused are natives [N.C.P., s. 7].

No Swazi court has jurisdiction, in the absence of express provision conferring jurisdiction, to try the following:—

(a) cases in which person is charged with an offence in which death is alleged to have resulted or which is punishable by death or life imprisonment;

(b) cases in connection with marriage other than marriage contracted under native law and custom except where and in so far as the case concerns payment or return of dowry.

(c) proceedings relating to witchcraft [N.C.P., s. 9].

(4) Jurisdiction—appellate.—Nil.

CONTROL OF COURTS

(5) Appeals from.—Appeals lie to the Swazi Court of Appeal [N.C.P., s. 31], and thence to the Higher Swazi Court of Appeal and from such court to the High Court of Swaziland.

(6) Review/revision.—(*i*) Civil proceedings of the Swazi courts may be revised by a Swazi Court of Appeal or a Higher Swazi Court of Appeal on application or its own motion within a period of 6 months of the termination of the proceedings [N.C.P., s. 29(1), (a)].

(*ii*) Criminal proceedings of the Swazi courts may be revised by the Judicial Commissioner, and every District Officer and Assistant District Officer as holder of a subordinate court [N.C.P., s. 28(1), (a)].

(7) Transfer.—(*i*) A party to a dispute who believes that a matter cannot be equitably adjudicated by the Swazi court, or that adjudication is unreasonably delayed or refused, may report the matter:—

    (a) to a Swazi Court of Appeal where the court concerned is a Swazi court;

    (b) to a Higher Swazi Court of Appeal where the court concerned is the Court of Appeal;

    (c) to the Judicial Commissioner where the court concerned is the Higher Court of Appeal.

The appropriate court may:—

    (a) refuse the application; or

    (b) hear the matter; or

    (c) direct the appropriate court to adjudicate upon the matter [N.C.P., s. 26].

(*ii*) The Judicial Commissioner and every District Officer and Assistant District Officer as holder of a subordinate court may transfer any criminal matter at any stage of the proceedings to a first class subordinate court or order the case retried by any other Swazi court [N.C.P., s. 28(1), (b), (c)].

(*iii*) The Judicial Commissioner or the High Court in exercise of appellate jurisdiction may order any case to be reheard before any other Swazi court or subordinate court of competent Jurisdiction [N.C.P., s. 33(b)].

(8) Inspection, supervision, etc.—(*i*) The Judicial Commissioner and every District Officer and Assistant District Officer as holder of a subordinate court has access to the records of Swazi courts [N.C.P., s. 28(1)].

(*ii*) The Paramount Chief, with prior approval of the Resident Commissioner, may provide by rules for the general administration and practice of the Swazi courts [N.C.P., s. 38].

LAW TO BE ADMINISTERED

(9) General law.—The Swazi court administers:—

    (*i*) the provisions of any Proclamation which the court is authorised to administer by the terms of the Proclamation;

(*ii*) the provisions of any law designated by an order of the Resident Commissioner;

(*iii*) the rules and orders of the Native Authority, Paramount Chief or a Chief under the Swaziland Native Administration Proclamation [N.C.P., s. 10(b), (c), (d)].

(10) Customary law.—The Swazi court administers: " the native law and custom prevailing in the Territory so far as it is not repugnant to natural justice or morality or inconsistent with the provisions of any law in force in the Territory " [N.C.P., s. 10(a)].

B. 2 SWAZI COURTS OF APPEAL

These are:—

(a) Judicial Commissioners' Courts;
(b) Higher Swazi Court of Appeal:
(c) Swazi Court of Appeal.

CONSTITUTION AND POWERS

(1) Establishment.—These courts are established by the Swaziland Native Courts Proclamation, 1950. The Paramount Chief may, with prior approval of the Resident Commissioner, recognise or establish any Swazi Court of Appeal or Higher Court of Appeal [N.C.P., 1950, s. 30]. The Judicial Commissioner means an officer appointed by the Resident Commissioner to carry out duties under the Proclamation and he is empowered to hold a first class subordinate court for the purpose N.C.P., s. 1].

(2) Composition.— (1) Establishment, *supra*.

(3) Jurisdiction—original.—For the Swazi Courts of Appeal— as defined by warrant, subject to the Proclamation. For the Judicial Commissioners' Courts—as subordinate courts of the first class [N.C.P., ss. 1, 6, 7, 30].

(4) Jurisdiction—appellate.—(a) The Swazi Court of Appeal hears appeals from Swazi courts.

(b) The Higher Swazi Court of Appeal hears appeals from the Swazi Court of Appeal.

(c) The Judicial Commissioner hears appeals in criminal proceedings from the Higher Swazi Court of Appeal [N.C.P., s. 31].

CONTROL OF COURTS

(5) Appeals from.—(*i*) Appeals from the Higher Swazi Court of Appeal in criminal proceedings lie to the Judicial Commissioner, and in civil proceedings to the High Court unless a Judge of the High Court orders such appeal heard by the Judicial Commissioner.

(*ii*) Appeal lies to the High Court from a decision or order of the Judicial Commissioner.

Appeal to the High Court is limited to cases where the amount of judgment exceeds £100 or where sentence is for imprisonment exceeding three months, or of corporal punishment of more than 8 strokes, unless a judge of the High Court in Chambers grants special leave to appeal [N.C.P., s. 31].

(6) Review/revision.—(*i*) The Judicial Commissioner and every District Officer and Assistant District Officer as holder of a subordinate court may revise criminal proceedings of a Swazi Court of Appeal. The Judicial Commissioner alone may revise criminal proceedings of the Higher Swazi Court of Appeal [N.C.P., 1950, s. 28].

(*ii*) The Higher Swazi Court of Appeal may revise the civil proceedings of a Swazi Court of Appeal [N.C.P., 1950, s. 29].

(7) Transfer.—See B. 1(7), p. 204, *ante.*

(8) Inspection, supervision, etc.—See B. 1(8), p. 204, *ante.*

LAW TO BE ADMINISTERED

(9) General law

(10) Customary law } As Swazi courts of first instance.

APPENDIX

DIAGRAMS OF COURT SYSTEMS

INDEX TO DIAGRAMS

PAGE

Basutoland	225
Bechuanaland	224
Cameroons, Southern	210
Gambia, The	209
Ghana	211
High Commission Territories	224
Kenya	215
Lagos	213
Liberia	214
Nigeria—	
Eastern Region	212
Federation of	211
Northern Region	213
Western Region	212
Northern Rhodesia	222
Nyasaland	223
Rhodesia and Nyasaland, Federation of	221
Sierra Leone	210
Somali Republic	220
Southern Rhodesia	221
Sudan—	
Civil Division	219
Sharia Division	218
Swaziland	226
Tanganyika	216
Uganda	217
Zanzibar	218

EXPLANATION OF SYMBOLS

O.	=	Original jurisdiction
A.	=	Appellate jurisdiction
R.	=	Revisory jurisdiction
T.	=	Power of transfer
I.	=	Power of inspection
C.	=	Power of confirmation
———		indicates a channel of appeal
– – – –		indicates a channel of revisory jurisdiction

Note.—All diagrams are to be read from top to bottom, courts of superior jurisdiction being at the head of each diagram.

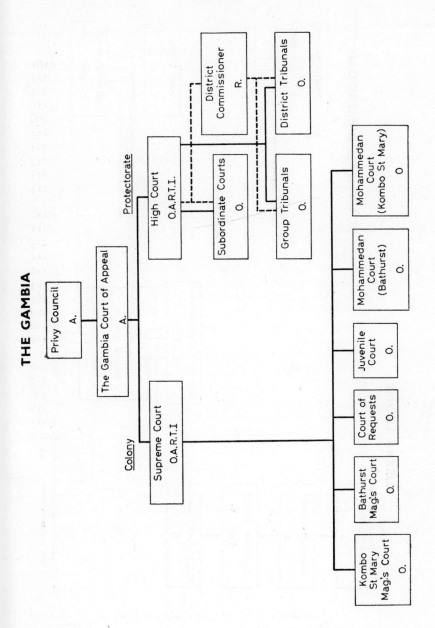

THE GAMBIA

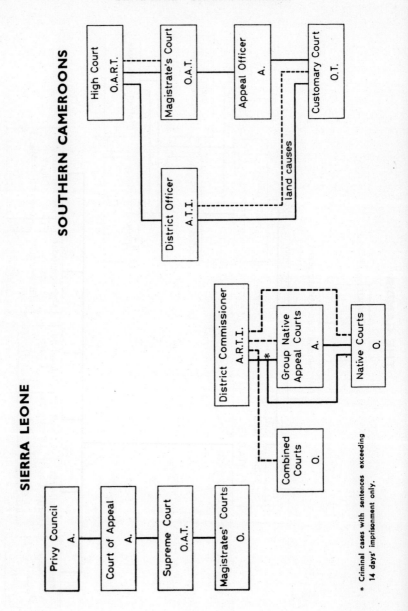

* Criminal cases with sentences exceeding 14 days' imprisonment only.

GHANA

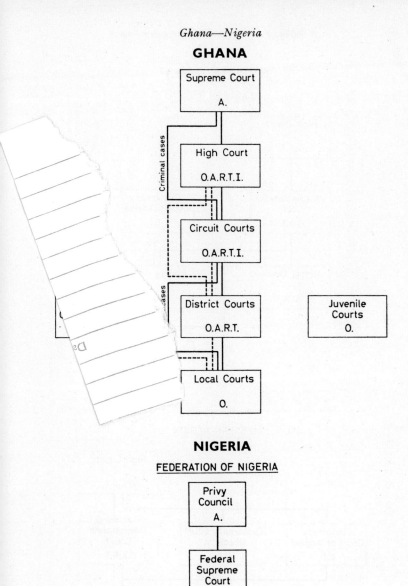

Supreme Court

A.

Criminal cases

High Court

O.A.R.T.I.

Circuit Courts

O.A.R.T.I.

District Courts

O.A.R.T.

Juvenile Courts

O.

Local Courts

O.

NIGERIA

FEDERATION OF NIGERIA

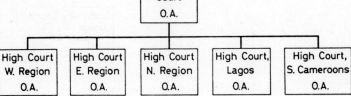

Privy Council

A.

Federal Supreme Court

O.A.

High Court W. Region	High Court E. Region	High Court N. Region	High Court, Lagos	High Court, S. Cameroons
O.A.	O.A.	O.A.	O.A.	O.A.

NIGERIA (cont.)

EASTERN REGION

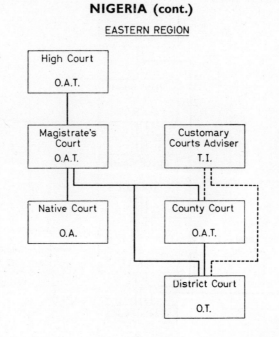

WESTERN REGION

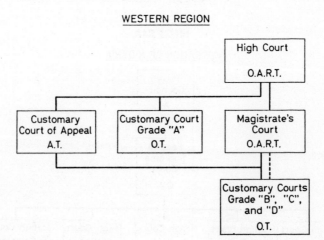

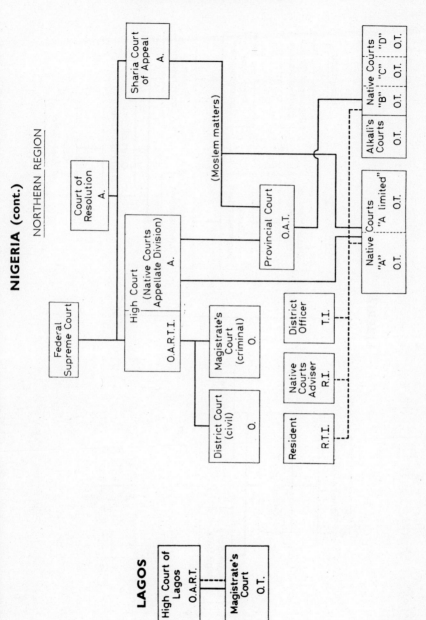

NIGERIA (cont.)

NORTHERN REGION

LAGOS

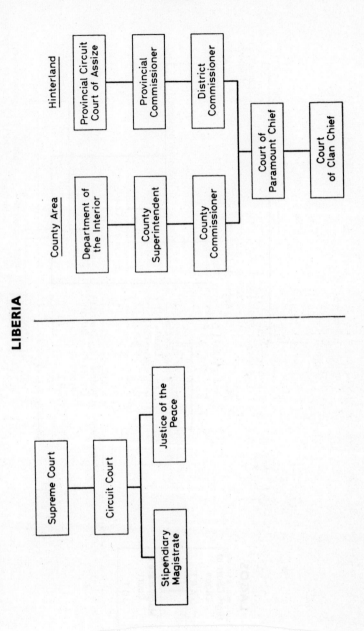

LIBERIA

Hinterland

Provincial Circuit Court of Assize	Provincial Commissioner	District Commissioner

County Area

Department of the Interior	County Superintendent	County Commissioner

Court of Paramount Chief

Court of Clan Chief

Supreme Court — Circuit Court

Justice of the Peace

Stipendiary Magistrate

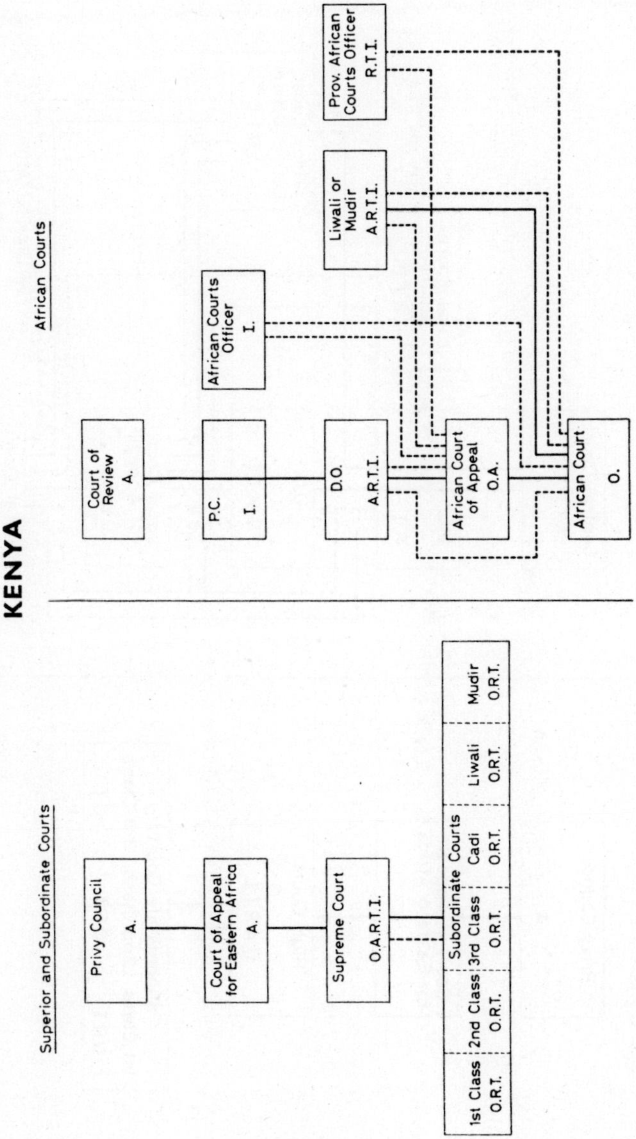
KENYA
Superior and Subordinate Courts
Privy Council A.
Court of Appeal for Eastern Africa A.
Supreme Court O.A.R.T.I.
Subordinate Courts
1st Class O.R.T.
2nd Class O.R.T.
3rd Class O.R.T.
Cadi O.R.T.
Liwali O.R.T.
Mudir O.R.T.
African Courts
Court of Review A.
P.C. I.
D.O. A.R.T.I.
African Court of Appeal O.A.
African Court O.
African Courts Officer I.
Liwali or Mudir A.R.T.I.
Prov. African Courts Officer R.T.I.

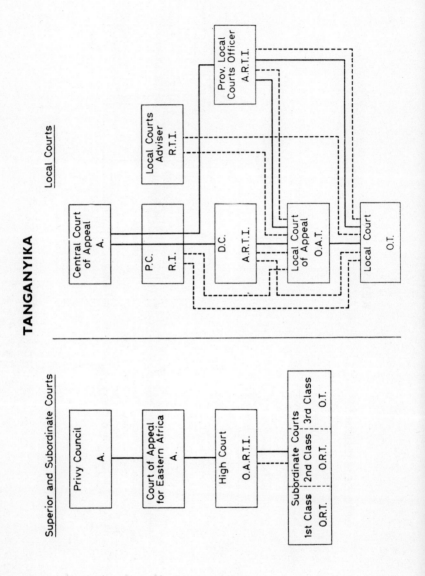

TANGANYIKA

Local Courts

Central Court of Appeal — A.

Local Courts Adviser — R.T.I.

Prov. Local Courts Officer — A.R.T.I.

P.C. — R.I.

D.C. — A.R.T.I.

Local Court of Appeal — O.A.T.

Local Court — O.T.

Superior and Subordinate Courts

Privy Council — A.

Court of Appeal for Eastern Africa — A.

High Court — O.A.R.T.I.

Subordinate Courts
1st Class — O.R.T.
2nd Class — O.R.T.
3rd Class — O.T.

UGANDA

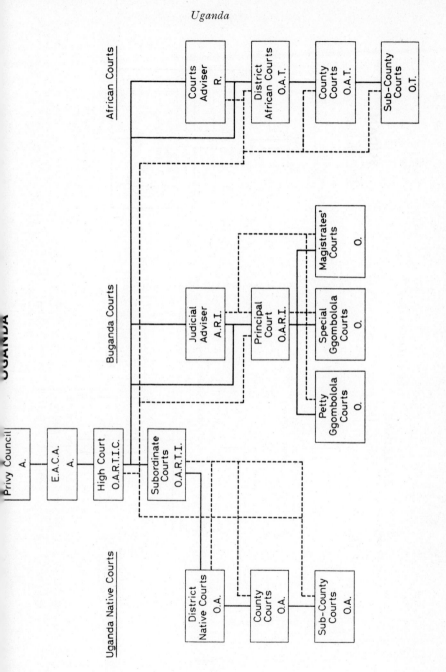

H*

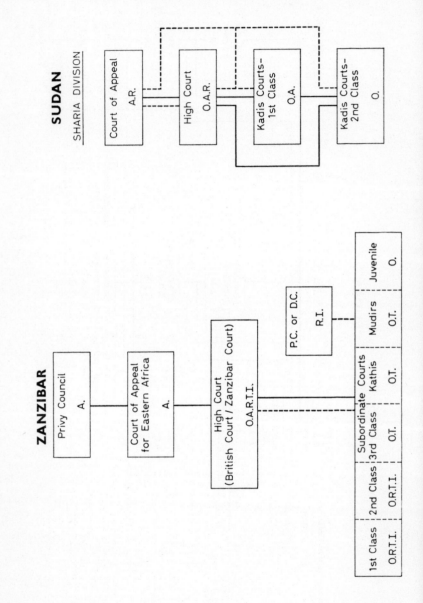

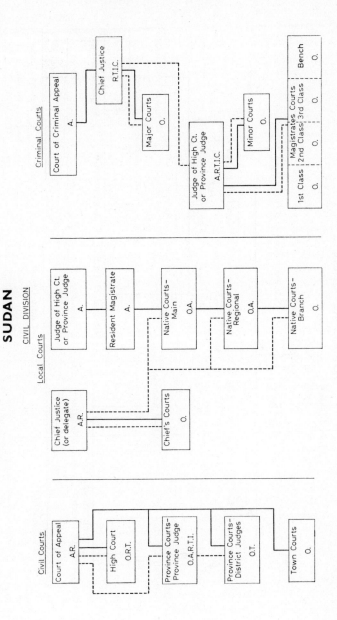

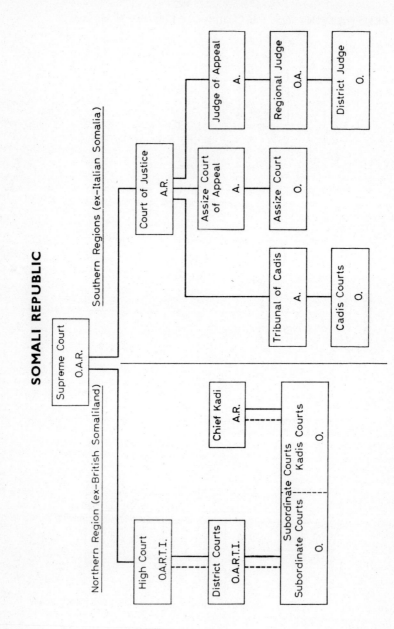

SOMALI REPUBLIC

Supreme Court
O.A.R.

Southern Regions (ex-Italian Somalia)

Court of Justice
A.R.

Judge of Appeal
A.

Regional Judge
O.A.

District Judge
O.

Assize Court
of Appeal
A.

Assize Court
O.

Tribunal of Cadis
A.

Cadis Courts
O.

Northern Region (ex-British Somaliland)

Chief Kadi
A.R.

Kadis Courts
O.

High Court
O.A.R.T.I.

District Courts
O.A.R.T.I.

Subordinate Courts
Kadis Courts

Subordinate Courts
O.

220

FEDERATION OF RHODESIA AND NYASALAND

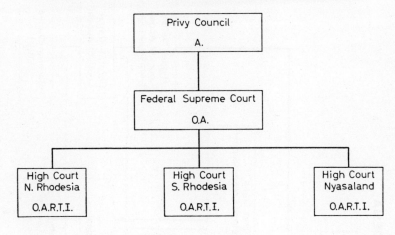

SOUTHERN RHODESIA

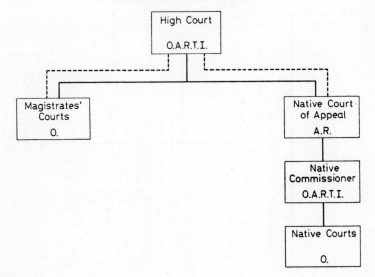

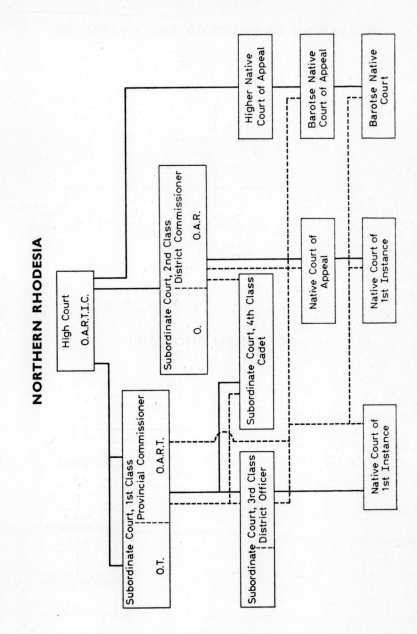

NORTHERN RHODESIA

NYASALAND

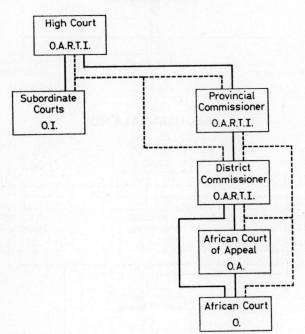

HIGH COMMISSION TERRITORIES

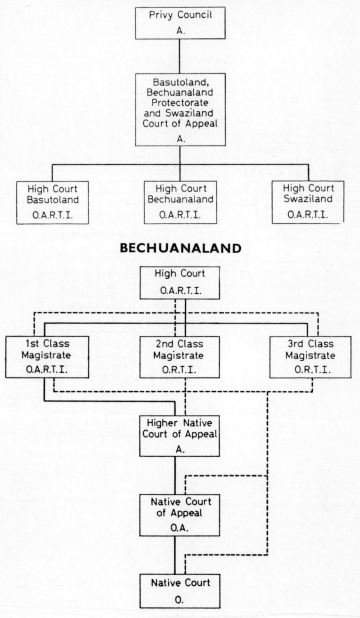

BECHUANALAND

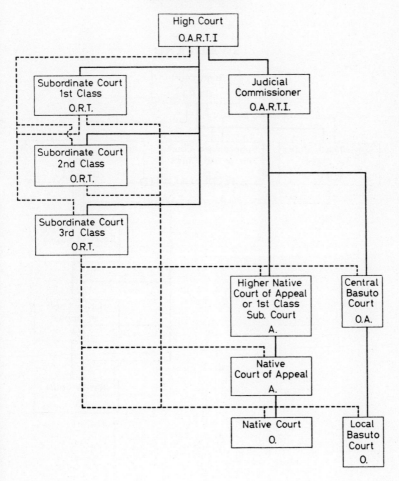

BASUTOLAND

High Court
O.A.R.T.I

Subordinate Court
1st Class
O.R.T.

Judicial
Commissioner
O.A.R.T.I.

Subordinate Court
2nd Class
O.R.T.

Subordinate Court
3rd Class
O.R.T.

Higher Native
Court of Appeal
or 1st Class
Sub. Court
A.

Central
Basuto
Court
O.A.

Native
Court of Appeal
A.

Native Court
O.

Local
Basuto
Court
O.

SWAZILAND

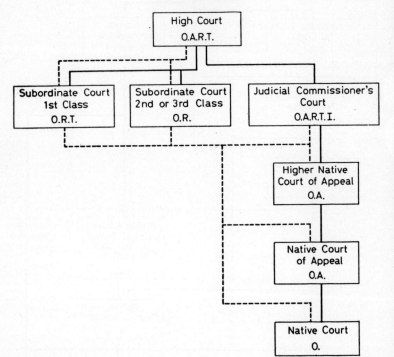